Fadhil Chalabi is the Executive Director of the Centre for Global Energy Studies, a London-based think-tank (founded and chaired by H.E. Sheikh Ahmed Zaki Yamani). Former Undersecretary of Oil at Iraq's Ministry of Petroleum, Fadhil Chalabi was Deputy Secretary General of OPEC from 1978–89 and from 1983–88 was OPEC's Acting Secretary General.

'Only a small number of people know that OPEC member countries have conflicting interests, which make decision-making extremely difficult. The people who recognise this...do not normally put in writing what they know, as it might conflict with the interests of the member countries they represent, or for other reasons. Chalabi is one of those rare individuals who truly understands OPEC from within and yet has always been extraordinarily frank, revealing what he knew even whilst still with the Organisation, which caused him difficulties at the time. He continued with this policy of frankness after leaving OPEC, and his book *Oil Policies, Oil Myths* reflects his forthrightness and great depth of his knowledge...an enormously unique and valuable book.'

H.E. Sheikh Ahmed Zaki Yamani, former Minister of Petroleum and Mineral Resources for Saudi Arabia (1962–1986), founder and Chairman of the Centre for Global Energy Studies.

'...an absorbing...highly professional analysis which deals with the complexities of change and turbulent events of international oil...throws new light on the roles of the leading actors and how decisions were made among the oil producing countries. He reminds us also that Baghdad in the 1950s and 1960s was not only a "cauldron" of political intrigue but also flourished as a centre for the arts – poetry, painting and music. He sees the end of cheap oil, the shift away from oil power, the opening up of energy markets and deals with the difficulties of rebalancing supply and demand...he chronicles events with a deep understanding of political policies and oil industry practices. Chalabi concludes that OPEC has a "vital role to play..."'

Dr Alirio Parra, former Minister of Oil for Venezuela

'Fadhil Chalabi offers a fascinating and essential history, told from the inside, of a turbulent and dramatic era of oil. He brings a unique and deep perspective – as the former Acting Secretary General of OPEC, as an economist, and as an Iraqi – into the decisions and events and personalities that shaped the oil world. He also brings new understanding of Iraq's decades of turmoil. He leaves no doubt how tomorrow's energy world will continue to be affected by the unfolding story he lays out in these pages.'

Dr Daniel Yergin, Pulitzer Prize-winning author of *The Prize: the Epic Quest for Oil, Money, and Power* and Chairman, IHS Cambridge Energy Research Associates

'An engrossing...behind-the-scenes account of politics and of the political background of international oil, with insights into decision-making in Iraq and OPEC...'

Dr Francisco Parra, former Secretary General of OPEC

'An excellent eye witness account...of the transition of control over oil resources from the dominant west to the OPEC countries, full of fascinating anecdotes...meetings with Saddam Hussein...the hijacking of OPEC oil ministers by Carlos the Jackal. Chalabi, a good friend of OPEC, struggled to reconcile his professional economist views with the realities confronting [its] diverse group of [member] countries... He warned his OPEC colleagues not to get carried away with the hype of unsustainable oil price spikes...instead to manage supply in such a way as to sustain competitiveness with alternative fuels and thus maintain...market share. Premature fuel switching and Iraq's new oil production escalation he sees as potential threats to OPEC... *Oil Policies, Oil Myths* is highly recommended reading for those connected with the oil industry, historians, policy makers, journalists...to learn more about this organisation's major impact on global energy and economic developments for half a century.'

Dr Herman Franssen, President of International Energy Associates, Senior Research Fellow at Center for Strategic and International Studies, Washington DC

'The story of oil by an intelligent dissenter and great expert. This book is a must for anybody wanting to understand a more rational set-up of the oil industry.'

Dr Marcello Colitti, former Energy Advisor to Chairman of E.N.I. S.p.A and former Chairman of Ecofuel S.p.A. (of the E.N.I. group)

OIL POLICIES, OIL MYTHS

Analysis and Memoir of an OPEC 'insider'

by

Fadhil Chalabi

I.B. TAURIS

LONDON · NEW YORK

Published in 2010 by I.B.Tauris & Co Ltd
6 Salem Road, London W2 4BU
175 Fifth Avenue, New York NY 10010
www.ibtauris.com

Distributed in the United States and Canada
Exclusively by Palgrave Macmillan
175 Fifth Avenue, New York NY 10010

ISBN: 978 1 84885 508 3

A full CIP record for this book is available from the British Library
A full CIP record is available from the Library of Congress

Library of Congress Catalog Card Number: available

MIX
Paper from
responsible sources
FSC
www.fsc.org   FSC® C013604

Printed and bound in Great Britain by CPI Antony Rowe, Chippenham

In memory of my beloved family: my grandmother, parents, two brothers and three sisters, each of whom, in his or her own way, gave me much love and care, and encouraged my education and career. Blessed be their souls.

I also dedicate this book to my dear children and grandchildren.

Contents

Illustrations

Figures

Tables

Abbreviations

AIOC	Anglo-Iranian Oil Company (renamed in 1935, formerly Anglo-Persian Oil)
API	American Petroleum Institute
$/bbl	dollars per barrel of oil
bn/B	billion barrels
BP	British Petroleum (formed in 1954 from AIOC)
BPC	Basra Petroleum Company
CFP	Compagnie Française des Pétroles (antecedent of Total)
CGES	Centre for Global Energy Studies
CNOC	China National Oil Corporation
CNRS	Centre National de Recherche Scientifique
CSIS	Center for Strategic and International Studies
DOE	Department of Energy
ECB	Economic Commission Board
EIA	Energy Information Administration
ENI	Italian State Oil Company
ERAP	Entreprise de Recherches et d'Activités Pétrolières merged with SNP in 1976 and later merged with Total.
ERDA	Energy Research and Development Administration
FLN	Front de Libération Nationale
F.O.B.	free on board
FSU	former Soviet Union
IEA	International Energy Agency
INOC	Iraq National Oil Company
IOCs	international oil companies
IPC	Iraq Petroleum Company

LTSC	Long Term Strategy Committee
mbpd	million barrels per day
MEC	Ministerial Executive Council
MIT	Massachusetts Institute of Technology
MPC	Mosul Petroleum Company
NATO	North Atlantic Treaty Organisation
NGL	natural gas liquids
NIOC	National Iranian Oil Company
NOCs	national oil companies
OAPEC	Organization of Arab Petroleum Exporting Countries
OECD	Organisation for Economic Co-operation and Development
OPEC	Organization of Petroleum Exporting Countries
PDVSA	Petróleos de Venezuela SA
p/b	per barrel of oil
PSA	Production Sharing Agreement
SNPA	Société Nationale des Pétroles d'Aquitaine
tbpd	thousand barrels per day
TPC	Turkish Petroleum Company
UNCTAD	United Nations Conference on Trade and Development
WAES	Workshop on Alternative Energy Strategies
WTI	West Texas Intermediate

Acknowledgements

My thanks and enormous appreciation go to my distinguished friends and Excellencies, listed below, to whom I am most grateful for having so kindly read my manuscript and made invaluable comments that were taken into account when drafting it.

My sincere thanks, therefore, for the very kind endorsement given me by His Excellency Sheikh Ahmed Zaki Yamani, former Minister of Petroleum and Mineral Resources for Saudi Arabia (1962–86), from 1989 founder and Chairman of the Centre for Global Energy Studies; for His Excellency Sheikh Ali Khalifa al-Sabah, former Minister of Oil for Kuwait 1978–90, former Finance Minister for Kuwait, and Chairman of Kuwait Petroleum Company, who took the trouble to make written observations chapter by chapter; for the very kind mention from Dr Alirio Parra, former Minister of Oil for Venezuela; for Dr Francisco Parra, former Secretary General of OPEC, who was very encouraging and helpful with his observations, and who was actively involved with OPEC's Long-Term Strategy Committee, chaired by H.E. Sheikh Yamani; for the very generous comments of Dr Daniel Yergin, Chairman and founder of IHS Cambridge Energy Research Associates, distinguished historian and Pulitzer Prize winner; for the helpful advice of Dr Abdul Amir al-Anbari, former Iraq Ambassador in France, UK and UN; for the perceptive comments of Dr Herman Franssen, President of International Energy Associates, Senior Research Fellow at the Center for Strategic and International Studies in Washington DC (serving also on the Energy and National Security Program and advisory board of Energy Intelligence); for the equally kind remarks of Dr Marcello Colitti, former Energy Advisor to Chairman of E.N.I. S.p.A and former Chairman of Ecofuel S.p.A. (of the E.N.I. group); for Dr Usameh Jamali of the Organisation of

Arab Petroleum Exporting Countries, who gave me excellent advice for my section on OAPEC; for Mr Mufid Mirza, CA, oil expert, for his very helpful comments on Iraqi oil politics; and for Dr Helga Graham, author and journalist, who in the first place encouraged me to write more about Iraq.

I must also record here my immense gratitude for the very generous time given by my personal assistant in research, Penelope Forbes (CGES Research Assistant). I am indebted to her for her dedication and skilful editing commitment, without which my book would have lost its momentum!

F.J.C.

Preface

Over the past four decades, few people have enjoyed a front-row seat at the development of the oil industry; even fewer people can narrate the story of this development better than Dr Fadhil Chalabi.

After attaining a law degree from the University of Baghdad, Dr Chalabi began his career amid an influx of intellectual ideas in 1950s Baghdad, when nationalism and the role of the state versus the dominance of 'imperialist' oil companies (arguments that prevailed in the capitals of many oil-producing countries) ignited the interest of young Iraqis in their oil resources. This also redirected Dr Chalabi's talents when, having obtained a scholarship to pursue his postgraduate studies in France, he began with economics but changed his focus to petroleum economics, on which he wrote his doctoral thesis, with particular reference to the history of the oil sector in Iraq.

Iraq in the 1960s was turbulent: there was one coup after another, and sometimes even one faction of one party turned against another faction of the same party. In this political environment he joined the Iraqi Ministry of Oil in Baghdad in various capacities, finally becoming Undersecretary for Oil. This led to his heavy involvement in formulating and discussing Iraq's oil policy, both domestically and internationally, as he represented Iraq on several OPEC committees, including the ever important OPEC's Economic Commission Board. It was while serving on the latter that he and I came into direct contact. We disagreed just as often as we agreed but, whether we agreed or not, we always went out together for a friendly dinner. Dr Chalabi's involvement with OPEC extended beyond representing Iraq to becoming OPEC's Deputy Secretary General and Acting Secretary General. Today, Dr Chalabi uses his extensive experience and knowledge to direct first-rate research at the Centre for Global Energy Studies, where he is Executive Director.

In the 1960s and the beginning of the 1970s, demand for OPEC's oil began to pick up vigorously as a result of weak oil prices and strong global growth. At the same time the situation in Iran under the Shah grew increasingly unstable. Looking for solutions to this unhealthy situation, Dr Chalabi, together with the late Dr Farraj (advisor to the Kuwaiti Ministry of Oil at that time), and a representative from Venezuela and I all met in Taif, Saudi Arabia under the chairmanship of Sheikh Ahmed Zaki Yamani. We feared that the sudden sharp and uncontrollable increase in oil prices in 1973 would prove unsustainable and lead inevitably to a serious decline in demand, which OPEC would be hard put to overcome.

We recommended gradually increasing oil prices in line with inflation and a factor reflecting growth in the world economy. But, alas, the Iranian Revolution in 1979 made nonsense of our recommendations and prices exploded again, leading to a sharp fall in demand for OPEC's oil, exactly as we had feared when we were in Taif. This was one of many critical episodes in the history of OPEC that Dr Chalabi witnessed first-hand and narrates in this book.

Unlike the rest of us in OPEC, Dr Chalabi's experience and knowledge, while discharging his responsibilities as both an Iraqi and an OPEC official, came under intense scrutiny and involved his own personal sacrifice. While we enjoyed the support of our national governments, he, on the other hand, as the Iraq Ministry's Undersecretary for Oil, had to learn to tread warily to avoid suspicion and brutal treatment from Saddam, whose ruthless intolerance of any divergence from his own opinion I witnessed on my many visits to Iraq. On occasions Dr Chalabi was unfairly suspected of serving an 'anti-nationalist agenda' simply because of his courage in speaking up and standing his ground.

Serving as Deputy Secretary General and Acting Secretary General of OPEC, he had to lead and mediate discussions among 13 oil ministers, some of them completely innocent of any knowledge of economics or familiarity with the oil industry. This was not without frustrations, as during such meetings some of these oil ministers came with a predetermined agenda set by their governments and, lacking the ability to defend these predetermined positions, tended to accuse anyone like Dr Chalabi of betrayal, simply because, no matter how logical his argument, it expressed a viewpoint that differed from theirs.

I will stop here and let you enjoy the history of OPEC oil and oil policies, as told by Dr Chalabi.

His Excellency Sheikh Ali Khalifa al-Sabah
Former Oil Minister of Kuwait (from 1978 to 1990);
former Finance Minister for Kuwait, and Chairman
of Kuwait Petroleum Company.

Introduction

As the year 1973 drew to a close the world was stunned by the news that the price of oil would increase by 400 per cent from its level of only four months earlier. This shattering news was announced from Tehran, where ministerial representatives of the member countries of OPEC (Organisation of Petroleum Exporting Countries) had gathered under the auspices of the Shah of Iran,[1] who pushed hardest for this pricing decision – which was ironic given that, at the time, he was considered the darling of the West.

Barely two months prior to that fateful meeting, ministers of the Arab petroleum-producing countries had met in Kuwait and decided, in support of Egypt's war with Israel, to reduce oil production as a means of exerting political pressure on America's pro-Israel policy. This decision provoked an immediate reaction not only from the world oil market, where prices rose dramatically, but also among Western political circles, given their deep concern for the security of oil supplies. It was amid these geopolitical tensions that the new Tehran price decision went ahead.

Marking the end of a long era of cheap oil, an era unruffled by price volatility, these two historical landmarks heralded the advent of expensive oil and a price volatility inherent with oil becoming commoditised, politicised and engulfed in an aura of geopolitical sensitivity (see Figures I.1 and I.2). Before these events of 1973 the world had scarcely heard of OPEC, which was not renowned as an oil price decision-maker. This is because the oil industry had been dominated for decades by seven major international oil companies (IOCs) by means of the concessions they held in the Middle East oil-producing countries, especially in the Gulf where the bulk of world oil reserves lie. After the collapse of the Ottoman Empire, from the early 1920s, Middle East oil was treated as the spoils of war, divisible by the First World War allies, Britain and France. With the USA exerting political pressure under the guise of its Open Door policy, American oil companies soon joined them.

Middle East oil was soon parcelled out in the form of long-term concessions to seven major oil companies, known as the Seven Sisters,[2] which included Anglo-Persian Oil (later British Petroleum [BP]), Royal Dutch Shell, and the American companies Standard Oil of New Jersey (later to become Esso then Exxon), Mobil, Gulf, SOCAL (Chevron) and Texaco. Later they were joined by Compagnie Française des Pétroles (CFP/Total), which became the cartel's 'eighth' sister. With their interwoven interests, these major oil companies established oil consortia (each consortium comprising two or more holding companies) and enjoyed exclusive concessions in a system that excluded competition.

An example of the Seven Sisters' concessionary model can be seen, par excellence, in the operations of the Iraq Petroleum Company (IPC). The IPC's holding company (set up as a consortium owned by some of the Seven Sisters) was committed to an investment plan for crude oil production in the area exclusively covered by the concession. In each case, the consortium would plan production targets relative to the shareholders' requirements for oil refineries and product distribution. In this 'upstream' phase of the industry the Seven Sisters established a system of close co-operation in which the extraction of crude oil involved nothing but inter-company exchanges. If any company within the consortium found itself short of crude oil it could buy from sister companies with a crude surfeit, in excess of their refinery requirements. Beyond these inter-company exchanges, the notion of a free market for buying and selling crude did not exist. Each company had its own downstream operations, i.e. refining and distributing networks so that its share of crude oil was transported to its own refineries.

Confining production and trading to exchanges within such a controlled network (with full integration in both crude oil and refined products) had correlative benefits that balanced each company's needs and, by the same token, maintained an overall market balance of supply and demand. There was no place for imbalance and price fluctuation. The companies simply 'posted' prices in Platt's Oilgram News bulletins, not for actual trading but to serve as a tax-reference price for the calculation of oil revenues paid to their host countries.

Such a system was made possible only by the long-term exclusive concessions granted by the host countries and the political weight of the major powers. This is why, as far as the host countries were concerned, the concession system could never be dissociated from a colonial-styled domination, which could be described as colonial plunder. The oil companies in the producing countries were resented as virtual 'states within a state' and many viewed with suspicion the oil concession system, regarded as an instrument for entrenching the transfer of wealth to the rich, aggravating already incongruous social disparities.

The first spark of 'oil nationalism' to spread among other Middle East oil-producing countries came from Iran, when Dr Mohammed Mosaddegh (elected Prime Minister of Iran in 1951) became the first architect of oil nationalisation in March 1951. The nationalisation measure proved abortive in conditions (to be discussed) that facilitated his removal from power by a *coup d'état* in 1953. Nevertheless, the very name of 'Mosaddegh' became semantically loaded: synonymous with heroic liberation. It inspired, ten years later, the stand-off between the Iraqi government and the Iraq Petroleum Company, prompting unilateral government legislation to recover for the state 99.5 per cent of the territory operated by the oil concessions. This will be discussed at length in Chapter 4, which also describes how Iraq, in spearheading the demise of the oil concessions, paved the way for OPEC's success and for its subsequent policies. Iraq's economy would pay a heavy price for promoting idealism over economic expedience. In this way, relative to other OPEC member countries, Iraq would become a net loser in terms of its market share.

Given Iraq's stand-off with the oil companies and similar developments in Libya and Algeria, it was soon evident that fundamental changes would swiftly dismantle the structure inherited from the colonial era. Meanwhile the major oil companies were quick to perceive investment opportunities outside the Middle East and Venezuela, especially with the price shock of 1973, which enabled the companies to take advantage of OPEC's new high-price regime, as it provided for them sudden viability for diversifying their investments into high-cost, *non*-OPEC oil areas. Hitherto, under the old low-price regime, these new areas were economically unfeasible, but with high prices they could prove lucrative.

A new era of expensive oil became a permanent feature, not only for the oil-producing countries, who were keen to liberate themselves from the old system, but also for the IOCs who viewed high prices favourably as a means of generating huge profits with which to reinvest in new, high-cost oil areas, such as the North Sea and Alaska. Without high prices, the companies would have been squeezed between mounting political pressure from the oil-producing countries and meagre investment opportunities elsewhere.

Seen in this light, it is highly unlikely that the momentous decision taken in Tehran in December 1973 to increase the oil price by 400 per cent came entirely out of the blue. Very few people were able to grasp this concept at the time and instead the assumption was that OPEC alone was to blame for the price shock. Outside the oil industry, many regarded the newly empowered OPEC as an alien phenomenon, whose soaring prices could presage galloping inflation and threaten havoc with the world economy. This alarm set the scene for OPEC's emergence as a powerful agent of change in the global economy. OPEC suddenly attracted media attention worldwide, as everyone wanted to know more about this 'ominous' organisation.

Apart from those in the industry, few realised that OPEC had been established 13 years earlier. Unaware of its existence at a time when the major oil companies were still in control of the oil industry, people were now keen to identify the implications of OPEC and analyse its motives. Media-inspired myths and legends abounded, ranging from the fearful concept of OPEC as a powerful oil cartel, posing a dark threat to the world economy, to fanciful depictions of a bunch of Bedouins sitting on oil wells, who, having taken over the oil industry, sought gigantic windfall profits that would transform their lifestyle from camel-riding to chauffeur-driven Rolls Royces and private jets.

OPEC's swift reversal of the old order gave rise to the question, frequently asked retrospectively, of how OPEC was able to defy the West without some degree of acquiescence from the dominant forces in the oil industry. Given their lack of serious opposition to the oil price shock, there is perhaps reason to suppose that a tacit understanding may have existed with the companies, without which OPEC would surely have encountered some obstruction to its swift and radical action, which in turn precipitated the sudden shift of IOC investments into those regions outside OPEC that were prohibitively expensive to develop under the old, low-price regime.

The transfer of oil supply management from the companies to OPEC brought fundamental changes to the structure of the world oil industry, in particular because oil became a primary commodity offered on a free market and hence was subject to price volatility. It was that shift of supply management to OPEC's national oil companies (NOCs) that gave rise to an inherent imbalance between supply and demand. The market is always hypersensitive to any change in supply and demand indications, such as the movement of stock build-up or expectations of world economic growth; and because of market sensitivity to geopolitical issues any negative geopolitical event has an immediate impact on the short-term demand/supply balance, and therefore impels market prices upwards. With the oil industry characterised by price instability, high oil prices became a perennial feature of OPEC's system. The spectacle of price volatility agitating the markets has become a market norm.

This contrasts sharply with the old concessionary regime's full integration of the oil industry, which systematically secured crude oil supplies by means of planned production that conformed with consumption requirements (as reflected at pump stations everywhere in the consuming countries). This system ensured a perfect balance between oil supply and demand on the world market outside the USA and the USSR. In the event of any major supply interruption, as during the Iranian Mosaddegh crisis, the oil companies averted market disruption by means of their self-adjusting integrated system that filled supply gaps by increasing production from other Middle East countries under their collective control, notably Iraq and Kuwait.

However, new developments led to the de-integration of the oil industry, with crude oil no longer planned in tandem with the variation in market requirements. OPEC was soon unable to cope with world market variations in supply and demand. If it had continued to lead the market in price formation, modifying conditions to minimise price instability, OPEC could have resolved the problem to some extent. But the chief impediment to this lay not only in the heterogeneity of OPEC's composition and its difficulty in reconciling the interests of its multiple members, but also in its lack of long-term vision or strategy. Above all, there has always been strong pressure within OPEC for achieving higher prices as a means of maximising oil revenues in the short run.

For five years after the 1973 events there were internal tensions within OPEC. Iran, joining a group of OPEC hawks, always pressed for higher prices, but was opposed by Saudi Arabia's call for moderation. The moment of truth for the high-price-mongers came with Iran's Khomeini revolution in 1979, as this unleashed a market spiral that swept aside any voices of moderation or economic rationale. Instead of considering the high price spikes as temporary phenomena, OPEC's hardliners pushed for the huge price escalations to be incorporated in OPEC's official price. By January 1981 OPEC's price had thus increased 12-fold from its mid-1973 level. This became known as 'the second oil price shock'.

Ignoring its moderate doves, OPEC members were by and large unaware of the consequences of these exorbitant prices, which simply encouraged consumers (especially in Western Europe and Japan) to conserve energy by resorting to more efficient energy use and by shifting to alternatives, in particular natural gas and nuclear power. Above all, as explained, the high prices led to massive investments in non-OPEC oil, made economically feasible by the high-price regime. It was not long before this competition from new oil impacted on world demand for OPEC oil, which was soon in sharp decline.

Before OPEC's NOCs assumed full management of their oil industry operations, the organisation had enjoyed a dominant market share of the world oil trade, and had a strong influence in market price formation. But new, competing, non-OPEC oil resulted in OPEC's market share of the oil trade falling to less than half. Instead of considering a logical solution to this problem, like reducing its prices, OPEC resorted to defending its high price through constant reductions in the volume of its output, by means of a quota system. This has served only to lose even more of its market share to the benefit of other oil and energy producers.

With this competition and erosion of OPEC's former lead in the market, the organisation surmised that its only leverage was its swift response in cutting production in order to defend the oil price whenever market conditions exert *downward* pressure on the price. Conversely, in the face of prevailing market conditions, including geopolitical events, that force the oil price *upward*, OPEC is typically slow to counteract this with increased output – so that the spiralling price is not stabilised or brought back to its previous levels. In this way, OPEC's failure both to manage supplies and define an optimum price with the aim of seriously achieving it, means that price movements tend to be constantly upward or else volatile. Hence, instead of being the price leader, OPEC's role has become confined to a 'crisis management' of the oil price, while it neglects long-term strategy.

Constant oil price volatility has, in turn, spawned an excess of speculation on the futures market, a trend in hedging that has only served to fuel the price volatility. Moreover, encouraged by the decline of OPEC's share in the world market, it is hedging that now plays a major role in market price formation. Stock markets dealing with a huge amount of hedge funds are sensitive to the market perceptions of buyers and sellers, and hypersensitive in anticipating geopolitical events and consequent oil supply interruptions in one country or another. These conditions force OPEC to follow the market rather than conduct it.

Over the past 35 years, with OPEC's inability to stabilise prices, the organisation has been unable to achieve the very *raison d'être* of its formation in Baghdad on 14 September 1960, when it was clearly stated in its first resolution (1.I.3) 'that Members shall study and formulate a system to ensure the stabilisation of prices by, among other means, the regulation of production, with due regard to the interests of the producing and of the consuming nations'.

OPEC's inefficient management of its production, stemming from its early failure to cope with market requirements, has made price turbulence an inherent factor. Latterly the price has been volatile, but dramatic market turbulence occurred when the OPEC basket price soared from $25 per barrel in May 2003 to over $140 in July 2008, with the West Texas Intermediate (WTI) reaching $147 per barrel on 11 July 2008, before the market crashed and prices plummeted in the last quarter of 2008 until early 2009.

This phenomenon in commodity trading arose because of OPEC's *two successive production cuts* despite the huge surge in oil demand and prices from 2004 onwards, caused by unprecedented strong demand-growth from Asia, in particular China. Ironically, OPEC showed a belated willingness to raise its production levels but only when it was already too late – as the unsustainably high oil price led to a dramatic price collapse, exacerbated by the world financial crisis, which began in the USA in September 2008, before spreading globally.

Having had to live with a 'third oil price shock' of almost $150 per barrel in July 2008, consumers en masse became wary and acutely conscious of saving energy and shifting to alternative fuels, a factor that will lead to a further reduction in the share of oil in the world energy mix, diminishing OPEC's oil-market share still further. While the increasingly competitive oil market further impeded OPEC's ability to steer the oil price, in the end it is OPEC's own pricing policies that have led to a dramatic fall in its share in world oil trade and at the same time propelled a radical transformation in the world energy mix.

Despite all the problems that OPEC faces with its loss of market share and failure to stabilise the market, the general public's abiding perception of OPEC is still as a powerful 'oil cartel' – which is, in essence, a myth. In this book I try to separate myth from reality, describing the interior process of OPEC's decision-making from the vantage point of an 'insider' who has lived with the *reality* of OPEC through historically crucial years. My account of OPEC, the oil industry and oil policies is interwoven with economic analysis and forecasts, history and also 'behind-the scenes' anecdotes that describe major events and the people involved, without political or personal bias.

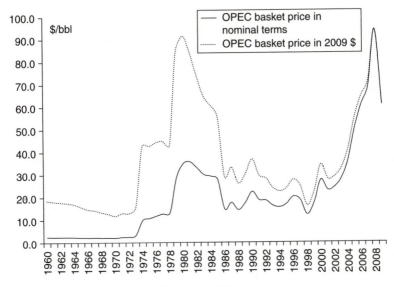

Figure I.1   Oil prices in nominal and real terms: 1960 to 2009
Source: CGES.

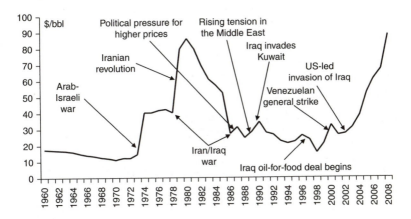

Figure I.2   Geopolitics and oil prices
Source: CGES.

1

The path that led me to the oil industry

I graduated in 1951 from Baghdad University's Law School, where several Egyptian and Iraqi professors taught after completing their postgraduate studies in France. This was primarily because of a post-war Francophile cultural orientation that influenced the humanities in particular. The law degree curriculum required two courses of economics, and my tutor, observing my keen interest, encouraged me to obtain an economics postgraduate degree in France, which was exactly what I had dreamt of achieving. This was not in line with the then prevailing academic opinion in Iraq, which held that the best economics degrees were from prestigious British or American universities. Degrees from Continental Europe, including France, did not enjoy the same esteem.

My motivation for studying in France came from my own great interest in French culture. Since my early teens I had been a passionate reader of Arabic versions of the French classics, also the works of Egyptian writers describing their experiences in Paris. A particular book, *A Bird from the Orient*, by the great Egyptian writer, Tawfiq al-Hakim, narrating his Parisian life, inspired my adolescent imagination and compelled in me a determination to experience life in that enchanting city. The book contained a quotation of Alfred de Musset, which had moved me so much that on my arrival in Paris among the first things I did was to visit the statue of this distinguished dramatist, novelist and poet, beneath which were engraved his own words: 'Rien ne nous rend grand qu' une grande douleur': nothing renders us as great as (or ennobles us more than) great suffering. Even with music, despite my homage to Vienna and Berlin as the greatest musical centres, I tended to look to Paris, especially when I enrolled at the Baghdad Academy of Music to take evening lessons in the cello with a French tutor, Monsieur

Taurer. Unable to realise my Parisian aspirations instantly after my graduation from law school (my family's finances being such as to necessitate a contribution on my part), I remained for a further five years in Baghdad, studying French language, literature, music and pursuing my intellectual and political interests.

This was an era when a keen, young, Iraqi generation strove eagerly for knowledge, and there was a stimulating intellectual life, inspired by Baghdad's very lively, contemporary, literary and artistic scene. From the end of the Second World War until the late 1960s Baghdad was a cauldron of political and ideological movements and flourished as a dynamic centre for the arts, with modern Arab poetry, masterpieces in classical Arab poetry and significant literary works in the genres of both novel and short story. While the Baghdad School of Painting and Sculpture was the forerunner of modern art in the Middle East, Baghdad also assembled the first philharmonic orchestra in the region and produced the most gifted performers of the Arab üd, the ancient forerunner of the lute. Study of this instrument at the city's üd school progressed enormously with new techniques from an eminent musician, Prince Haider of the Royal family, a fine cellist, who applied Western musical methods to this originally oriental instrument. Meanwhile Iraq's fine art, without becoming dissociated from its Iraqi roots, fell under the spell of French and post-expressionist German schools, while modern Arab poetry was enormously influenced by the great modern European or American poets, especially T.S. Eliot. For younger generations, reading and discussing world literary masterpieces became an obsession, and in certain Baghdad coffee shops – the Café Suisse and the Café Brazil – Iraqi intellectuals gathered to discuss political issues and the philosophy behind literary or artistic movements, such as Sartre's existentialism. As they were avid readers of Western literature, notably Tolstoy and Dostoevsky, it is not surprising that Baghdad soon became a melting pot of Western ideas and philosophy, including that of Karl Marx. Even centre-left democrats were influenced by the British Labour Party and its Fabian roots. Such was my generation's enthusiasm for Western culture that eminent personalities from abroad were in constant demand, invited to give lectures to which multitudes rushed to secure seats. I recall one day the great French Arabist, Louis Masignon, giving a lecture on sophism, and the hall was packed from top to bottom with his eager audience, and many people willingly stood at the back, from where it was almost impossible to hear. Influenced by so much Western political thought, Baghdad became a hub of political turmoil in its search for democracy and freedom. I became involved in all these activities, without, however, forgetting my dream of going to France for my postgraduate studies.

The prevalence of this pro-Western outward thinking, so typical of that period, had been indirectly fostered by the post-Ottoman era of strong economic and social development, during which Iraq became a unique case among the oil-producing countries in using its oil revenues rationally for investment and development. Following the 1952 profit-sharing agreement with the oil companies, which led to a substantial increase in oil revenues, the Iraq government created a Development Fund to which 70 per cent of oil revenues were channelled for exclusive expenditure on development projects. The Ministry of Development acquired the best Iraqi expertise for a style of management radically different from that inherited from the Ottoman era, and any expenditure from this Fund was strictly subject to the approval of the Development Board, chaired by the Prime Minister. No other OPEC member country applied this rational and unique method for allocating oil income. It became also an efficient means of preventing over-expenditure on consumer requirements, instead assigning the bulk of oil revenues for modernising infrastructure, including roads, dams and education.

When I observed the decadence that crept into Iraqi politics a decade later, as a consequence of the reckless politics that regrettably came to characterise the new regime after the revolution of 14 July 1958, and compared the progressive Iraq I knew of 60 years ago with what became of my country under Saddam Hussein (and after him), it revealed just how the civilising process is capable of regressing into barbarism, even in a country that in ancient times reached an apotheosis of civilisation.

Meanwhile, back in 1956, the great day at last came when I was granted a two-year scholarship for a postgraduate degree, for which I needed to obtain two higher *diplômes d'études superieures*: one in political economy and the other in economic sciences. For this stage of my study I chose the University of Poitiers, as one of France's most prestigious universities, not too far from Paris.

Poitiers, forming as it did part of the old French tradition and – like Tours – having been an ancient cultural centre of France, its university is one of the oldest cultural and theological centres. It is therefore not surprising that Poitiers French is held to rank among the best. (While resident in Poitiers, my first son was born, and given the unusual Arabic name, 'Talik', meaning 'the one who is unbound', which I borrowed from Percy Bysshe Shelley's great lyrical drama *Prometheus Unbound*.)

The great Battle of Poitiers in AD 732 was, of course, decisive in preventing the spread of the Arab–Islamic civilisation to the rest of Europe, after the Arabs and Moors had captured Spain and Portugal. As Charles Martel drove the Arab army out of France back into Spain, Poitiers for the French came to represent an instance of *gloire* in their history. As this was a turning point in reversing the great wave of Arab Muslim expansion, Poitiers represents for the Arabs one of the blackest moments in Islamic history; and before I had left for France, a friend of my father, discovering my intended place of study, exclaimed: 'of all the cities in France you have chosen Poitiers, which is associated with Arab defeat!'

Another reason for choosing France for my PhD was that, at the time, the French university system had a greater degree of flexibility (compared with its Anglo-Saxon counterparts), in that it permitted law graduates to switch to postgraduate studies in economics within a relatively short period, and this saved me time. For foreign students the minimum time for two diplomas was three or even four years, but fortunately, thanks to proficiency in the French language and also knowledge of English (in which the best economics literature was to be found), I was able to get the two diplomas in less than two years. According to the terms of my scholarship, I had to return to Iraq to work for the Ministry of the Economy for a period of two years before I could acquire a further scholarship for my PhD degree. Before returning to Iraq, my plan had been to continue my studies in London at the LSE, as by then I had two diplomas in economics.

This plan was interrupted by Iraq's political revolution on 14 July 1958, in which Iraq's royalist regime was toppled by a *coup d'état* staged by an army officer, Abdul al-Karim Qassim. The monarchy of King Faisal[1] was deposed and replaced with a republic, in the establishment of which the political left played a major role. At the time, I found this event inspiring and felt motivated into returning to Iraq to work for the Ministry of the Economy. Although I never actually enrolled in a political party, left or right, I was generally sympathetic to leftist movements as they represented the only effective opposition to the monarchical regime. During my two years in Baghdad before returning to France, my position in the Ministry gave me some valuable experience participating in trade negotiations with government delegates of various countries, and I was involved in implementing the new regime's economic policies, including the increase of trade with socialist countries which, under the old royalist regime, had been entirely excluded.

My second departure for Paris was in early October 1960, and on arrival I asked to meet with the best and most renowned of economics professors in France, Maurice Byé, to whom I professed my hope for his supervision. Initially he accepted my chosen topic, which (in compliance with my contract with the Baghdad Ministry of Economy) was 'Iraq's foreign trade and balance of payments'. The three-month period he gave me for writing the first chapter I spent studying various theories of foreign trade and balance of payments problems in developing countries, reading extensively English literature on the subject. Then, leaving my first chapter with the Professor before proceeding any further, I went to see him on the appointed day to discuss my work. His grim comment came like a thunderbolt, telling me that although I had made a serious effort to follow what had already been written, I had brought nothing new or original to the topic to qualify me for writing a PhD thesis in economics. He added that he could not continue with me if I insisted on this topic and that I would be better off looking for another supervisory professor.

Bearing in mind that my scholarship was for a two-year duration only and that I had only one and a half years left, and that changing one's professors would be seen as a sign of rejection by the professor for an inadequate performance, I asked Professor Byé's advice about what to do. It was then that he urged me to write on oil because, as an oil country, Iraq's balance of payments depends almost entirely on its oil revenue. He then added, by way of encouragement, that what stood in my favour was the very limited amount of material that had been written in France on oil and that he could infer from what I had so far written that my English reading was at least competent. But his suggestion startled me, as I knew absolutely nothing about Iraq's oil affairs, which were shrouded in secrecy; and those privileged to work in oil (within the Ministry of the Economy) were attached exclusively to the Minister. Others in the Ministry of Economy knew absolutely nothing about their own country's oil affairs. Not surprisingly I was at a loss, but the professor cut my prevarication short by saying 'either you write on oil or look for another supervisor'. I replied without a moment's more hesitation that I would indeed write on oil. I feared it could involve great personal risk, but I preferred this to having to search for another professor. Despite my grave misgivings at having to embark on such an inscrutable topic where Iraq was concerned, the adrenalin caused by the pressure of having only a short time left in which to complete my new thesis created in me a degree of focus, zest and inspiration, which helped my research.

The first book I ever read on the subject of oil was a French translation of Paul Frankel's *The Essentials of the Petroleum Industry*, an impressively well-researched work published in 1946 in the UK. My next was a book written in French that was influenced by a famous report submitted to the US Senate in 1952: *The International Petroleum Cartel*, which explained in ample detail the interlinking of the major oil companies' interests, depicted as typical of an international cartel, the existence of which in the USA would have been regarded as a breach of US Anti-Trust Laws. For this reason US President Eisenhower had intervened to prevent this report being published. Nevertheless it was later released and caused a big stir, especially as the act of writing the report appears to have been politically motivated by opposition to the American oil companies' vast interests in Middle East Arab countries.

Naturally I obtained a copy of this volume and read it with a consummate eagerness, but it neither provided nor inspired any original material on oil itself, and was useful only for background knowledge. Just by chance I had the opportunity of gaining access to a government library attached to the French Ministry of Industry's Département de l'Hydrocarbure, which dealt with oil affairs and was near my residence in the Montparnasse quarter. I met the director there and explained my predicament, and he kindly assisted by granting me access to their departmental library. I felt a great surge of relief, like an oppressive weight suddenly lifted from me. I was able to read its many useful publications and reports written in English. The lady in charge, whose namesake was the great French composer, Poulenc, discovering I was from the Arab world (of which she had previous experience), kindly helped in allowing me to take literature home for study at the weekends. Stirred by a keen passion to explore all there was to know about oil, I exhausted all the possibilities of that library, which gave me new horizons that I could only have dreamt of. I also found the Centre National de Recherche Scientifique (the CNRS) to be another source for world petroleum information. It was there that I discovered 'the unknown' and was able to write the first part of my dissertation on the structural changes in the international petroleum industry, the weakening of the major oil companies' domination of the industry and the dawning of a new era towards a relatively competitive market structure.

When I took this first 250 pages to my supervisor, he, glancing at the volume of work, commented encouragingly, and asked me to meet him two weeks later at the Conseil Sociale et Economique (a government unit), where he was an adviser on foreign trade issues, including oil affairs. On arrival I waited anxiously for the professor, who was in a meeting. An hour later he came towards me in the reception area, his face radiant with happiness. 'Monsieur Chalabi,' he beamed, 'what you have provided so far is very important and virtually sufficient to grant you the degree. You have made a compelling contribution to French literature on oil. I congratulate you.' I could hardly believe my ears when I heard this accolade and expressed my gratitude, then explained to the professor that I must work on two further sections: one about OPEC (founded in Baghdad a year earlier, 1960) and the problems inherent with the pricing of oil; the other about Iraq's oil industry – to form the third and final part of the thesis. From his standpoint of advisor to the Conseil and with his knowledge of Iraq's great oil potential, he made an observation that deeply influenced my approach to the oil industry: 'Your country has an abundance of oil. Is it not in your own interests, as Iraqis, to develop this vast wealth and sell oil at a lower price? You would then derive the large amount of foreign currency that your country needs for its economic and social development, which would then take off to a degree far beyond that of other Middle East countries.'

To his memorable words I replied that the companies had low-ered the price of Middle East oil, even before the profit-sharing agreement of the early 1950s, which had changed the basis of the posted price for Middle East oil, making it far cheaper than US oil. It is known (I continued) how the companies initially fixed the posted price of Middle East oil as equivalent to the price of American oil, minus the freight rate. In calculating the latter, the companies cre-ated what is referred to as a watershed point, for which Naples was chosen initially, lying as it does between the Middle East and the United States' eastern seaboard. The companies then moved this towards London then back to New York. If one deducts the freight cost for this greater distance, one finds the price of Middle East oil relatively very low. To this the professor replied that on the basis of Iraq's oil being so cheap to produce, it was in my country's interests to secure as many markets as possible, commensurate with Iraq's vast reserves.

These wise words uttered by Professor Byé (who sadly died pre-maturely of cancer) still ring in my ears today. When I see what has happened to Iraqi oil, I recall the many studies, after mine, that revived the old saying that Iraq sits on a lake of oil; which is no myth or whimsical *façon de parler*, as studies have repeatedly shown that Iraq has virtually the same oil potential as Saudi Arabia. When I look at Iraq's recent history I am reminded of irresponsible political measures that have hampered the expansion of Iraq's oil industry – all a result of political out-bidding by over-ambitious politicians, always eager to prove that wresting the oil industry from the hands of oil companies serves their country's best interests.

Returning to the era of my PhD, when I gave Professor Byé my next tranche, which concerned oil pricing, he again remarked that this was sufficient with which to grant the degree; but an insatia-ble curiosity spurred me to write a third part focusing on Iraq's oil affairs. Realising how much I had learned about my country's oil industry, I was now leading on from what had already been writ-ten in English. Then came one of the most joyous days of my life, 18 December 1962, thanks to the unexpected praise heaped upon me by the *juri* (examining board) in their assessment of my degree, not only by the board's chairman, my supervisor, but also by two other professors, especially Professor Bartolli who was particularly impressed by my analysis of the extent to which Europe, especially

Italy, lacked access to the Middle East's cheap oil, and how this had led the Italian Mattei to inflict the first fracture in the hegemony of the major oil companies, who had been providing Italy with more expensive oil – until the Italian State Oil Company (ENI) offered better terms to the oil-producing host-countries in the Middle East and Africa. The examining board granted my work the highest accolade with 'très bien retenue' and it was sent on to the arbitration committee to be nominated among the best dissertations of the year. CNRS offered to publish it at their own expense, but as I had to leave Paris for Baghdad on 1 February 1963, there was no time to remain in Paris long enough to meet the CNRS's terms and conditions for publication. Meanwhile a letter offering an interview arrived from Texaco France, to which I did not reply as my return to Baghdad was uppermost in my mind. A friend of mine saw this letter and was amazed when I failed to reply, passing up – as he pointed out – such a promising opportunity, the chance of a good job in Paris. I told him that my ambition above all else was to work in oil-rich Iraq, especially as the Iraqi government was about to form a national oil company.

It was ironic that a mere six days after my departure from France and arrival in Baghdad, a violent *coup d'état* was staged by the Ba'ath Party on 8 February 1963, during which General Abdul al-Karim Qassim was killed and all left-wing sympathisers were subjected to a McCarthy-style witch hunt. I was not a communist, but was considered a leftist sympathiser. Ten days later I found myself arrested while at the Ministry of Economy, from where I was marched to the 'security premises' of the intelligence police. Here I was held prisoner for four days, a grim ordeal with more than 50 captives crammed into a room designed to hold only a few. Later it was a relief to find ourselves transferred to the Baghdad Central Prison where our miserable conditions were alleviated by the luxury of proper prison facilities: water, relatively clean conveniences, even a shower! We were joined by a crowd of intellectuals, university professors, scholars, former ministers and high-level government officials. After six weeks in this more 'pleasant' prison, I was released once it was ascertained that I was not a communist.

Upon my release, I was able to rejoin the Ministry of Economy, but conditions had greatly deteriorated. My office status had been downgraded. I was confined to a small room with no work, and no one dared visit me for fear of being suspected of left-wing sympathies. I continued biding my time at the Ministry reading until suddenly there was another military coup, which ousted the Ba'ath Party. While I was seated in my isolated office, the door suddenly opened and the new minister, Mr Aziz al-Hafedh, strode in, accompanied by the administration officer. As we had not met before, he asked me questions and I told him I had finished my studies at French universities. The minister (a graduate from the UK in chartered accountancy) expressed surprise to find that, as a graduate from France, I was reading a British journal, *The Economist*. I replied that I was interested in both languages, and explained that I was reading as I had no work, having been stripped of my responsibilities for political reasons – as the administration officer accompanying the Minister knew perfectly well.

It was at this time that the United Nations established a new agency, the United Nations Conference on Trade and Development (UNCTAD) specifically to deal with emerging economies, referred to at that time as 'Third World issues'. All its documents were sent to Iraq's Ministry of the Economy which was in charge of foreign trade. I had enough time to read and summarise in Arabic all UNCTAD's numerous reports dealing with development and various aspects of trade in the developing countries. I also made recommendations as to the position Iraq should take in the conference. My work fortunately seemed to impress the new minister, who normally showed disdain towards economists from French universities, and he seemed even surprised to find an economics graduate from France who had a good capacity for economic analysis. My relations with the Minister strengthened over time and I became his de facto advisor, to the resentment of more senior staff.

Meanwhile, when Iraq was setting up its national oil company, an Iraqi petroleum engineer was appointed its director, whose name was Ghanem Uqaili, with whom I was acquainted from the days when he had been seconded to OPEC in Geneva, before the organisation moved its headquarters to Vienna. As I was in the throes of finishing the final part of my thesis, it occurred to me to discuss various aspects with some OPEC officials, including the Venezuelan, Dr Francisco Parra (with whom I later had a very good friendship). To this end I met Mr Uqaili in Geneva where we discussed Iraq's oil industry in the context of my thesis, and when he became director of the new state-owned Iraq National Oil Company (INOC) I met him again and put myself forward as a candidate for the company. After Uqaili had spoken to the board of directors about my case, he was very courteous to me but explained that despite being aware of my competence the decision was one of rejection 'based entirely on political grounds'. I later learnt that my name had been rejected by the board members because I was still suspected of being a communist. There was a very strange political atmosphere in Iraq at this time, as it was considered that any person who was in the least intellectually active must be of a leftist political persuasion. Even if you became simply a *friend* of a Marxist you were immediately branded as such. If you published an article in any of the other party's newspapers – those of the nationalist movement, for example – then you were equally branded and assumed to be a partisan. If one dared, after 1958, to talk of any positive aspect of the royal regime, one was immediately mistaken for a royalist sympathiser or a reactionary. This type of branding was typically adopted by those who feared the threat of competition from certain individuals.

It was at that precise moment that I decided I must leave Iraq. To this end I applied for a post in UNCTAD through the United Nations office in Baghdad, and to my pleasant surprise a letter arrived from the UN Headquarters in New York, asking me to send a copy of my PhD thesis. I sent my only copy, asking them to return it to me afterwards. It did not take more than a few months to receive a letter from the UN Headquarters offering me the job of economics officer in Geneva in UNCTAD, which it was agreed I would commence in October 1966.

To begin with I welcomed my new post in Geneva as a great reprieve, a respite from the politically tense atmosphere of Iraq, as well as a meaningful event in my life. However, although I was motivated and worked very hard, gradually I began to feel that the UN provided no intellectual challenge or stimulus, as most of the reports one had to write were descriptive, requiring no analysis of ideas on policy recommendations. A feeling of frustration crept up on me when I began to observe so many people of various nationalities who had no real work to speak of but were there simply because of a geographical quota system.

Being involved in the primary commodities division, I passed much of my time researching and writing about commodities including petroleum; but I found the information on oil consumption, production and trade to be limited and basic: adequate only for someone with no information on the subject. One day I went to see the Division's second-in-command, who was from the USA, and asked him why UNCTAD did not discuss such matters as the pricing of oil, given that the agency was founded with the aim of improving trade terms for Third World countries and primary commodities exports. I added that trade terms for oil were deteriorating in real value: its prices, having been reduced twice, were now frozen; while the prices of manufactured goods imported into the oil-producing countries were rising, thus causing adverse trade terms for the oil exporters. As my words fell on his unattuned ears, the man grew surprised and then quite resentful. He replied abruptly that this was not the required business, that we should not be interfering with such sensitive issues and that oil prices were a matter for the oil companies.

Here was an instance that confirmed my belief that working in the UN could end up as meaningless, lacking as it did any infiltration of new ideas. But my UN salary was far higher than my income had been in Iraq, my family and I found life in Geneva very pleasant, we liked our comfortable apartment and agreeable neighbours. (On our floor there was a Russian, also working in the same UN agency. He and his wife were very fond of my younger son, Jafar, who, with his dark hair and alert eyes, was very popular among the children there, especially with his natural talent for mimicry.) With our family feeling so settled, my wife and I were in no hurry to leave.

Then, towards the end of 1967, I received a letter from my former minister in Baghdad, Mr Shawaf, who, having become a personal friend, took me into his confidence about sudden big changes in Iraq's oil industry. He urged me to return as he felt I could do well taking up the post of Director General of Oil Affairs in the Oil Ministry. He explained there had been a political 'purge' in which most senior people had been replaced. This was because negotiations between the government and the oil companies had been called off by certain politicians and the military (as will be discussed in detail in Chapter 4).

This post that he recommended had been held by Mr Abdullah Ismail, an influential man in Baghdad, who was now accused of being a British spy by the Soviet TASS news agency, in a report made by the famous double agent, Kim Philby – who now fled to Moscow from his base in Beirut. In Baghdad this gave the pretext for a thorough pro-Nasser 'purge', forcing the old senior staff to resign and be replaced with a set of pro-Egypt people. A new oil minister was appointed, an outspoken pro-Nasserite; a Mr al-Jadr was appointed president of the new state-owned INOC; while my friend, Dr Hassib, became a very influential member of its Board of Directors.

When I read this astonishing letter from Shawaf, I found myself on the horns of a dilemma. I was torn between accepting the offer in Iraq on the one hand and, on the other, remaining in Geneva with job security yet professional mediocrity. Whenever I sought advice, I was told I would be mad to leave Geneva and the UN for an unknown future of dramatic *coups d'etat*, especially in countries involved with the oil sector, in which (especially in the case of Iraq) politicians could so easily find themselves badly 'burnt' or made a scapegoat of. One of the people who made a great effort to convince me not take such a risk was Iraq's brilliant Ambassador to the UN, Dr Yassen, a very well-known lawyer and diplomat, who considered my decision to return to Iraq an act of pure folly.

When the presidential decree naming me as the Director General of Oil Affairs finally came through, the Charge d'Affaires of the Iraqi Embassy in Bern, who had been a fellow-student of mine at law school in Baghdad, tried his best to warn me, sounding very worried, reminding me that all those working in oil faced an unknown future, adding that so many in Iraq dreamt of being in my place in Geneva. How could I want to leave and return to Iraq? But for me oil was like a magnet, my desired goal ever since writing my PhD on the subject. Political reasons alone had prevented my joining the INOC. Despite a good income and lifestyle in Geneva, the intellectual stimulation and professional challenge that I sought were totally lacking. Yet, given the warnings I received of the probability of a coup, the fear of finding myself in prison or unemployed made me hesitant.

It so happened that a former Minister of Oil from the royalist regime, Dr Nadim Pachachi, a friend of my elder brother when both were students at London's Imperial College prior to the Second World War, came to Geneva. He came from a very well known family in Baghdad, and was now working as an advisor to Sheikh Za'yed of the United Arab Emirates of Abu Dhabi, as well as being an oil consultant for the Libyan government. I went to the prestigious Swiss Hotel de Bergue to see him and explain the situation. He looked at me and said, 'Well, what are you waiting for?' He promptly advised me to accept the offer and return to Iraq where working in oil would open new horizons, not only in Iraq but internationally. He reminded me of the mediocre future with the UN, where the best you can get is a directorship and then the moment you turn 60 you will be obliged to retire. By then I was 37 years of age and I felt my career was at a critical turning point, but I explained to him the political risks that might harm me and my family. He told me not to worry – as even if I were to lose my oil position in Iraq I would find opportunities elsewhere. 'Go immediately and don't even hesitate,' he continued, 'You could have a very good future, but I must warn you that working in oil is like a disease ... it becomes part of you, like falling in love with a woman, and once involved you can never tear yourself away!' Despite having to accept a drop in salary to one sixth of my UN salary, in the end I was persuaded by this man of wisdom and experience, whom I trusted because of his personal friendship with my brother. He reinforced my conviction that oil was the right métier for me.

When I went to tender my resignation, the Head of the Primary Commodities Division, a kind Australian, Mr Judd, was surprised: 'Are you unhappy here?' he asked, 'I was thinking of promoting you. You are the only Iraqi in UNCTAD. Why on earth are you leaving?' When I explained the matter he said, 'Well, you know your interests better than I do, but you can stay here and earn a good salary and when you terminate your services you'll have a good pension.' He was a genuine person and it was with a heavy heart that I declined, while thanking him profusely. My decision was not an easy one, despite Dr Pachachi's exhortations.

Having left Geneva in March 1968, on arrival at the Oil Ministry in Baghdad I found myself warmly welcomed back to Iraq by the new Oil Minister Ali al-Hussein, who very kindly congratulated me for having earned a good reputation abroad – as when the ministry had enquired of me, apparently all had recommended me highly for professional and moral integrity – which was indeed gratifying to hear! His 'number two' in the Ministry, Mr Gulam, was also present, an extremely courteous man who understood people and how to deal with them. He had no real background in oil, but I found him very supportive.

Only a few weeks later, everyone sensed something was on the verge of happening. Aware of this air of expectation I attended an official reception and, seated among people I knew who held prominent government positions, I was startled to hear them deriding the country's political situation. It was very strange coming from those in high places with crucial responsibilities. Meanwhile the Minister, who belonged to the pro-Nasser group (purported to be anti-Ba'athist), demonstrated unexpected courtesy towards a number of Ba'ath officials, who thus gained a stronger foothold in the Oil Ministry.

This worried me initially, given that the Ba'athists, in their February 1963 coup, had imprisoned me on my return from Paris. Soon, however, I noticed that these particular Ba'athists were surprisingly friendly towards me, even consulting me on political issues, in particular the relationship between the government and the foreign oil companies, then reaching its peak of tension. In Iraq, oil had by now become a political commodity for politicians to outbid each other, and the criteria for 'national interest' involved necessarily confronting the companies and their concession system – that legacy from colonial rule. For my part, I was too keenly aware of the primordial importance for Iraq of *economic* benefits and had no time for political confrontation for its own sake when Iraq's own economy was at stake.

But the political situation was suddenly explosive with talk of an imminent military coup. I approached the Oil Minister, Ali al-Hussein, who was most kind in listening attentively to my concerns about having brought my family back from Geneva with the aim of serving my country, only to find there were now rumours of a *coup d'état*. There was a touch of sadness in his eyes when he now informed me that the Prime Minister, Mr Yahya, had received an envoy from President Nasser, in Cairo, advising him of an American plot to stage a coup with a Ba'athist façade, while the real plotters were deemed to have CIA connections. My worst fears were confirmed and I instantly recalled the advice of friends and colleagues in Geneva who had warned me of unpredictable political upheavals that I might find myself thrown into if I returned to Iraq.

I told the Minister that I should either return to the UN in Geneva or else teach oil economics at Baghdad University. In his friendly, outgoing manner, he showed a genuine readiness to do everything he could to help me along whatever path I chose.

But only a few weeks after this discussion, at dawn on 17 July 1968, we awoke to the clatter of machine guns and the sound of tanks nearby, as our house was not very far from the Presidential Palace. So, here then was the expected coup, and our very weak, ineffectual head of state, President Abdul Rahman A'ariff, was removed and flown by private plane to his exile in Turkey. In his place the military Ba'athist, Ahmed Hassan al-Bakr, was appointed. In reality, those who had instigated this coup were non-Ba'athist top military personnel, among whom was the head of military intelligence, al-Naif, rumoured to have CIA connections. This man became Prime Minister, while another, similarly 'rumoured' (according to senior personnel) to be CIA-connected, became chief of the presidential guard. Without these two 'collaborators' it is doubtful that the coup would have ever succeeded. I turned up at my office only to find that the Ministry was minus its Minister. Though his name was announced for the new cabinet, he was by then living in the USA. In his place they brought in a temporary former minister, with whom I was acquainted.

Just over a week later, on 31 July 1968, we were told that Prime Minister al-Naif was to visit the Ministry and wished to meet all the director generals, which meant I had to attend. When he arrived, he asked one of us to speak, and here Abdullah Ismail made himself known (the one whom I had replaced on my return from Geneva when, as mentioned, he was removed from his post during the 1967 pro-Nasser coup). The Prime Minister, who was acquainted with Ismail's brother in the military, asked him to speak. Abdullah Ismail began a tirade against those who had 'destroyed the oil sector and who had ousted knowledgeable, decent patriots and replaced them with communists'. He continued in this vein, raging at what had happened in the INOC and in the Ministry. Prime Minister al-Naif listened very attentively but after a while he advised Ismail to be patient, as things were about to revert 'to the way they were before, and very soon'.

As it turned out he was wrong, but at this stage I kept very quiet, feeling that Ismail's reference to communists replacing 'patriots' included an oblique (and unjustified) reproach towards me personally. The message came like a slap in the face, and I was so certain that from now on I was *persona non grata* that when I returned to my office I emptied my drawers of papers and memos, put everything into sacks and drove home. All the way home I was wondering how to explain things in a letter to my UN boss, the nice Mr Judd, and ask for his help so that I might return to the safety of UNCTAD and Geneva.

However, as it happened, things turned out very unexpectedly. That very evening, on 31 July 1968, we were sitting in the cool of the garden watching television. Suddenly the new President al-Bakr filled the TV screen and behind him stood a tall, young, dark-haired man in military uniform, bearing a machine gun, who we later learnt was Saddam Hussein – he who was to play such a fateful role in Iraq's history.

al-Bakr in his TV address talked of 'traitors' and 'plotters' and 'agents of imperialism' who had infiltrated the Ba'ath revolution in order to destroy it from within; and that the Ba'ath party itself had hatched a plan to eliminate them. In this context he mentioned first the name of the Prime Minister, al-Naif, whom I had only just met earlier that afternoon. We later learnt that the latter had been invited to lunch at the Presidential Palace by the new President, but on arrival was arrested, escorted under arm by Saddam Hussein and sent by military aircraft to Spain as the Iraqi ambassador. The story of how this happened was told in a quasi-official biography of Saddam entitled *Saddam Hussein: The Militant, the Thinker and the Man*, by Emir Eskander (for which, it was said, this biographer was handsomely rewarded with a very large sum), whose many biographical details were reminiscent of Al Capone stories, the Chicago gangster of cinema fame.

What disturbed me was knowing that, without al-Naif, the Ba'ath Party would never have come to power. Later this man was assassinated one night when coming out of the Intercontinental Hotel in London. This was for fomenting opposition to Saddam. Meanwhile, back in 1968, just listening to al-Bakr was like another sharp slap in the face. Knowing only too well what the Ba'athists were like, I felt exasperated and muttered to myself, 'You reckless fool – coming back to this quagmire!'

Two days later, a new cabinet was formed, but with a different, far more conciliatory political message based on seeking co-operation from all political tendencies, in particular the left-wingers (as the victims of the first 1963 Ba'ath coup). The President announced that all sentences against leftists or communists were to be commuted, and all those exiled or expelled for political reasons were similarly reprieved and their jobs reinstated. Later, a friend of mine, Mohammed Selman Hassan, a well-known leftwing economist (with a PhD from Cambridge University, England) informed me that he had been invited to join the new government as Minister. At the time he was teaching in Kuwait, and he was brought to the Presidential Palace by military jet. He did not accept the cabinet offer and instead asked the President to allow him to teach at the University. Overnight I found myself suddenly esteemed instead of brandished as a Marxist. I was even promoted and made a member of the new Board of Directors of INOC. I was astonished returning to the Ministry of Oil to find Ba'athist eyes turned on me with this degree of respect. Later, I was appointed to the board of Iraq's Central Bank, membership of which was another unexpectedly prestigious position.

The new Ba'athist Oil Minster, Dr Rashid al-Rifa'i, had engineering degrees, including a PhD, from British and American universities; but, though highly intelligent, he nurtured some sort of complex that I found mystifying. I made allowances both for his background, which was humble, and for the fact that an accident had left him lame; but try as I might to placate him, his manner towards me remained inimical. Mercifully his antagonism was at odds with the benign attitude shown me by my government. It was after Rifa'i and I participated on a televised panel, concerning the development of Iraq's sulphur deposits, that his hostility seemed to fester into hatred. My exposé on the TV panel displeased the minister, for whom the sulphur project was one of his pet achievements. Prior to the Ba'athist acquisition of power, a great fuss was made over the sulphur issue when a former US Secretary of State, Bill Anderson, had arrived in Iraq with a proposal to develop this resource. He had been recommended by Egypt's Nasser, with whom Anderson had personal connections. The project assumed great importance as many held that sulphur could earn for Iraq as much foreign currency as oil and would help reduce the country's dependence on oil exports. But as soon as the Ba'athists were in power their paranoia led them to suspect that the ongoing talks with Bill

Anderson constituted a 'plot' hatched by CIA agents to exploit Iraq's new source of wealth. This prompted the brutal Ba'athist regime to hold a sham of a military tribunal, and heads literally rolled – the heads of over 40 innocent people, some of whom were prominent officials. The regime then gave the sulphur project to a Polish firm.

As I had thoroughly scrutinised the feasibility study prior to the TV panel, I was able to explain the economics of this sulphur project and how much foreign exchange Iraq could, according to various scenarios, acquire; and I pointed out that, compared with Iraq's revenues from oil, the revenues to be derived from sulphur were minimal. This came as a surprise to a public awaiting positive news about this great new myth, the new source of income that would reduce Iraq's dependence on oil exports. Annoyed, Rifa'i promptly transferred me from my position as Director of Oil Affairs (in which I had been looking after oil policies, the government's relationship with the oil companies and OPEC matters) to the post of Director of Economic Affairs, leaving me (with knowledge of English) with just OPEC matters to deal with and no policy decisions whatever.

It was then, in the autumn of 1968 in Baghdad, that I attended for the first time an OPEC Ministerial Conference. Later on I travelled with the minister to Tehran to discuss a report prepared by the consultant Economist Intelligence Unit on the co-operation among NOCs of OPEC countries. I had studied very carefully the voluminous report before reaching Tehran, where I seemed to be the only one at the meeting discussing it; and so when we attended the next OPEC meeting in the summer of 1969, held in Doha, Qatar, the Economist Intelligence Unit report was re-examined and discussed in more detail, which gave me the first opportunity to speak on the matter to the Ministerial Conference. On our return to Baghdad we spent two days in Kuwait at the invitation of the Kuwaiti minister, Abdul-Rahman al-Ateeqi, a most pleasant person. It was the first time I had seen Kuwait, a city state, and I was impressed by its buildings and the sense of abundance, modernity and Westernisation. This made me reassess at once the unfairly condescending attitude of Iraqis towards the 'Bedouins'. My third, and last, trip to Vienna with my difficult boss was in June 1969 to attend the OPEC ordinary summer meeting.

Rifa'i was then replaced, in January 1970, by a new minister, who was at the time Chairman of INOC of whose board I was a member: a Dr Sa'doun Hammadi, a Ba'athist veteran with a good education, having obtained a PhD degree in economics from the University of Wisconsin, USA, prior to which he was a graduate from the American University of Beirut. Observing my performance as a member of the board of the National Oil Company, this new minister was extremely supportive, and appointed me to be directly under him exclusively to deal with the problems and the disputes arising between the Government and the oil companies. He seemed to be a very strong leader and, at first, not unduly fanatical as a Ba'athist, although he remained a fanatic when it came to the concept of widening Arab unity. He repeatedly stressed that for him what mattered were efficiency, good performance and a sense of patriotism. The first thing he did when he came into the Ministry was to hold a meeting with the staff, during which he said (to the resentment of the Ba'athist staff) that a true patriot is one who serves his country well and is not necessarily a party man, but rather his service, honesty and performance is what counts. From the day this Minister took office until the day he left in late 1974, I found myself intensively involved in policy-making problems. I travelled extensively with him and became very involved in OPEC Ministerial Conferences, which helped me gain some recognition.

From 1968 onwards, my involvement in the oil industry and related matters was consummate: firstly in 1968 as Director of Oil Affairs at Iraq's Ministry of Oil, before being appointed Permanent Undersecretary for Oil in 1973; then spending two years with the Organization of Arab Petroleum Exporting Countries (OAPEC) in Kuwait, as Assistant to the Secretary General; and later moving in 1978 to OPEC as Deputy Secretary General for almost 11 years, five years of which I was appointed Acting Secretary General (1983–88).

When I finally departed from OPEC in mid-1989, from August of that year I was the Executive Director of the Centre for Global Energy Studies (CGES), a non-profit energy research institution based in London, established by the former Oil Minister of Saudi Arabia, Sheikh Ahmed Zaki Yamani.

My professional life with oil has thus remained an essential part of my existence, and in this way the prophecy of former-oil minister, Nadim Pachachi, was true: that oil would open up international opportunities for me, but that once involved with oil I would be unable to abandon it. His analogy of 'falling in love with a woman' is apt, except that with oil it has been a love that never wanes! After my experiences of 'living with oil' for well over 40 years, these memoirs attempt to describe some epoch-making events, how they happened, the people involved and the consequences.

2

Why OPEC? Confrontation or common cause?

At the invitation of the Government of Iraq, delegates from five major oil-producing countries – Iran, Kuwait, Saudi Arabia and Venezuela, together with their host country Iraq – met in Baghdad and, on 14 September 1960, announced the formation of OPEC. This historic event came as a response to the oil companies twice reducing what was then called the 'posted price of oil' – at the time unilaterally set by seven major IOCs, known as the 'Seven Sisters' or the 'international petroleum cartel'.[1]

The previous year, in February 1959, this cartel had made its first cut to the posted price of oil, reducing it by as much as US$0.18 per barrel for Gulf oil, so that the price fell from US$2.08 to US$1.90 per barrel. In August 1960, a second price cut, reducing the price by a further $0.10 cents, was imposed unilaterally – first by Esso, followed by other oil companies. Meanwhile, over this two-year period, the price of manufactured goods had increased by 9 per cent, affecting the balance of payments of countries dependent on imported products.

Therefore the most immediate objective for the OPEC delegates was to safeguard their governments' oil revenues against further erosion resulting from any bid by the companies to cut the oil price yet again. According to the profit-sharing agreements drawn up in the early 1950s, between Middle East oil concession holders and host countries' governments, the latter's per-barrel revenue of exported oil was determined at 50 per cent of the official posted price, less half the cost of producing that barrel. Any upward or downward fluctuation in this oil price affected the government per-barrel income correspondingly. When the two price cuts were imposed by the oil companies, these countries' revenues per barrel were reduced by more than 15 per cent, relative to the price prior to the cuts.

From the early 1950s onwards, this official posted price – a fixed price, unilaterally set and posted by the companies in the daily bulletin, *Platts Oilgram* – was more of a *tax-reference price*, on which host countries based their taxes, rather than a real market price derived from the exchange of oil between buyers and sellers in a free market. For the companies, the tax paid to host countries, together with production costs, determined the operators' *tax-paid cost*, i.e. the cost incurred by the oil companies as a result of lifting one barrel of oil, plus tax and royalties paid to the host governments.

For this reason OPEC's first resolution reinforced the need to avoid price fluctuations, in the interests of maintaining oil price stability. This resolution also emphasised the necessity of restoring prices to the pre-1959 level and stipulated that the companies should not undertake unilateral changes to the posted price without prior consultation with and agreement of the host countries.

OPEC's five resolutions were thus predicated on certain broad objectives: namely, that the organisation would devise a price system that secured market stability – by various means, including the regulation of production – with the aim of protecting the interests of both oil producers and consumers and of guaranteeing the stable oil revenue of the former. OPEC also announced that its fundamental purpose was to co-ordinate the oil policies of its member countries in order to safeguard their interests, both individually and collectively.

All those cognisant of OPEC affairs are well aware of these initial primary objectives. What has not been discussed, however, is the actual necessity for the existence of OPEC, not only from the oil producers' viewpoint but also for the sake of price stability and growth of the oil industry, conditions that served equally well the interests of the oil companies. The dominant position of the latter by the late 1950s was being undermined by aggressive competition from emerging new companies, vying for a market share in direct competition with the established major companies.

A false impression prevailed in some (even OPEC) circles and even lingers today: that the formation of OPEC was an act of confrontation with the major oil companies, aimed at asserting the legal rights of the oil-producing/exporting countries. It is not surprising if this impression was conveyed by the rhetoric of certain oil demagogues, such as Sheikh Abdulla al-Turaiki, former Oil Minister for

Saudi Arabia, who had played a major part in the formation of OPEC in 1960.

The fact is that the creation of OPEC was considered necessary for *both sides*: the oil producers and the major oil companies, for the sake of price stability and fostering a healthy growth of the world oil industry at a time when it showed signs of weakening. Had the oil companies foreseen any element of confrontation or possible threat to their interests, they still wielded enough political clout in those days to have thwarted the development of this new organisation, especially given the political situation of many of its member countries, some of which were at that time still British protectorates, in which BP (of which the British Government was the majority shareholder) operated, as was the case in Kuwait, Qatar and Abu Dhabi. Similarly American political influence in Saudi Arabia and Iran could have played a role in rooting out the organisation in its infancy, had the US been so inclined; but no opposition emanated from any quarter; nor did the major oil companies raise any objection to OPEC's first resolution preventing the oil companies from undertaking changes to posted prices, which, according to the terms of their oil concessions, the companies were still within their rights to set. On the contrary, there was even an air of co-operation in the way the oil companies complied with OPEC's resolution pertaining to prices, notwithstanding that it clearly represented a unilateral decision that was set to overhaul radically the terms of the old concessions.

In the circumstances, the companies' reaction was curious, and an important question lingers: why in the first place did the oil companies undertake their two successive cuts to the posted price of oil? They must have foreseen that this action risked provoking a defensive rebuff from the oil-producing countries. Their 'response' was incipient, as OPEC was its outcome, and the story of this historic response from the oil producers requires at the outset a brief description of the state of affairs then prevailing in the oil industry and of salient developments that occurred in the second half of the 1950s.

To begin with, an essential factor should be borne in mind. If left entirely to free market forces, without any intervention in supply regulation, the oil industry would be susceptible to a high degree of price volatility. Without ensuring an even-handed balance between supply and demand, the oil market would be chaotic and subject to price wars among the producers, each endeavouring to protect its own share in the world oil market, regardless of the extent to which the price fell – as long as the selling price covered the operational costs per barrel, which are normally very low compared with the capital investment costs involved in establishing a new production capacity. In the event of a price war (as happened in the late 1920s, when the oil price fell to 20 cents per barrel in the USA) the producer considers the capital costs incurred for the installation of its producing capacity as *sunk* capital, relative to the importance of retaining an undiminished market share. After a lead time, very low prices cannot provide the necessary capital investment for adding the new capacity needed to meet growing consumption. With insufficient production capacity to meet demand growth, severe shortage and soaring prices would ensue. Such sharp fluctuations would be detrimental to the stability and growth of the oil industry.

The industry's need for a structural mechanism to secure an ideal balance of supply and demand led, in the USA, to the establishment of the Texas Railroad Commission, which took the requisite measures for preventing either surplus or shortage in the oil market, and thus avoiding sharp price volatility. This same consideration motivated the major oil companies into agreeing on joint measures to secure full control of production and export from the key oil-producing areas, especially from the Middle East Gulf.

This happened at the initiative of the then chairman of Shell, Sir Henry Deterding, when Shell, Standard Oil of New Jersey and Anglo-Persian Oil (later BP) met in secret in August 1928 (at Achnacarry Castle in the Scottish Highlands), arriving at an agreement by which they sought to prevent an excessive and detrimental degree of price competition. They resolved to collaborate over policy principles pertaining to efficiency and optimisation of oil industry markets, and this they achieved by ensuring the joint planning of production. The outcome was called the 'Achnacarry' – or 'As Is' – Agreement of 1928, and it was implemented with considerable success owing to the structure of the oil concession system, which granted the companies direct control over investment programmes, production, pricing and exports from the oil-producing areas. The As Is Agreement shaped, in 1928, the structure of what would later be termed – in a 1952 US Senate subcommittee report – the 'international petroleum cartel'. Throughout this period, the host government's sole influence, beyond its role of tax collector, lay in employment regulations aimed at promoting local technical expertise (a policy which in Iraq became known as 'Iraqisation').

This Seven Sisters' concessionary cartel system was the main feature of the oil industry after the First World War, and in the Middle East it began with the partition of territory, formerly part of the Ottoman Empire, into spheres of influence as political mandates. It was this that gave the concession system its legacy of colonial domination and a structure that afforded the concession holder a monopolistic right in the exploration of oil, its discovery, development and production. The concessions were not granted to individual companies but to holding companies, owned by the major oil companies with varying percentage shares. The holding (non-profit-making) company's role was to invest capital in oil production and distribute it to the shareholders – according to their respective shares – at a price equivalent to the cost of producing a barrel of oil, plus a nominal amount per barrel to cover administrative costs.

The shareholders in a holding company in one country also had shares in holding companies in other areas, in such a way as to lead to a linking of their interests in the *upstream phase* of the oil industry, i.e. crude oil production or what is referred to as 'horizontal integration'. This promoted the rigorous joint planning of crude production, securing each shareholder's crude requirements for its own refineries and distribution networks in consuming areas. Figure 2.1 shows the complex horizontal integration and percentage-ownership links of the major IOCs vis-à-vis the major oil-producing companies.

The oldest and best example of this feature of horizontal integration in the *upstream* of the oil industry was the Iraq Petroleum Company (IPC), which formed part of the Seven Sisters. The IPC was previously, between 1925 and 1931, known as the Turkish Petroleum Company (TPC). The story of the IPC ended when it was nationalised in 1972 by the Iraqi Government, but, prior to the oil nationalisation measure, it had comprised first the British, French and Dutch, then American, shareholders in a holding company. The production of the holding company was decided on a joint-planning basis for a certain period, in accordance with the shareholders' crude requirements, in order to meet their *downstream* needs, i.e.

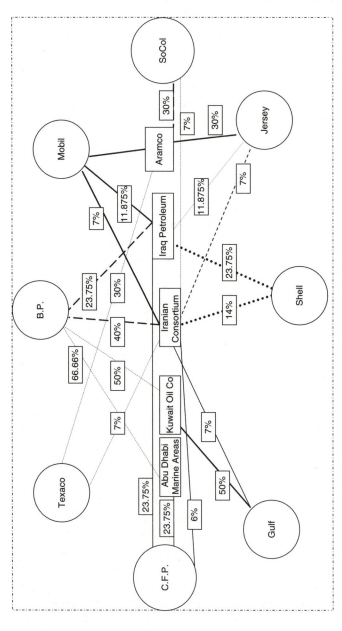

Figure 2.1   Ownership links between major IOCs (including Compagnie Française des Pétroles) and major crude-oil producing companies in the Middle East, 1966 (percentage of shares held)

Source: Penrose, E., *The Large International Firm in Developing Countries: The International Petroleum Industry* (London, 1968).

refineries and distribution networks. As Figure 2.1 shows, the shareholders held shares in holding companies in other countries. For example, apart from its 23.75 per cent share in the IPC, BP (formerly Anglo-Persian, renamed Anglo-Iranian in 1935 and BP in 1954) owned large shares in Qatar and Abu Dhabi, and it had owned Iran's entire oil production; although after General Zahedi's toppling of Mosaddegh regime in August 1953, BP's share was subsequently reduced to 40 per cent as a result of a settlement by which it was agreed to distribute the remaining 60 per cent among other cartel members in varying percentages.[2]

Along with its share in the IPC, BP also held 50 per cent of Kuwaiti oil, while the American company, Exxon (formerly Esso), held a share of the IPC and a 30 per cent share of Aramco in Saudi Arabia, and also 7 per cent in the Iranian Consortium. Similarly, Gulf Oil, which owned 50 per cent of the Kuwait Oil Company, held a 7 per cent share in the Iranian Consortium; while Texaco had 30 per cent in Aramco, and 7 percent in the Iranian Consortium. Apart from its share in the IPC, Mobil held a 10 per cent share in Saudi Arabia and 7 per cent in Iran. Meanwhile, Compagnie Française des Pétroles (CFP/Total) held a 23.75 per cent share in the IPC and 23.75 percent in Abu Dhabi and Qatar, as well as a 6 per cent participation in the Iranian Consortium.

This co-operative interlinking of the Seven Sisters' interests in the upstream of the oil industry, which facilitated their control of crude supplies (in balance with their needs for refined petroleum products at the downstream consumer end), did not prevent competition arising from various 'restrictive rules' (to be elaborated in Chapter 4). For example, the big companies, like BP and Exxon, which sought to preserve their dominant, competitive strength relative to smaller sister companies, had access to cheap crude in excess of their downstream requirements, and were thus in a position to sell a surplus quantity of crude at a 'fixed' price to a smaller sister company that lacked access to crude for its downstream requirements, such as Shell and CFP. This and other such restrictive practices have been amply described by Professor Edith Penrose[3] as well as in the earlier-mentioned 'Joint Control over Foreign Oil' report presented in 1952 to the US Senate by its subcommittee.

In synchronisation with their 'horizontal' integration, each of these shareholding companies was 'vertically' integrated in the sense that the crude oil to which it had access was shipped to its own refineries, which, in turn, were in line with the company's selling networks of petroleum products. With this total integration throughout the crude oil-production phase, the international oil industry cohered perfectly. The companies' horizontal and vertical integration prevented any possibility of a price war among sister companies, as their crude production was kept in balance with requirements on an international level. There was no place for either crude surplus, which would lead to a price collapse or crude shortage, leading to high prices.

It was the Seven Sisters' adroitly balanced crude production planning – as exemplified by the IPC's five major shareholders – that enabled their supply regulation to achieve its optimum balance of supply and demand even in exceptional circumstances. For instance, no oil shortage occurred when the supply of Iranian oil was interrupted after the oil nationalisation measure of Mosaddegh's government in 1951, because the oil companies were able to increase production from Kuwait, Iraq and Saudi Arabia to replace Iran's oil shortage.

The Seven Sisters' stranglehold over the international oil industry, by means of their co-ordinated, integrated system, was of major significance in preventing – until the 1950s – a world oil trade, in the sense of buyers and sellers on a free market. Apart from rare exceptions, no free market for oil existed at this time, and crude oil moved within the system from one company to another in the form of an *intercompany exchange*, not as real trade, as we know it. As already pointed out, the posted price was more or less a fictitious price to serve not only as a taxation reference for host governments but also as a price for intercompany exchanges (at 'cost' plus half the posted price).

However, from the late 1950s, the predominance of these major oil companies came under threat. Their absolute control in their concessionary areas, sustained by their compact system of rigorously regulated crude oil production, began to be challenged by independent oil companies, and this would become more marked by the end of the decade. Besides ENI of Italy,[4] independent 'newcomers' began to invest outside the monopoly of the Seven Sisters and were linked to systems financially at variance with the cartel. At this time, new producing areas were discovered, as in the case of Libya where, as well as Exxon, there was Occidental, which was becoming a major player in its own right. Such developments resulted in crude oil being produced independently, outside the cartel system controlled by 'the majors', and offered for sale to independent refiners with no access to crude oil.

Competitively priced crude oil from the USSR began to make its way onto the free market. For Soviet oil to move on the market, it needed to offer attractive discounts. Other factors came into play, one being the measure taken by the USA to limit crude oil entry on the market in order to protect its own oil industry. Many independent American oil companies with access to foreign crude oil were thus deprived of selling on the US market – a situation that led to their being forced to sell surplus crude outside the cartel.

A limited free market price began to take shape in the form of discounts on the posted prices that had been set by the major oil companies. Next a new pattern of tax relationship emerged with the entry of the newcomers investing in new oil areas, such as Libya, where the government's per-barrel share was not calculated on the 'fixed' official posted price but rather on the basis of a price realised on the free market, which invariably undercut the posted price. When a market-realised price fell, the host government's per-barrel share fell accordingly, and the tax cost for the new producer was correspondingly lower, thus providing a good margin of profit for a new investor with which to reinvest new production capacity.

This fostered growth in the free market, where crude oil is physically and freely bought and sold. The larger this market, clearly the less the share of the Seven Sisters, whose output share in world production (outside the USA and USSR) was now being undermined by these new investors. According to Professor Penrose,[5] in 1950 the Seven Sisters owned 85 per cent of the crude oil production in the world outside Canada, the USA, Soviet Russia and China. By 1960, this share had fallen to 72 per cent, to the benefit of the newcomers, whose share had grown from 15 to 28 per cent. The share of the Seven Sisters in refinery capacity fell in a far more pronounced way: from 72 to 53 per cent during the same period. This benefitted the new, independent companies because more independent refineries required more crude oil outside the cartel's circuit.

The USSR's massive discounts on its crude generated further fierce competition, on top of the cut-throat competition from the newcomers. The hegemony of the major oil companies was now in jeopardy. They were forced to cut their posted price in order to reduce the tax-paid cost. This cut was pushed for by Esso (Exxon) and supported by the other companies. Hence the two cuts in the posted price, in 1959 and 1960, were a counter-measure to the increased market share of the newcomers.

In other words, one can argue that, had this fierce competition of price cuts in a free market not been curbed by some form of restrictive regulation, the continued slashing of prices would have led to a level of competition harmful to the industry and to the major oil companies themselves.

At this juncture, therefore, the formation of OPEC could not have been more timely, as it put an end to a damaging scale of competition that was affecting adversely the oil industry itself, as well as the position of the major oil companies. OPEC's first step was to enlarge its membership. Shortly after its foundation, Qatar joined the organisation, followed by Indonesia, Libya, the Emirate of Abu Dhabi, Algeria, Nigeria, Ecuador and Gabon. (Both Ecuador and Gabon left OPEC in the 1990s, but Ecuador rejoined in 2008.) This enlargement of OPEC's base served to strengthen the position of the producers vis-à-vis the oil companies. OPEC then took various measures that greatly helped to put an end to the price erosion.

These involved, among other things, the unification of the tax system: the levying of tax from the oil companies operating in member countries' territory in such a way as to make levies similar to those applied in the Gulf, i.e. using not a realised market price but rather the 'fixed official posted price' as a reference price for the calculation of tax and royalties. This measure put an end to the tax system in the new areas, where tax and royalties were being paid by new investors on the basis of lower realised market prices – the system that had given the new companies a competitive edge over the major companies. OPEC thus succeeded in curbing the newcomers' ability to invest in expanding capacity and acquire an enlarged market share at the expense of the major oil companies.

In response to OPEC's resolution, Libya amended its tax system, putting it in line with the Gulf's. This instantly had the effect of limiting the expansion of the new companies' investments, as they now had to pay higher taxes than before. OPEC's price-structure reform not only served the oil-producing countries by consolidating price stability and hence their oil revenues, but also at the same time enormously benefitted the major oil companies by preserving their dominant position in the oil industry, which would no longer be eroded by new independent companies.

Another measure taken by OPEC, of no less significance in consolidating the price structure, was the amendment of the tax regime, so that payment of royalties was treated separately from taxation. The 1952 'fifty–fifty' agreement (between the governments and the oil companies) had decreed that the government share was calculated at 50 per cent of the posted price. But in 1964, OPEC declared to the companies that the 50 per cent was to include *both tax and royalties*, and that the investor was to pay a 12.5 per cent royalty to the landowner, irrespective of taxable profits. OPEC asked the companies to pay first the 12.5 per cent royalty and then 50 per cent tax on the profits. The companies conceded to this with the proviso that the royalty be 'expensed' as part of their production costs (given that the government share is 50 per cent of profit minus costs). Royalties, as a cost, increased the government share by 6.25 per cent of the posted price. This meant that the net share of the host countries from royalties would be 50 per cent (of the posted price) and then increased to 56.25 per cent.

Although this increase had to be implemented gradually by allowing temporary, decreasing discounts to the companies, it nevertheless had the effect of consolidating the price structure by increasing the tax-paid cost. The measure had the effect of strengthening the level of realised prices because the higher the tax-paid cost, the higher the price floor, which would then make discounts more difficult.

OPEC's achievements were, at this stage, already remarkable. Its primordial aim had been to put an end to price cuts, but it also achieved a strengthening of the price structure that safeguarded the mutual interests of oil-producing countries and major oil companies, allowing the latter to retain their leading role in the industry while weakening the role of the newcomers. Without OPEC's reforms and consequent curb on free market expansion, a plethora of newcomers would have jeopardised market stability. Penrose records that *after* the creation of OPEC 'the share of the major oil companies in the upstream part of the industry increased from

72 per cent in 1960 to 76 per cent in 1966. Similarly, in the down-stream operations, their share increased from 53 per cent to 61 per cent, respectively'.[6] The shares of the newcomers declined correspondingly from 28 to 24 per cent in the upstream activity and from 47 to 39 per cent in the downstream. OPEC had effectively reversed the trend of new independent companies increasing their share in downstream operations.

Many observers concluded that in its first decade OPEC did little to change the international oil relationship because it failed to achieve the initial objective of the organisation when it was founded in Baghdad in 1960: which was to restore the posted price to its level prior to the companies' cuts of 1959 and 1960. Some assumed that during those first ten years OPEC did little to implement the general principle (which is internationally recognised) of the sovereign right of the state over its resources. But this view is both naïve and inaccurate. The measures that OPEC took constituted a complete overhaul of the oil concession system. Prior to OPEC's existence, host countries were not equal partners in their own industry, as their role did not exceed the levying of taxes from the oil companies which, according to the terms of the concession, enjoyed absolute freedom to decide whatever suited their own interests in all oil industry matters in the territory covered by concessions.

OPEC's first ten formative years changed for the better its relationship with the oil companies in a way that served the interests of both. It is true that during its first few years OPEC remained a dormant partner, but the partnership evolved into an active one, with OPEC shifting from simple tax collectors into active, negotiating partners determining prices.

The catalyst for OPEC's evolution was its cardinal Resolution 90 of June 1968 (discussed below), followed by its February 1971 Tehran Agreement with the companies over the pricing of oil (described pp. 48–67). This was followed by two complementary Geneva agreements adjusting the oil price against the fluctuation of the US dollar. This mutual co-operation between OPEC and the oil companies peaked with negotiations to implement the principle of state participation in the oil concessions. As will be discussed later, the aborted agreement nearly concluded with the Aramco shareholders by Saudi Arabia's Oil Minister, Sheikh Ahmed Zaki

Yamani, could have opened a new dimension of fruitful and con-structive co-operation between the oil producers and companies.

From the time of OPEC's inception in September 1960, its early years prepared the terrain for subsequent developments. The first of these was the stand-off between the Iraqi Government and the shareholders of the IPC and its affiliates, which ended in unilateral legislative action on the part of the Iraqi government to recover all the territories held under the concessions, as will be discussed in Chapter 4.

Iraq's futile battle with the oil companies was significant in later empowering OPEC and shaping its future policies, notably when OPEC adopted Resolution 90 (of June 1968). This was the Declara-tory Statement of Petroleum Policy in Member Countries, the source of all later developments that finally brought about the rupture in the co-operative partnership between OPEC and the oil companies, which signalled changing investment interests of the companies and a consequent rupture of their partnership with OPEC, to the detri-ment of the OPEC producers rather than the companies. Among Resolution 90's most significant items, later to have far-reaching effects on this relationship, the following appeared under a sub-heading entitled 'Resolution Concerning Mode of Development':

> Member governments shall endeavour as far as possible to explore and develop their hydrocarbon resources directly. The capital, specialists and promotion of marketing outlets required for such direct development may be complemented, when necessary, from alternative sources on a commercial basis.

Resolution 90 became the most influential factor in shaping the future of the oil industry and oil policies. Declaring its emphasis on member countries' investments in the upstream oil industry being made by the state, and no longer by the companies, unless procuring services on a commercial basis, OPEC essentially laid the foundation for a state takeover of the oil industry. This corner-stone principle of OPEC showed a direct influence from Iraq's own experience, as the Iraqi government had already announced that the development of its giant North Rumala oil field in Basra was to be undertaken directly by the state-owned INOC. Later INOC concluded an agreement to develop that field with the help of the Soviet Union. OPEC's 1968 Resolution 90 thus triggered new developments for the 1970s in the form of nationalisation, or government takeover by mutual agreement. In the same vein this Resolution permitted member countries to resort to outside operators but on the basis of 'reasonable remuneration, taking into account the degree of risk involved' and with governments retaining 'the greatest measure possible of participation in, and control over, all aspects of operations'.

This principle of state participation was embodied by Resolution 90: 'Where provision for government participation in the ownership of the concession-holding company under any of the present petroleum contracts has not been made, the government may acquire a reasonable participation on the grounds of the principle of changing circumstances'. Again this notion takes its origin in the Iraqi case (see Chapter 4) which concerned the stand-off with the oil companies. The principle of government participation was envisaged and urged by Sheikh Ahmed Zaki Yamani, notably in a lecture at the American University of Beirut in 1965. He felt OPEC should act collectively, and this it did when negotiations were later conducted by Sheikh Yamani himself on behalf of OPEC.

The Resolution also included a key item on 'Posted Prices or Tax Reference Prices' that would have far-reaching effects on the international oil industry, forming the basis of OPEC's decision in 1973 to take over the pricing of oil from the companies. This is because that key item made provisions for the then revolutionary concept of oil prices being determined by producing countries instead of the oil companies. It even recommended that the government should take into account the relationship between import prices for 'manufactured goods' and the price of oil exports.

Resolution 90 importantly reaffirmed the right of OPEC countries to exercise permanent sovereignty over their hydrocarbon resources, in accordance with the General Assembly Resolution of the UN of 1966; also that all member countries should determine the best means of safeguarding their interests and implement a co-ordination and collective 'unification' (or a unified theory) of petroleum policies, in accordance with OPEC's original statute.

Among the other principles embodied in the Resolution was the necessity for the revision of contracts on the basis of changing conditions. In matters of oil pricing, Resolution 90 enforced the maintenance of the real price and its protection from world inflation.

Its 'Item 3' stipulated that 'All existing contracts and agreements should be subject to revision, on the legal basis of changing circumstances'. That is to say, the conditions of oil concessions concluded in the 1920s or 1940s were no longer operative. The changed circumstances themselves justified this inevitability.

Historically speaking, therefore, OPEC's Resolution 90 was instrumental in heralding a fundamental change in the oil industry and in oil companies' policies. In hindsight we can see how all ensuing developments have taken their points of origin and reference from this Resolution.

The coming chapters, which are instalments that follow on from this radical change, will examine the 1971 Tehran Agreement, the price shocks of the 1970s and various nationalisation measures taken by OPEC countries, as well as other momentous events that took their cue from OPEC's Resolution 90.

3

New winds begin to blow

As was discussed in the previous Chapter, during the first ten, formative years of its life, OPEC was able to consolidate its performance and, through various measures, achieved a degree of stability in oil pricing, though failing, at this earlier stage, to restore the price to its level prior to the companies' cut of 1959.

When OPEC's ordinary meeting took place in Vienna, on 8 and 9 July 1969, everything seemed normal – except for one especially notable event that would play a major role in OPEC's future, which was Algeria's admission to the organisation as its tenth member. I arrived in Vienna with the Ba'athist Oil Minster, Dr Rashid al-Rifa'i, to attend the meeting, my second OPEC conference. My delight at being in Vienna, resplendent with its legacy of the old Hapsburg dynasty and Austro-Hungarian Empire visible everywhere in its architecture, statues and monuments, stirred in me a veneration for the distinguished city that had nurtured great master composers – Mozart, Beethoven, Schubert, Brahms, Mahler, whose art has given the world such pleasure.

After a period of hesitation, the Algerians had decided to join OPEC as they considered that its principal members were too heavily influenced by, and far too obliging towards, the major IOCs. This was at a time when Algeria was already following a 'national oil policy' in an attempt to develop its oil independently of the oil companies. It was noticeable how large the Algerian delegation was compared with other member countries' delegations, which normally consisted only of the oil minister and just one or two aides. The Algerians, by contrast, numbered about ten, among whom there was the president of Sonatrach (Algeria's national oil company), Sid Ahmed Ghozali, who would later play an important political role, and Noureddine Ait Laoussine, who at that time was chief of Sonatrach's marketing arm.

This Algerian delegation, arriving for its first attendance of an OPEC meeting, was headed by their Oil Minister, Belaid Abdesselam, a prominent member of the ruling Front de Libération Nationale (the FLN), a party belonging to an influential group very close to President Boumidien. Belaid Abdesselam, with his fair complexion, serene blue eyes, unhurried and calmly majestic gait, exuded an air of self-confidence. He was, in fact, a revolutionary from the mountain tribes called the Kabyl, and his apparent calm concealed an extraordinary degree of extremism when dealing with oil affairs.

Following the Six Day War between Egypt and Israel in 1967, Algeria had nationalised several small, independent American oil companies that same year. For this reason they considered themselves 'pioneer liberators of oil from the clutches of Western oil companies'. Also with the Algerian delegation was Sheikh Abdullah al-Turaiki who, having been sacked by King Faisal from his post as Saudi Arabia's Oil Minister, had established a consulting office in Beirut. I knew this man in Baghdad, where he was a consultant to the Iraqi government. Notwithstanding al-Turaiki's help in establishling OPEC in 1960 when he was Saudi Arabia's oil minister, he was a dangerous demagogue and caused much damage to Arab oil by politicising it with meaningless yet harmful slogans through his monthly bulletin, entitled 'Arab Oil Belongs to the Arabs'. His tirades at the Arab League's annual oil conferences were heavily influenced by the political stance of Egypt's Gamal Abdel Nasser.

Even before OPEC's Ministerial meeting was convened, its entire proceedings were nearly threatened by Abdullah al-Turaiki's presence. The Saudi delegation, headed by Sheikh Ahmed Zaki Yamani, made it clear to everyone that if al-Turaiki personally attended this official meeting the Saudi delegation intended to boycott it. The reason for this was that al-Turaiki, after being sacked by King Faisal, was *persona non grata* in his native Saudi Arabia as he was a staunch opponent of the Saudi regime and, in the name of Arab unity, had supported the Egyptian–Arab expansionist policy promoted by Nasser, who was already at odds with Saudi Arabia because of the Yemen War.[1] It would have been unthinkable as well as gravely insulting for the Saudis had al-Turaiki attended the official meeting, seated with the Algerians on the other side of the table. The Algerians, on the other hand, insisted that, as a consultant to their government, he had every right to be included in their delegation. Mediators came in to resolve the problem, notably Iraq's Ba'athist Oil Minster, Dr Rashid al-Rifa'i, and the Libyan representative, Ibrahim al-Hangari (Undersecretary for Oil prior to Gaddafi's regime change), both of whom succeeded in convincing the Algerian delegation *not* to include al-Turaiki at the official meeting of the conference.

Apart from this incident, what struck me was the solemn atmosphere that shrouded the Algerian delegation, already reflecting a heightened degree of self-esteem as newcomers. This was no doubt linked to the legendary sacrifice of one million Algerian 'martyrs' who had given their lives in the war of liberation against French colonialism. Nevertheless, that aura of pride projected by the Algerians would later become a catalyst in aggrandising the role that Algeria would play in OPEC policy decisions, despite its secondary place relative to the big producers, Saudi Arabia, Iraq, Iran, Kuwait and Venezuela. Algeria's proven petroleum reserves amounted to less than 1.5 per cent of OPEC's total recoverable reserves, and its national technological expertise at that time lagged behind that of Iraq, or Iran under the Shah.

Apart from welcoming Algeria into the family of oil producers, little else was discussed beyond routine, administrative matters; but the inclusion of Algeria was a crucial component of OPEC's policy of broadening the partnership, as this enlargement, by means of including smaller producers, was necessary to strengthen the organisation's negotiating position, particularly in the early stages. Later, when OPEC took command of oil pricing (from the companies), after various state ownership measures, Algeria and Libya (the latter under Gaddafi) adopted major roles that seemed disproportionate to their relatively limited reserves and lower production levels, and both countries, in particular Algeria, exerted pressure on OPEC's major oil producers in order to guarantee their own interests.

Soon after the Vienna OPEC meeting in 1969, a dramatic military *coup d'état* was staged in Libya. On 1 September that same year, King Idris of Libya was ousted and power was seized by the military junta, at the vanguard of which was a young army colonel by the name of Muammar Abu Minyar al-Gaddafi. Libya under its

nationalistic new leader, Gaddafi, would have far-reaching consequences for OPEC and the oil market. As was the case with many
coups of this nature, the 'conspiratorial' mentality prevalent in
Arab culture received the news with instant suspicion that foreign –
probably American – interests lay behind Gaddafi's coup. Apart
from Iraq's military coup in July 1958, which no document so far
unearthed has ever suggested had foreign links, several other political coups including Syria's were, according to Miles Copeland,[2]
either instigated or supported by the CIA.

Libya's oil investments and the structure of its oil industry
were always of a different order from the Gulf's. Oil companies
had a direct contractual relationship with the Libyan government:
Exxon, for example, along with several independent companies,
one of which was the pre-eminent American Occidental, owned
by the great tycoon and art collector, Armand Hammer. Instead
of the Gulf's oil concession system, as exemplified by the Seven
Sisters, with shareholders (of non-profit holding companies) lifting oil, virtually exempt from government interference, Libya,
by contrast, experienced several major head-on disputes with oil
companies over the pricing of its oil, prior to the Gaddafi coup.
The companies had arbitrarily decided to price Libyan crude oil
at a level almost equivalent to Iraq's Kirkuk oil, exported from the
east Mediterranean terminals, but without taking into consideration the quality and geographical advantage of Libya's oil, with
its proximity to Europe. Libyan crude oil, being almost sulphur free
(containing as it does a much lower percentage of fuel oil), is very
light and of a far higher quality than heavy Kirkuk crude. Its value
ought always to reflect this. It was said at the time that Dr Nadim
Pachachi, the former Iraqi Minister of Oil, in his capacity as advisor
to the Libyan government, had convinced the latter of the wisdom
of accepting the companies' pricing formula in order to give Libyan
oil a competitive edge over Middle East oil in European markets.
This led to very substantial increases in Libyan production, which
began to have adverse effects on the country's oil fields, a fact that
later led Libya to produce less.

When the pre-coup Libyan government had then demanded
that the companies adjust the price upward, restoring its real value
commensurate with its geographic and 'quality' advantages, the
oil companies obstinately refused. The government then found

itself receiving diminished oil revenues under protest until the new military rulers forced the companies to conform with government demands. It so happened that when, in September 1970, OPEC's Secretariat issued a uniform code for sound optimum production practice in order to preserve the oil fields (a pro forma resolution for the conservation of hydrocarbon reserves), Gaddafi used this code as a basis for an across-the-board cut, reducing production from all companies operating in Libya.

I vividly recall when, in my capacity as a Director of Oil Affairs representing the Iraqi government, I attended a meeting of IPC directors with their shareholders in Lisbon, Portugal, at which the company representatives were infuriated over the Libyan government's tactics. One of them, a Mr Sutcliffe of BP, a tall man exuding a gratuitous arrogance, turned to me and exclaimed, 'Just look at this Colonel Gaddafi – trying to blackmail us by reducing production! We'll disappoint him because we're in a position to do without Libyan oil.' By talking in this presumptuous vein, this man (whom I knew only too well through earlier negotiations in Baghdad) showed how unaware he was of changed circumstances that had transformed the old colonial guard into a relic of the past. He was unaware of the fact that Gaddafi could succeed in his target by simply breaking the weakest link in the chain – the independent companies that had no alternative sources of crude oil outside Libya.

Because of a supply tightness in the market (when prices of oil products were rising, especially in Western Europe) the independent oil company, Occidental, found itself in dire need of more crude from Libya to meet its refinery requirements. This left the company with no choice but to comply with the Libyan government's demands for an upward correction to their oil pricing, a compliance that served to bolster the young Colonel Gaddafi in his dealings with other oil companies which, contrary to Mr Sutcliffe's overconfident predictions, were now forced to emulate the example set by Occidental – when, for example, the latter accepted the Libyan government's increase in tax ratio from 50 to 55 per cent. This in turn boosted the price of Libyan crude, reflecting more realistically its advantages.

Libya's bold demands under Gaddafi heralded the new winds of change that were blowing through OPEC. By 1970, a major change had occurred in the relationship between the oil companies and their host countries, as if the latter had won a major victory, entirely through Libya's action. This marked a redefining moment in the history of the oil industry, and a very different atmosphere now prevailed within OPEC, which began to redefine itself as a newly empowered entity.

For the first time the organisation could consider a collective entry into negotiations with the oil companies (which in the past had always refused to negotiate collectively with OPEC). Whenever agreements on 'expensing of royalties' had been concluded, the companies (while agreeing to the principle) had insisted on bilateral agreements, between individual oil company negotiating directly with individual OPEC member country, despite the formula being identical.

Next, OPEC's Caracas meeting, held in December 1970, was to mark the decision of OPEC members to authorise 'a negotiating committee' that would represent OPEC member countries bordering the Gulf, and which would be invested with principles and influence, if not control, over the oil price and the tax ratio.

To get to Caracas we boarded the then Venezuelan Airlines in Madrid, where it was extremely cold in December of that year, and so I was dressed in heavy winter apparel with little idea of the hot weather awaiting us in Caracas. Still wearing my heavy clothes when I emerged from the plane into a blast of hot air and oppressive humidity, I nearly fainted. We stayed at the Sheraton Hotel in the area called La Guerra, which is a resort for tourists to enjoy swimming in the Caribbean. The city of Caracas was itself higher than La Guerra but it was decided not to hold the ministerial meetings in the capital for security reasons. At the time, extremists were engaged in guerrilla warfare and were in the habit of kidnapping prominent people, ambassadors or ministers. The government settled on the Sheraton in La Guerra as a safer option for the delegates, both as venue and accommodation, being easier for their security patrols to monitor. Only the opening session was held in the capital, where the President of the Republic gave his opening speech. I asked one of the escorts of the delegation to accompany me into the city to buy light, summer clothes. The next day, on arrival at the opening session, the ambassadors of the various Arab countries that were accredited to Venezuela, informed OPEC's Arab ministers that the Ambassador of Israel was present with other Israeli diplomats. This predicament risked turning into a major crisis, as the Arab oil ministers, who formed the majority in OPEC, resolutely refused to attend the session with the Israeli ambassador present. Since the beginning of the Arab–Israeli conflict, the policy of Arab countries was to boycott Israel and anything related to it. The hostility of the Arab oil ministers greatly embarrassed the Venezuelan government, which seemed oddly unaware of – and hence unprepared for – the intensity of anti-Israeli sentiment engendered by their conflict. This delayed the opening session until Venezuela's Foreign Minister convinced the Israeli ambassador of the wisdom of leaving, disinclined though he was to depart.

The President of the Republic of Venezuela during this period (from 1969 to 1974) was Rafael Caldera. Caldera, a moderate Christian Democrat, became President for a second term, from 1994 to 1999, after a certain paratrooper named Hugo Chávez had attempted to orchestrate a *coup d'état* in 1992 against President Carlos Andrés Pérez. The coup failed, Chávez was caught and imprisoned for two years, but he was pardoned by the benign Caldera, who by then had been re-elected as President, and in order to pacify his country had granted an amnesty to guerrilla militants in an attempt to incorporate them into the democratic political process. Caldera's benevolent policy proved most fortuitous for Hugo Chávez, whose release marked the initiation of his own successful pursuit of power by democratic election. But once Chávez found himself elected, he was evidently very keen to entrench his power – along with an endless flow of anti-American rhetoric.

Incongruous though our hotel setting was for such a serious event as this OPEC meeting (a beautiful, relaxed holiday resort with its direct access to the Caribbean Sea), it was nevertheless here – as 1970 drew to a close – that we began our crucial session that would influence the oil industry more than any OPEC measure so far taken at that stage. Firstly, it was decided that the new 'negotiating committee' comprising oil ministers from Iran, Saudi Arabia and Iraq (as representing OPEC members bordering the Gulf) would commence talks with the oil companies in Tehran as soon as possible. For this purpose the Iranian Oil Minister, Dr Jamshid Amouzegar, by virtue of being the host country's minister, became the de facto spokesman, not only for the Committee but also for OPEC. The committee was authorised to fix an across-the-board increase in prices and amend the tax ratio in the manner that Libya had. There were odd discussions about what kind of across-the-board increase the price should take. There were two trends of thought: on the one hand, the moderates, represented by Sheikh Ahmed Zaki Yamani, Saudi Arabia's oil minister, who declared that he would be happy with an increase of 16 cents per barrel; and on the other, the hawkish side, namely Libya and Algeria, who were asking for a larger increase. The decision was finally to authorise this Negotiating Committee to fix the amount of the increase and also to amend the tax ratio.

With the Iranian minister heading the Committee, Tehran was chosen as the venue and January 1971 was set for negotiations to begin with the oil companies. The choice of Tehran was a thorny issue for Iraq as tensions between Iran and Iraq had reached boiling point. The Iraqi Oil Minister, the (late) Dr Sa'doun Hammadi, expressed his reluctance and embarrassment at having to negotiate in Tehran in the circumstances, though later felt no regret. I encouraged him not to think of Tehran as the problem but to focus only on Iraq's interests, agreeing to terms that could benefit Iraq, including resolving the government's disputes with the oil companies in pricing Basra crude oil, which the companies had pegged at a lower level than its real value. I agreed with him that our presence in Tehran was awkward, especially at a time when the Shah was fomenting, or at the very least aiding, rebellion among Iraqi Kurds in the north and providing the Kurdish guerrillas with money and arms, to help destabilise the Iraqi regime. It was at this time that a French engineer, working in a small Iraqi oil field near the border, had been kidnapped by the Iranians.

Our Iraqi delegation was undeterred and participated very actively during these crucial Tehran negotiations. The event gave me a unique opportunity for learning and reporting to the ministers. During the course of the negotiations we flew various times to Tehran in a military aircraft and on arrival the Iranian Minister always greeted us at the airport with unfailing courtesy.

During the course of the Tehran negotiations, OPEC people were struck by the prospect of a whole new dimension opening up before their eyes. Here, at last, representatives of the oil-producing nations could discuss important issues on an equal footing with the oil companies. This was different from the old times when the oil-producing countries, as 'hosts' to the companies, were little more than tax collectors, leaving to the companies the full management of oil operations. There was now an OPEC technical group designated for discussions with technical staff from the oil companies, while the ministerial Committee addressed pricing and policy decisions with the companies' directors. It was my first tough experience with OPEC negotiations, but I coped with it fairly well, and on a technical level I played an important role, while also acting as a rapporteur, bringing cases to the ministerial committee. This helped me acquire solid experience in oil pricing, taking into account quality and geographical location, and how to calculate the value of crude oil in the exporting terminals, 'netting back' the price of products in the main consuming areas – namely Rotterdam and East Coast USA – after deducting the cost of refining crude oil, transporting it, etc. In this respect I found the Tehran experience a personally valuable one, not only being called on to report directly to the ministers, which provided an opportunity to establish good rapports (and be noted or even appreciated); but above all it gave me a first-hand knowledge of oil market operations and the economics of the international oil industry. Among the technical people actively participating in the technical discussions, there was an Iranian, Dr Parvis Mina, who had valuable experience, as well as a civilised refinement, altogether an excellent, very courteous person, with whom a good friendship formed, lasting even today. After Ayatollah Khomeini's revolution in 1979, Mina left Iran and now lives in Paris.

In January and February 1971, I travelled so many times to Tehran during this round of negotiations with the companies that I had ample opportunity to acquaint myself with this remarkable city, with its streets bearing the distinguished names of Persian history and literature, such as the avenue named after the great Persian poet, Hafez. Our Iraqi delegation, headed by Dr Sa'doun Hammadi, used a shuttle between Baghdad and Tehran, which facilitated our purchase of Iranian goods, and to this day I treasure my Persian carpet, not only for its magnificent colours and craftsmanship but also because I associate my acquisition of it with those remarkable times. I had longed to see this ancient city since my childhood, for which my experience as a visitor to Tehran now revived nostalgic feelings, having been born in the north of Baghdad in a city called Kadhimain, one of the four centres where Shiites from Iran visited the shrines of descendants of the prophet Mohammed. The most prominent of these was Karbala, where the prophet's grandson Hussein was slaughtered and buried, and in Kadhimain itself (where Persian exists alongside the Arabic language, especially in the 'Astrabadi Bazaar' or marketplace) there are the tombs of two Shiite imams, descendants of the prophet Mohammed, to which Iranian women made pilgrimages, some deciding to stay, just to be near these shrines. Many worked as servants, as was the case in our home. In early childhood, I would listen uncomprehendingly to their chatter, as, with the exception of my father, none of our family spoke either modern Farsi or the old Persian. One of my early childhood memories was being taken by my father to the Turkish public baths, where, obscured by steam, Iranians could be heard singing, the acoustics of the bathhouse giving their melodies a haunting resonance that I found moving, accustomed as I was to hearing records at home of oriental (mostly Egyptian) songs and music.

The shining star of our Tehran negotiations was our host country's Iranian oil minister, Dr Jamshid Amouzegar, who was spokesman not only for the OPEC countries bordering the Gulf but for the entire organisation. He was an intelligent man and a very good speaker, though as Minister of Finance he had only partial knowledge of oil affairs, which he tended to treat as a tax issue. On the Committee with Amouzegar was Saudi Arabia's minister, Sheikh Ahmed Zaki Yamani, and Iraq's minister, Dr Sa'doun Hammadi. The Kuwaiti minister, Abdul-Rahman al-Ateeqi, was present though not a Committee member, an amiable man sporting a thick, dark moustache, aptly nicknamed by company representatives as one of the Marx Brothers. Representatives from Qatar and Abu Dhabi joined us, but OPEC's Secretary General, Dr Nadim Pachachi, was absent owing to an acute bout of influenza. In his place he had sent a representative from the Secretariat, Dr Abdul Amir al-Anbari.[3] At the time my surmise was that Pachachi had abstained from the Tehran meeting because the Iranians had earlier vetoed his appointment as Deputy Secretary General, accusing him of being 'a pro-company man', but apparently this was not the case.

During the four rounds of negotiations difficulties arose, mainly because of the lack of a common language and also OPEC member countries and their representatives were not fully acquainted with the issues, as they had never been directly involved in oil affairs. They had a very limited knowledge of the pricing and marketing of oil, and knew only about oil tax levies, which provided the main revenue with which to finance their budgets. For the companies' part, some delegates represented an older generation that tended to have a patronising attitude towards certain OPEC member states, some of which were still British protectorates under the mandate system, such as Qatar and Abu Dhabi. All things considered, not surprisingly the first round of negotiations reached a stalemate and was nearly derailed when the oil-producing countries' representatives held out for a minimum across-the-board increase (estimated at the time to be US$0.34 per barrel), in addition to increasing the tax ratio by 5 per cent. Various other issues were also raised concerning member countries' specific problems with the oil companies.

The Tehran negotiations were characterised by much sabre rattling, and as soon as the oil ministers presented their demands, the companies responded with much less than the producers were asking for. Negotiations, reaching a stalemate, were adjourned to another date, so that the company representatives would have enough time to consult their superiors. At last, in February 1971, while the fourth and final round of negotiations were on track, the deadlock was broken by government representatives taking a final position that the companies either 'take it or leave it'.

This showed how the Tehran experience had imbued OPEC delegates with a newly found self-confidence, and how it represented a perceptible change in the relationship between producers and companies. There was no trace now of the old anachronistic colonial hauteur of a bygone era that I had experienced earlier in Baghdad with the BP representative (Sutcliffe) and IPC London executive (Geoffrey Stockwell), who had inexcusably failed to take seriously the Iraqi government's representatives.

By this stage of the negotiations, and with the arrival of OPEC ministers from outside the Gulf, the atmosphere was becoming theatrical, involving the Shah in a meeting (in the parliament building) set up by 'protocol people' in order to agree what the minimum demands should be. We waited for some time before the Shah arrived. Our seats, tagged with our names, were set at a lower level than the Shah's majestic throne, which was studded with precious stones and with good reason called the 'Peacock Throne'. Suddenly a great fanfare announced the arrival of this king of kings, who with great swagger paraded his entry like a pageant, such was his air of self-aggrandisement, as if owning the whole world. A hush ensued and Minister Amouzegar solemnly took the parliamentary speaker's chair to explain the final position of the negotiating team. This heralded another scene of great solemnity with each OPEC minister taking the floor in turn to express his government's position vis-à-vis the negotiations. All ministers were speaking 'in one language' in that their governments supported the final position of the Committee's negotiating team. It was agreed that given any instance where oil companies exerted pressure on a country by boycotting its oil, other OPEC countries would undertake not to oblige the companies by increasing production to compensate for the supply gap resulting from the boycott.

I was as intrigued by this revolutionary decision, as much as I had been baffled by the theatricality of the whole scene preceding it. At that time it was quite extraordinary for countries that were not yet independent solemnly to assume a pose of absolute autonomy, given that their relationship with the oil companies had amounted to little more than the role of tax collectors. It was fascinating to see the Tehran meeting in February 1971 as the harbinger of change, a new wind blowing everything in reverse. The Tehran outcome empowered OPEC and reversed the dominance of the oil companies. It was the first sign of a collective engagement in oil politics, and it would revolutionise energy policies in the industrial world, whose oil-based economies for decades had been guaranteed strong growth by the secure flow of very cheap oil. The spectacular economic growth of Western Europe and Japan was due largely to artificially cheap oil from the Middle East, which effectively subsidised their economies, aiding their recovery after the Second World War. This had been to the cost of the oil-producing countries, which had virtually no resources other than oil.

So that we had the Iraqi government's sanction for the ministerial announcement at the Tehran meeting, Minister Hammadi asked me to fly to Baghdad to obtain authorisation from Iraq's Vice President, General Amash, who, as al-Bakr's second-in-command, was responsible for the government's oil policies. As there was no direct flight between Tehran and Baghdad, I took an Iranian plane to Abadan and then flew to Kuwait for a connecting flight. On arrival in Kuwait, I requested from the Kuwait Airlines desk a ticket for the next available flight to Baghdad, soon to depart, but was told that the plane was already full. In view of the urgency of securing General Amash's approval for the Tehran announcement, I approached the Iraqi Embassy in Kuwait, where a smart, heavily moustached man introduced himself as the labour attaché. He may also have been attached to the Iraqi intelligence service for when I apprised him of the situation his reply was as instant as it was laconic: 'No problem. You will fly on a Kuwait Airlines flight, which will depart very soon.' He swiftly disappeared and half an hour later returned bearing a first-class ticket for the very same flight that I had been informed (and had explained to him) was 'full'. 'Here you are, sir, and have a good trip to Baghdad,' was all he said. I was so puzzled at how this Iraqi Embassy attaché could pull strings and secure my seat from a fully booked *non-Iraqi* airline, that I asked him, and his response was equally baffling: 'No problem. I just asked them to request one of their passengers to delay his trip.' It made me wonder just how influential the Iraqi Embassy in Kuwait must have been.

On arrival in Baghdad, I met General Amash, who had been expecting me, and before I could even begin explaining the situation, I was chastised for keeping him waiting when he was 'starving', and told that we 'oil people' always brought problems. After informing him of the Tehran proceedings, I secured his authorisation, and then asked if he could arrange a plane to hasten my return to Iran. This he did, and I arrived in Tehran just in time for my minister to express his government's position along with the others.

The oil companies did accept OPEC's minimum demands and they signed the Tehran Agreement on 15 February 1971. Retrospective to 1 January that year, this agreement was binding for five years, after which period it was to be renegotiated. In addition to an across-the-board price increase (amounting to 35 cents per barrel) as well as an increased tax ratio, Iraq also benefitted in correcting the price of its oil to the Basra price, which hitherto the oil companies had refused to do. The agreement stipulated an annual increase of 2.5 per cent to offset world inflation and an annual increment of 5 cents per barrel, per year.

The evening before the Tehran agreement was signed, we were sitting with the Iranian oil minister, Jamshid Amouzegar, who looked extremely tired. I happened to make an observation about the agreement to the effect that it would likely restrict OPEC negotiators exporting their oil from the Mediterranean; and, as far as Iraq was concerned, this was a vitally important point, as the larger part of Iraqi oil exports went via the Syrian pipeline to the east Mediterranean terminals. At this Amouzegar grew furious, having misinterpreted my observation as an accusation, which was not at all my intention. I apologised profusely, but fearing that a problem could arise for Libyan, Saudi and Iraqi oil exported from the Mediterranean, Amouzegar continued his harangue, blaming me for not appreciating all his efforts. His manner embarrassed both me and my minister. Others intervened, notably the amiable Kuwaiti minister, Abdul-Rahman al-Ateeqi, who reassured the Iranian minister that Chalabi was 'a man of good intention and experience' who had painstakingly contributed to the technical side and to the success of the negotiations. At this Minister Amouzegar at last calmed down.

The next day brought a great victory for the OPEC producers, and to celebrate the signing of the Tehran Agreement, that evening an elaborate dinner was held by the Iranians, attended by all the signatories – the companies and OPEC oil ministers. There was much food and drink, and very good French wines, and it was altogether a pompous and lavish affair, during which the Iranian minister, Amouzegar, took the microphone and gave a charming speech about the agreement, its significance in auguring a co-operative relationship between the producers and the oil companies. On our return to Baghdad we went directly to the Presidential Palace of the Republic to meet President Ahmed Hassan al-Bakr, to whom we explained the new agreement and what it could mean for Iraq's oil revenues, at a time when the government's finances were at their lowest ebb.

President al-Bakr and his second-in-command, General Amash, were almost ecstatic at the news. For the government, this agreement brought joy at a time when the relationship with the oil companies had soured and was at its worst. The IPC companies were failing to meet the terms of the concession agreement, which made it mandatory that they increase production from the territory left them for their operations. Iraq's oil production was thus badly neglected, left to stagnate to the advantage of Iran, Saudi Arabia, Abu Dhabi and the others.

With this resultant loss of Iraq's oil revenues, the situation prior to the new Tehran Agreement had become so dire that once, in 1970, I was recalled to attend an urgent meeting, chaired by the President, to resolve a problem of obtaining $30 million for an agricultural project, which was extremely urgent but for which there was no budget appropriation. President al-Bakr asked how more funding from oil could be obtained, at which Minister Hammadi suggested that the President allow me to explain. My answer was that, as long as any mutual understanding between the government and the IPC was blocked, there was no hope of increasing oil production – and hence revenues for Iraq, because the companies, in face of the Iraqi deadlock, had shifted their production expansion programmes to Saudi Arabia, Kuwait and elsewhere at the expense of Iraq. The meeting had ended in consternation, lamenting the trifling amount of $30 million for a country said to sit on a lake of oil, as has always been the Iraqi legend.

Therefore, when we returned from Tehran and presented President al-Bakr with the news of a substantial increase in store for Iraq's oil revenues, his facial expression transformed from moroseness to elation, and he even laughed with joy at the prospect of counteracting the earlier IPC refusal to increase production.

The next day, in my office, I was surprised by the sudden arrival of a messenger from the Presidential Palace, clutching an envelope in his hand. When I opened it I found some 500 Iraqi dinars (then about US$1,500). It was a gift from the grateful President, but my instant reaction was not to accept it. I told my minister, Hammadi, that I had no intention of doing so, as accepting this money would be legally unsound and not in accordance with accounting procedures and regulations, especially as it had been sent without an official letter. At this Hammadi smiled and advise me to accept it, as any refusal on my part could be misinterpreted as offensive, betraying an attitude of condescension towards the President. I reluctantly accepted his argument, but disliked being forced to accept such an archaic, antiquated expression of 'appreciation'. But, after all, the President was a Bedouin, despite his military rank, and for a Bedouin such a gesture of gratitude was culturally ingrained, an ancient tradition of generosity. It so happened that at that time I was in debt from the construction of a house on a piece of land, sold by the government to its employees at a very cheap price. Despite my protests, I was truly grateful for this windfall as it helped me to repay most of my debt!

No sooner had the 'first act' of the new OPEC opera in Tehran finished, the curtains were raised on the second act, which entailed negotiations with the companies on the issue of oil exported from the Mediterranean. As Iraq exports most of its oil through the Syrian pipeline to the east Mediterranean, and Saudi Arabia also exports some of its oil to the east Mediterranean to Sidon in Lebanon, it was decided that both the Saudi Minister, Sheikh Yamani, and Iraqi Minister, Dr Hammadi, would travel to Tripoli to consult the Libyans (and possibly the Algerians) over the most appropriate tactics in our collective negotiations with the oil companies. I joined both ministers Hammadi and Sheikh Yamani, who was accompanied by his Undersecretary, Mr Mohamed Joukhdar (formerly a Secretary General of OPEC by rotation).

It was the spring of 1971 when we boarded a small Saudi private jet from Beirut. I sat at some distance behind the others as I was engrossed in Miles Copeland's book, *Game of Nations*, especially – as mentioned – on the subject of military coups in the Middle East and the role played by CIA agents (in particular Kim Roosevelt[4]). This book, which had been recently published, had caused a considerable stir. Sheikh Yamani soon beckoned me, calling out, 'Why are you seated so far from us? Come and sit with us!' I explained how I was very absorbed in Copeland's book and he replied that he could understand, having read it himself. Next thing we flew into a sandstorm, while approaching Tripoli airport, and it was impossible for the pilot to see the runway for landing. Through the window I could observe the pilot's repeated endeavours to land and how, realising he was in the wrong area, he would quickly climb again to correct his bearings. I nervously watched the aircraft's wing dipping, fearful that it might touch the ground at any moment. Hammadi's and Joukhdar's faces had turned white with terror. Sheikh Yamani remained very calm and talked to them in an effort to take their minds off the ordeal. I noticed him twice going to the cockpit and returning as if nothing had happened. He later told us that this was a bid to get the pilot to land at the nearest Tunisian airport (Jerba) but the captain had replied that there was insufficient fuel for this. I quelled my fear by reciting verses from the Qur'an, which Muslims, as a rule, do when facing death. After a miraculously safe landing we met the Libyan minister, al-Mabrook, and a large team of assistants, doctors and an ambulance all prepared for disaster.

The next day we met Libya's 'number two', a Lieutenant Abdul Salam Jaloud, and my first impression was of a quite small, unkempt man shouting in a strong Libyan accent while beating his fists uncontrollably on his desk in an angry outburst. 'Our oil! Our oil!' he shouted, thumping his desk, 'it's the blood in the arteries of those countries in the West and yet they grab it so cheaply! What if we cut off their supplies?' Libya, we immediately discerned, was seeking a higher price increase than the Tehran Agreement had allowed for. It is to be recalled that Libya had pioneered aspects that had helped move OPEC into its 'new era'. Imbued with their own success and in their sense of leadership of OPEC, the Libyans scrutinised the Tehran Agreement with a critical eye.

Despite Libya's crude oil being of a far superior quality than Gulf oil, the companies were under-pricing it by means of the API (American Petroleum Institute) system[5] according to which light crude, despite yielding a higher percentage of gasoline, was priced without any consideration of its superior quality or sulphur content. This disadvantaged the almost sulphur-free Libyan crude. According to the API degree system, very light oil from North Africa was priced higher than other crudes by US$0.2 per degree of API, so that Libyan oil of 41.API was 10 cents more expensive than Arab Light. This was a negligible amount that did not reflect the true value of Libya's light crude, especially when taking into account the value of the refined products from this crude.

In view of its hard line on the price increase for Mediterranean crudes, Libya conducted unilaterally its own negotiations with the oil companies instead of following the Tehran pattern of collective negotiations with other OPEC members. It was Libya, therefore, that took the initiative and signed with the oil companies what became known as the Tripoli Agreement. This agreement, struck in March 1971, radically changed Libya's oil-pricing structure, for the first time boosting its price by 10 cents per barrel as a 'sulphur premium', reflecting at last the quality of its oil and its geographical location.

The trip to Libya was not my first, as I had already visited the country at the request of General Amash following the 1969 coup to observe the outcome of the new government's oil policy. Despite the fact that Tripoli was a modest city it was very beautiful with its Italian marble balustrades, especially along the promenade which, surrounded by trees, encircled the curve of the bay, giving different angles from which to view the ever-changing blue sea. Having enjoyed very much walking along this promenade, on subsequent trips, I noticed a distinct deterioration, especially in 1987, during an OPEC ministerial mission, staying only overnight in order to meet with the same 'number two', Jaloud, who by then seemed to have regained his composure.

On my return from Tripoli to Baghdad, I flew with Minister Hammadi in an Iraqi military cargo aircraft, with only two or three passenger seats. After another hazardous trip, losing height, with a continuous, loud mechanical vibration, when we at last landed in Baghdad the captain reassured us that it was God who had saved us, as the technical fault in the engine was grave and the aircraft could have plunged at any moment had we not landed just in time! The captain had informed the airport tower without telling us about the dangerous situation. We later learnt that, on his safe arrival, this captain's family offered a sacrificial lamb, an Arab Islamic practice which, of course, takes its origin from Abraham's sacrifice of a lamb in place of his son – upon the intervention of God after His 'test of faith'.

Having reached the conclusion that collective negotiations with the companies were ruled out concerning OPEC oil exported from Mediterranean ports, and that Libya was to 'go it alone', it was thought that Iraq and Saudi Arabia should co-ordinate on their crudes exported from the east Mediterranean: Banias, and Tripoli and Sidon in Lebanon. For this purpose it was decided that Minister Hammadi and I would go to Riyadh to meet Sheikh Yamani, who, as he was now separated from his first wife, was living in a suite attached to the main hotel in the city. He welcomed us, and discussions began. He held the opinion that we should implement the same across-the-board-price increase decided in Tehran, as well as other provisions. After the discussions I remember Yamani talking to us about the old ruins in the south of the Arab peninsula, inhabited by ancient tribes, Aad and Thamoud, mentioned in the Qur'an as the people who carved houses for themselves in the rocks of the mountains. I showed my interest in this topic and told him of my wish to go and see this place one day. At this Hammadi looked surprised, as the Iraqi government, secular in outlook, assumed incorrectly from my earlier, youthful Marxist leanings that I had no religious affiliation. Just because I appeared not to observe some Islamic duties (weekly attendance of the Mosque, overt prayers, fasting during Ramadan or abstention from wine or any alcohol) this did not mean that I was not devoted to reading the Qur'an, which I still am. Ever since the shock of the 1967 Six Day War (during my time in Geneva), I had observed a daily ritual of reading the Qur'an after taking a shower. This revered and wonderful book is charged with great spiritual strength and a fundamental knowledge of human nature, so that during the reading process one draws from it a sense of great metaphysical power lying behind our universe, relative to which man feels he is but a small drop in a great ocean.

In March 1971, when Libya had signed its Tripoli Agreement, Minister Hammadi asked me to return to Riyadh to meet the Saudi Minister and tell him that Iraq accepted the Saudi approach to pricing east Mediterranean crude oil. Before returning (that same day) to Baghdad, I asked the man accompanying me from the Saudi Ministry to drive me through parts of Riyadh. He asked what I would prefer to see. Having little time to spare, I expressed a wish to see first and foremost the old palace of the House of Saud, which is no longer residential. After driving only about 15 minutes, we reached the area where the old palaces are situated, the exterior walls of which were of an extremely simple construction of baked bricks; but what struck me on arrival was the severe poverty of people living in the area. Their living quarters were made mostly from large, empty tin containers stuck together with mud mixed with straw, and this was in a region where summer temperatures can rise to over 50°C in the shade.

I took the military aircraft back to Baghdad; and there, according to an agreement reached with Sheikh Yamani, it was decided that each country should sign separately an agreement with the oil companies, appropriate to the understanding reached between the two countries. When we informed the IPC management of our readiness to sign an agreement on Iraq's crude oil exported from the east Mediterranean, it was the IPC London executive mentioned earlier, Geoffrey Stockwell, who came to sign on behalf of the companies. While we were talking and agreeing on the text, which was then made ready for signature by Stockwell and the Iraqi Minister, Hammadi, there was suddenly an electrical power failure and we were plunged into darkness. During the power cut, people brought in candles and placed them in front of Stockwell and the minister. The English sense of humour was demonstrated by this man who professed how happy he was to be signing the agreement in the romantic atmosphere of candlelight. He enjoyed his joke, while everyone, except Hammadi, joined in the laughter.

Not long after signing this agreement in October 1973 something unexpected happened. To everyone's surprise, the US government suddenly announced that it was to cease the official convertibility of the dollar to the gold standard. According to the Keynesian-inspired conclusion of the Bretton Woods Agreement of 1944, the dollar had become the world international reserve currency, to which other currencies were pegged at fixed rates, with the dollar being convertible to gold at a rate of $4 per 1 oz of pure gold, anyone holding dollars had the right to buy gold at this rate. As the real value of the dollar was in decline, the US government decided to devalue it by 8.5 per cent. This was a momentous decision for the oil producing countries as it devalued the oil prices negotiated at the Tehran Agreement. It was for this reason that OPEC suggested amending the latter agreement with a view to preserving the real value of oil. Given that the price of oil is denominated in dollars, and most oil market transactions are in dollars, the purchasing power for oil for other currencies had been considerably reduced.

In fact, the dollar had been under increasing pressure since the end of the 1960s as a result of a growing deficit in the USA's trade balance. This meant that fixed exchange rates (according to the Breton Woods Agreement) had ceased to reflect market realities, as the financial markets showed that the value of the dollar was falling. The effect of this on oil exported by OPEC depended on each member's trade pattern and the extent to which trade was concentrated in Europe or Japan, rather than with the USA. Those countries heavily dependent on US products were less affected. To this end, OPEC decided at the Caracas conference (December 1970) to take steps to protect the real price of oil against the devalued dollar.

Negotiations recommenced in Geneva with the oil companies to amend the 1971 Tehran Agreement and restore the purchasing power of the barrel. After delaying tactics, obfuscation with IMF data and general prevarication, finally the oil companies accepted the principle of protecting the oil price against variations in dollar exchange rates. On 20 January 1972, the important Geneva agreement was signed, which would become known as Geneva I (preceding a second Geneva agreement). The Tehran pricing was corrected by a formula devised for protecting the real price from currency fluctuations. For this purpose, a basket of nine major currencies (including the Deutschemark, sterling, French and Swiss francs and the Japanese yen) was chosen to monitor the extent of the decline in purchasing power, i.e. it was measured by the value of the currency basket. When, relative to this basket, the value of the US dollar declined, the oil price increased so as to retain the purchasing power of the oil barrel.

That evening, on the 20th, just after the agreement had been signed, another Iraqi delegation arrived in Geneva to participate in OPEC discussions concerning government participation in Middle East oil concessions and the historic implementation of OPEC's Resolution 90 of 1968. I was in my hotel room on the eve of my departure when the Iraqi delegates arrived from Baghdad. Among them was my friend Adnan Janabi, who came in and announced the happy news that my wife had just given birth to our fourth child, my daughter Dounia, and so we spent my last evening sipping French cognac in celebration.

Subsequent events in world money markets and the later decision to float currencies proved the inadequacy of the Geneva I agreement, and this led OPEC to negotiate another agreement in order to apply the new and mathematically complex mechanism for correcting the price in relation to the basket, to which the dollar itself was added. A second agreement, on the issue of the dollar, was also signed there called Geneva II.

In the coming pages we shall see the extent to which Iraq's oil politics and disputes with the companies contributed to the development of OPEC policies, especially after the Tehran Agreement of February 1971.

4

Iraq's oil politics: precursor of the demise of the concessions

Western rivalry for the control of Iraq's oil dates back to the late nineteenth century, when in 1890 Deutsche Bank of Germany succeeded in securing the agreement of the Ottoman government to build a Berlin–Baghdad railway, offering mining rights in 20-kilometre areas on both sides of the railway. In 1912 the TPC was established, which to begin with was jointly owned by Deutsche Bank and Anglo-Persian Oil Company. But after the First World War and Treaty of Versailles (June 1919), control of Iraq's oil fell to both Britain and France, and in the subsequent San Remo agreement of 1920, these two allies partitioned between them the now defunct Ottoman Empire. In this they were joined by the USA through their Open Door Policy.

Thus Western involvement in Iraqi oil effectively began with the establishment of the TPC as a holding company owned by the following shareholders: the Anglo-Persian Oil (the forerunner of BP), Royal Dutch Shell and Compagnie Française de Pétrole (CFP, which later became Total). Each acquired 23.75 per cent in shares, and similar percentage shares were acquired by two American companies: Mobil and Standard Oil of New Jersey (later Esso/Exxon). The remaining 5 per cent went to Calouste Gulbenkian, the original founder of TPC, nicknamed 'Mr Five Percent' (who, with his influence with the Turkish government, was courted by banking and other vested interests).

These five major shareholders of the TPC were interrelated within the Seven Sisters, whose exclusive oil concessions prevented an important free market trade in oil until the end of the 1960s. The concession system granted an exclusive right to explore, extract and export oil, leaving other investors unable to compete within the concession area.

In 1925, when the Iraqi government granted an oil concession to the five major TPC shareholders, one of its key conditions was the 'relinquishment' of those territories where concession holders failed to find or develop oil. This agreement involved the provision of various 'lots' of land, to be explored and developed within a certain time frame, at the end of which the territories would be returned to the government if the companies had not fulfilled their obligations. The relinquishment aspect was crucial in giving the government some leverage in getting territories developed, and if necessary by alternative companies. (Later, the Red Line Agreement was signed by the TPC on 31 July 1928, prohibiting any of its shareholders from seeking oil concessions independently in the former territory of the now defunct Ottoman Empire.)

In 1932 Iraq gained its full independence and admission to the League of Nations as a sovereign state, officially ceasing to be a League of Nations mandate under the administrative supervision of the British government. But Iraq's new rights proved more theoretical or *de jure* than de facto, given that Britain, retaining military bases and oil interests, effectively still controlled the country. This was exemplified by the manner in which the TPC oil companies had got the Iraqi government to agree, in 1931, to an exclusive 75-year concession for the whole area northeast of the Tigris, in which the relinquishment terms for undeveloped territories were now even abrogated, thus giving the company an absolute monopoly in the area. The Iraqi government had felt obliged to waive its right to the 1925-agreed principle of relinquishment as a quid pro quo for British support (at the League of Nations) for Iraq in its sovereignty dispute over Turkey's attempt to claim the Wilayet province of Mosul – the same Iraqi territory in which the supergiant oilfield of Kirkuk is located. With Britain's commanding position in Iraq's nascent statehood and its support in this territorial quarrel, the Iraqi government, under Prime Minister Nouri Pasha, felt it had little choice but to go along with the new agreement, despite fierce opposition from many Iraqi politicians. With this new agreement, shareholders converted the old TPC to the IPC.

In 1938 there was another major surrender on the part of the Iraqi government when it granted a concession for the entire territory south of Baghdad to the Basra Petroleum Company (BPC), owned by the same shareholders of the IPC. Prior to this, a concession had been granted to the Mosul Petroleum Company (MPC) for the northern part of Iraq, west of the River Tigris. All Iraq's territories thus fell under the monopoly of the IPC, denying the Iraqi government the right to invite other companies to develop its oil.

In this way, Iraq's oil presents a unique case in the history of the international petroleum industry. Although it is widely agreed that the country has abundant oil reserves, Iraq's real potential remains a big unknown because exploration and development were hampered for so long. Published data concerning the magnitude of reserves place Iraq after Saudi Arabia and Iran with the third largest proven reserves. But research undertaken by the CGES in collaboration with Petrolog suggests that Iraq's discoverable reserves may be twice its published reserves of 115 billion barrels (bn/B). Studies conducted by Iraq's Ministry of Oil give an even higher calculation. Whatever the case, Iraq's potential oil reserves are now estimated to be second only to Saudi Arabia's, and could even be equal.

This uncertainty in assessing the true magnitude of Iraqi reserves is the outcome of prolonged stagnation in exploratory efforts. In the entire world, no oil industry has been as disadvantaged as Iraq's. Since the discovery of the giant Kirkuk oilfield in 1927, Iraq has witnessed a total of only 15 years of intensive exploration during two periods. The first period, 1952 to 1961, saw the discovery of the giant Rumaila oil field in the south together with many smaller oilfields such as Zubair. During the second period, 1973 to 1980 (the year of the outbreak of the Iraq–Iran war), Iraq witnessed a period of intensive exploratory effort, resulting in the discovery of many giant oilfields, such as West Qurna, Halfaya, Majnoon, Nahr Umar, which in a matter of seven years added a prodigious 45 bn/B of new reserves. The magnitude of the discoveries gave credence to the legend that Iraq sits on a lake of oil.

This evident neglect of Iraq's oil industry stems firstly from certain restrictive methods of investment and development regulations of the foreign IPC concessionaires in the 1930s and 1940s when, after the discovery of the giant Kirkuk oilfield, virtually no investment was made in exploration and development. Anglo-Persian (in 1935 renamed Anglo-Iranian, antecedent of BP) and Standard Oil (antecedent of Esso) had access to plenty of crude oil outside Iraq and therefore preferred to hold the Iraqi concessions in reserve, but the French company, CFP, needed more oil and was keen to push on with developing Iraq's oil. These divergent interests among TPC concession holders further delayed the discovery and development of new oilfields in Iraq.

Then a second factor followed: Iraq's unrealistic oil politics in the 1960s provoked unnecessary deadlock with the companies, a situation that led to the transfer of exploration activities to other oil-producing countries. But, above all, from 1980 onwards it was Saddam's wars and prolonged UN economic sanctions that undermined Iraq's oil development.

Dealing first with the concession era, restrictive regulations arising from the IPC shareholders' divergent interests resulted in a serious stagnation of oil investment in Iraq, compared with counterpart development in Saudi Arabia and Iran. Anglo-Iranian (BP) had vast crude oil interests in Iran, surplus to its downstream requirements, i.e. refineries. Meanwhile, the American company, Exxon-Mobil, was keen to promote crude oil production in Saudi Arabia. The object of these two companies was *not* to increase investment in Iraq, which would have benefitted both Shell and the French company CFP, given their crude deficit, relative to their downstream requirements.

This meant that CFP and Shell, deprived of more access to cheap 'cost oil', had to buy crude oil from BP at a price much higher than the cost oil lifted in accordance with the concession agreement. The stronger IPC partners imposed these restrictive rules against the expansion of Iraq's oil industry so as to safeguard their own operations and thwart the competitive positions of CFP and Shell, whose instinct was to expand their operations in Iraq with the aim of securing cheaper crude for their expanding oil refineries. It was the conflicts of interest among shareholders which, giving rise to complex, restrictive regulations, in turn stifled Iraq's oil development – to the benefit of Saudi Arabia's and Iran's oil industries. In 1949 oil production in Saudi Arabia and Iran reached 0.477 million barrels per day (mbpd) and 0.561 mbpd respectively; whereas Iraq's production in the same year amounted to a mere 0.090 mbpd, despite the fact that Iraq's oil had been discovered ten years earlier than Saudi Arabia's. During this period of stagnation in Iraq, its oil revenues even dwindled, while Saudi Arabia's increased to $5.5 billion and Iran's to $3.7 billion.

In her book on the international petroleum industry,[1] Professor Edith Penrose describes IPC conflicts of interest giving rise to an extremely complicated system that severely hampered the progress of Iraq's oil industry. By contrast, in Kuwait, both Anglo-Iranian and Gulf had unrestricted access to oil through their joint owner-ship of the Kuwait Oil Company. If a similarly liberal agreement had been applied to Iraq 'the latter's output would have grown very much faster, and...the pressure to explore elsewhere felt by CFP...Shell and Mobil...would have been reduced'.[2] In contrast to the Kuwait agreement, under the 1948 Heads of Agreement, expan-sion of Iraq's oil industry was handicapped by the restrictive rules governing IPC operations, favouring – as explained earlier – the larger shareholders. Plans were agreed for the production of Iraq's crude oil for the whole consortium, with each shareholder contrib-uting to the investment according to his or her ownership share, and thus acquiring crude oil at cost. In accordance with the 1948 Heads of Agreement, a five-year plan was drawn up on the basis of each shareholder's nomination for crude oil reflecting the down-stream requirements: i.e. the distribution networks of refineries and products. The resulting balance between supply and demand – as a feature of the IPC regulatory system – was at that time emulated by concession systems elsewhere, until this model was overtaken by the 'Fifty–Fifty' profit-sharing agreement in 1952.

One positive feature of the major oil companies' integrated system was that supply interruption was avoided. Despite Mosaddegh's nationalisation of Iran's oil in 1951, the risk of oil shortage was averted by increasing production from Iraq and other oil-producing countries. The IPC then swiftly embarked on an ambi-tious expansion programme of exploration in Iraq and discovered the supergiant Rumaila oilfield, as well as other (smaller) oilfields. The group increased production from the South and constructed the Khor al-Amaia deep water terminal in the high seas of the Gulf, to which giant tankers could have access. As a result, by 1961, Iraq's oil production, at 1 mbpd, almost drew level with Iran's 1.2 mbpd and Saudi Arabia's 1.48 mbpd.

The year 1952 witnessed a major change in the history of Iraq's oil industry when an agreement was struck between the Iraq government and the oil companies in the application of the Fifty–Fifty profit-sharing agreement, which had by then been extended throughout the Middle East oil-exporting countries. In the aftermath of the Second World War, the USA devised a fiscal system to encourage American oil investments outside the USA by providing incentives to the oil companies with what was termed at the time a 'depletion allowance', the effect of which was to reduce US tax liability of American companies producing oil abroad wherever they had to pay higher taxes to the host governments. The Fifty–Fifty agreement had the effect of increasing oil revenues for the oil-producing countries, and also led to a rapid expansion of Iraqi oil.

During the royalist regime, the Iraqi government and the companies were beset by a number of outstanding issues, raised by the government as litigious, including the question of relinquishing territories, held under the monopoly of the companies and left unexplored and undeveloped. The government managed to steer clear of outright confrontation with the companies, from whom they were receiving oil revenues (despite their reservations). But strained relations with these companies reached deadlock after the revolution of 14 July 1958, when the old royalist regime was overthrown by a military *coup d'état*, headed by Abdul al-Karim Qassim, who seized power and established a republic.

By now the Iraqi negotiating team had a long list of grievances with the IPC group, some of which were insignificant, while others were of key importance, such as a 20 per cent government participation in the group's capital, and the companies' relinquishment of undeveloped territories. The participation claim on the part of the Iraqi government was based on the old 1920 San Remo agreement (involving, as mentioned earlier, Britain and France). This agreement provided that in the event of the oil companies listing shares on the stock market, the government of Iraq, or Iraqi individuals, would be entitled to 20 per cent of the shares. This same provision was again repeated in the agreements of 1925 and 1931, but their wording of this provision was such as to render it a 'dead letter', given that the IPC, as a non-profit holding company (owned by the British, American, French and Dutch companies), did not list shares on the stock market.

The government's negotiating team seemed unaware that its various demands would (according to the concession terms) involve an overhaul of the concession system for the entire Middle East region – and not just Iraq. Iraq stood alone in its bid to get the companies to concede to demands that were not even considered feasible until 15 years later, when OPEC achieved success as a collective negotiating power. This was because each concession agreement was hampered by a 'most favoured nation' clause, so that any privilege that Iraq obtained from the companies would have to be applied throughout the Middle East concession system. This very aspect encouraged the companies not to yield to Iraq's demands because, from the companies' perspective, to sacrifice Iraq, leave its oil industry undeveloped and instead expand elsewhere in more favourable conditions was far preferable to accommodating Iraq's demands and then being faced with the complications and tedium of remoulding the entire concession system accordingly.

Notwithstanding the injury to Iraq's stagnating oil industry, Qassim's regime made demands that turned a new page in the history of the international oil industry, as they highlighted grievances that were for the most part genuine and legitimate. This had the effect of discrediting the IPC and the existing concessionary framework, just at the point where OPEC would pick up the baton of leadership from Iraq in a quest to change the relationship between the oil companies and host governments. That Iraq was ahead of its time in spearheading a fundamental change that would hasten the demise of the concession system is noted by Penrose, who also records how Iraq had to pay a heavy price, with its oil industry being penalised by the companies (which had the backing of their powerful governments):

> One of Iraq's major objectives was to break the existing pattern of profit-sharing and ownership in the major concessions in the Middle East. Iraq paid a stiff price for being ahead of her time... [given that the country] obtained neither an increased share of the profits nor a share in ownership... The pattern was not to be broken for ten years... the companies, though continuing to produce, failed to expand Iraqi output significantly... When they did start increasing output, the increase was well below that of other exporting countries in the Middle East. Ten years later other countries were still receiving substantially greater per barrel revenues from oil and Iraq was still locked in serious conflict with the companies, while Iraqi national production from the expropriated areas was only just beginning.[3]

Throughout the process of renegotiations with the oil companies the approach of the Iraqi government's negotiating team was inept and lacked vision – especially in the way the team put aside important priorities affecting the future of Iraq's oil. The team did not avail itself of opportunities that were within its grasp. Its failure to seize the chance of achieving positive results and developing Iraq's oil industry prevented the country from being a major player among the other oil producers.

In particular the government's regulatory team neglected a rational solution of the issue of relinquishing undeveloped territories, which had already been raised with the companies towards the end of the royalist regime. After the revolution of 1958, whenever the question of the percentage of territory-relinquishment was addressed and the companies were prepared for agreement, the government team then escalated the percentage. Having initially asked for an immediate relinquishment of 50 per cent of the territories covered by the three concessions (amounting to the entire territory of Iraq), they then increased this to 60 per cent, then 75 per cent and even 90 per cent. The final position of the government was pronounced by Abdul al-Karim Qassim himself, having dictated a draft letter to be addressed by the companies to the government, expressing their readiness to relinquish 75 per cent immediately and a further 15 per cent a few years later.

Perceiving that this demand was acceptable to the companies (who, according to Penrose, were ready to relinquish even 90 per cent of the territories), Qassim was on the point of announcing the success of the first round of negotiations when his tough negotiating team insisted that unless the companies accept the principle of government participation in 20 per cent of the companies' capital there could be no satisfactory conclusion. This obdurate moving of the goalposts brought negotiations into instant deadlock. As a result, the government promulgated, in 1961, Public Law no. 80, by which the Iraqi government recovered 99.5 per cent of territories covered by the three concession agreements, leaving to the companies only the territories in active production, which amounted to 0.5 per cent, in both the north and south.

The oil companies objected to the government's unilateral legislation as a breach of the 1925 and subsequent agreements. They requested that the matter be referred for international arbitration, and that any amendment to the agreement be made only by mutual consent. But the demand for arbitration was ignored by the Iraqi government. This rebuff inevitably renewed the deadlock.

The companies were backed by their powerful governments (the US, the UK, France and the Netherlands), whose official stance was to treat the 'invested-in' territories recovered by the government as 'disputed territories'. This exposed the Iraqi government to the risk of litigation. As a result, the Iraqi government was unable to conclude any agreement with other foreign investors to develop Iraq's huge oil reserves, which were now abandoned and left in the ground. For their part, the companies froze any expansion in production from their allocated oilfields, with the result that Iraq's oil production stagnated, to Iran's and Saudi Arabia's gain.

The year 1965 saw a fresh round of negotiations between Iraq's post-Qassim government and the oil companies. A draft agreement was reached, but not ratified, between the two sides, by which the companies declared their recognition of Law no. 80 with the proviso that para. 3 of the law be implemented to the effect that the government would cede to the companies part of the recovered territories equal to that allocated to the companies by the same law, i.e. another 0.5 per cent of the recovered territories. The significance of this part of the draft agreement was that the additional territory to be restored to the companies would comprise the oil-rich northern area of the giant Rumaila oilfield, discovered by the companies but so far left undeveloped. The newly drafted agreement stipulated that the government would retain 99 per cent of the territories together with a jointly owned national company, Baghdad Petroleum: to be owned by the INOC and the shareholders of the IPC (with the exception of Exxon), with the aim of developing about 7.5 per cent of the recovered territories; and with the proviso that it be reduced every three years by 25 per cent. While, INOC would retain one-third of the capital of the new joint company, the oil companies, for their part, undertook to increase substantially Iraq's oil exports from the territories allocated to them.

Had this draft agreement been fully ratified, it would have given a whole new dimension to the development of Iraq's oil industry. During that post-war period, oil consumption in Western Europe and Japan increased at extremely high rates, with consumption in

Western Europe doubling almost every ten years, while Japan's consumption grew even faster. Meanwhile INOC, established in 1964, could have undertaken joint ventures with individual oil companies from Japan, Italy, Spain, Germany and the USA to develop some of Iraq's prolific oil reserves, which were readily discoverable, without causing problems with the companies or their governments.

However, the draft agreement was aborted because pro-Nasser or 'Nasserite' army officers threatened Iraq's President Abdul Salam A'ariff with a *coup d'état* if he dared ratify the agreement with the oil companies. They objected chiefly to the proposal to hand back to the oil companies the northern part of the Rumaila oilfield, which was considered the most oil-rich and which they insisted should be developed directly by INOC. These Nasserite politicians and army officers argued that the proposed new agreement would be against national interests and contravened Law no. 80 of 1961, which for Iraq's oil politics had become a symbol of nationalist aspirations.

Nasserite influences, prevalent in Iraq, were not as salient among Iraq's more pragmatic oil-exporting neighbours; and for Iraq this 'oil nationalism' proved self-defeating. Although Iraq's hypersensitivity towards foreign oil companies understandably stemmed from the old era of 'colonial rule' when oil concessions were imposed by the British after the First World War, this over-politicisation of its oil ensured not only stagnation of Iraq's oil industry but also oil's treatment henceforth as a political commodity with which to outbid other politicians and political parties.

The promulgation of Law no. 80 in 1961 and the non-ratification of the 1965 agreement with the companies were driven by political sentiment, without any consideration of Iraq's economic benefit. Instead of taking advantage of what was economically beneficial and realistically available, Iraq allowed its oil politics to be influenced by impractical nationalistic ideals and slogans, with the result that Iraq became the loser, as if it had even opted to serve the interests of the other Gulf producers. This illustrates how self-defeating Iraq's oil politics had become.

Iraq's share of total Gulf oil production had been 18 per cent. By the time of Law no. 80, Iraq's 1 mbpd oil production (as pointed out) had almost caught up with Iran's and Saudi Arabia's (1.2 and

1.48 mbpd, respectively). Yet over the next nine years, thanks to disputes in negotiations between the government and the companies, Iraq's production by 1972 dwindled to an 8.3 per cent share of total Gulf production, or 1.5 mbpd, compared with over 6 mbpd in Saudi Arabia and over 5 mbpd in Iran (at the time of the Shah); while Iran's share of Gulf oil increased to 28.7 per cent and Saudi Arabia's to 34.4 per cent.

This was the high price that Iraq paid for defiance and idealistic bluster. Of all OPEC's member countries, Iraq for decades remained a net loser in market share and revenues. But Iraq's experiences of relative 'disempowerment' became the dynamic that empowered OPEC, because the country, for its pains, had paved the way in dismantling the Middle East oil concession system by staking its claims, all of which – including government participation, increased tax rates, increased prices, expensing of royalties – were embedded in OPEC's Resolution 90 of June 1968 (see pp. 42–47). This declaratory statement of petroleum policy was implemented in 1972, by which time OPEC's Resolution 90 had become a historical landmark.

In the meantime Iraqi 'oil nationalism' fostered irrational elements in the new republic's oil policy and drove oil politics to extremes at a time when it could attain nothing of benefit for Iraq. Mosaddegh's nationalisation of Iran's oil industry in 1951 encouraged the Iraqi opposition party, during the time of Iraq's royalist regime, to place oil nationalisation at the forefront of its political objectives.

Hence, in 1952, when the royalist regime signed the 'Fifty-Fifty' profit-sharing agreement with the oil companies, Iraq's political opposition fought it, undeterred by the fact that, by then, Mosaddegh's nationalisation attempt had been thwarted by the seven major oil companies' regulatory integration and control, which prevented nationalised oil being sold on a free world market (see pp. 36–40 and Figure 2.1). Deprived of oil revenues, Iran's economy collapsed. This situation facilitated a CIA-backed *coup d'état*, headed by the 'anti-Mosaddegh' General Fazlollah Zahedi, who secured the Shah's return to Iran.

Thus, from the early 1950s, despite Iran's nationalisation endeavours proving abortive, oil nationalisation became a political slogan for prominent Iraqi opposition leaders, in particular for the leader of the Iraq National Democratic Party, Kamel Chaderchi, who was unrealistic in championing nationalisation when it was clearly impracticable at the time.

Compared with their oil-producing/exporting neighbours, the Iraqi people at heart tended to be more politically driven, having had reason to be suspicious of Western oil companies – an attitude that persists until now as a legacy from the occupation of Iraq as a British mandate after the First World War. Strong anti-British sentiment led to local rebellion against British rule, culminating in 1920 with a popular armed uprising, proudly cherished by the Iraqi people, and this preceded the independence achieved 13 years later.

I well recall an episode in which political fervour took precedence over economic commonsense, showing how even economic benefits could be completely overshadowed in the Iraqi political mindset. After the formation of OPEC, the interests of oil nationalism were frequently voiced. During its formative years, one of OPEC's achievements (see pp. 33–44) was the 'expensing of royalties', the effect of which was to increase the government's share in the price of oil. To this end, all OPEC member countries, with the exception of Iraq, signed an agreement with the companies. Iraq refused to sign because, central to the whole issue, there was a dispute concerning the price on which royalty expensing was to be calculated. As is known, in the case of Iraq, the oil companies exported oil through the pipeline to the East Mediterranean export terminals, which meant that the official 'posted price' of Iraqi oil at those terminals included the transit fees paid to Syria and Lebanon.

According to the 1952 Agreement between the Iraqi government and the oil companies, the price on which government revenue was calculated was not the official posted price at Banias, Syria, but a price called the 'border price'. This was the posted price in the East Mediterranean, minus transit fees to Syria and Lebanon. These fees, which then amounted to about US$0.40 per barrel, were more or less equivalent to the cost of shipping oil from the Gulf to the East Mediterranean terminals: which is to say that the official price reflected the freight advantage of Iraqi oil exported from those terminals.

The government's financial arrangement with the companies, therefore, had no bearing on the posted price in the East Mediterranean but had everything to do with the border price. Yet the Government was adamant that it would not sign the royalty expensing agreement unless the oil companies conceded that the calculation of the royalty be based on the posted price at the east Mediterranean ports. The companies did not agree, stating that the government's per barrel share was calculated not on the posted price in Banias but on the border price and, therefore, the expensing of royalties should be based on the latter and not on the former.

The Iraqi government approached the firebrand consultant Abdullah al-Turaiki (former Saudi oil minister, alluded to earlier as having played a key role in founding OPEC in 1960) to give his advice on this and another issue concerning a dispute with the oil companies. He submitted two reports expressed in his demagogic style and when I read them I detected basic inconsistencies. This firebrand (and there are many like him, though the Arab world has more than its fair share) advised the Government to insist on the posted price in Banias as the basis for the expensing of royalties. My own view was different, conforming with the oil companies' standpoint, which adopted the border price for the sound reasons explained.

I wrote a long memorandum to the then Iraqi oil minister (Ali al-Hussein) about al-Turaiki's assertions, pointing out that they contradicted the 1952 agreement, while the companies' position remained consistent with it. More important, I argued that even if the companies agreed to take the posted price of Kirkuk oil at Banias as a basis of royalty expensing, it was not in the government's interests because this would have meant that the cost per barrel incurred by the companies in lifting Iraqi oil from those terminals would have been higher than similar oil, taking into account both quality and geographical location. In other words, the insistence on the East Mediterranean posted price as a basis for expensing royalties made Iraqi crude oil less competitive and more expensive than other crudes, reducing the companies' motivation for increasing oil production in Iraq, at the very time when the Iraqi government was complaining about the companies' failure to increase production. My observations were based simply on reality and commonsense and, as it happened, coincided with the companies' line of reasoning.

Because the Iraqi government's finances were already dire by this time, I included in my memorandum an important point about creating incentives for the companies to produce more Iraqi oil via the Syrian pipeline, and that this would involve accepting the companies' offer, which was, after all, in line with our government's 1952 concession agreement. I added that this would have the effect of *not weakening but instead strengthening* the competitive edge of Iraqi oil over other crudes. To illustrate my point, I drew up two comparative tables: one based on royalty expensing that took the posted price in Banias, and the other taking the border price, as stipulated in the agreement of 1952. These comparative tables demonstrated exactly how much more expensive the Banias option made Iraqi oil, and how this would deter the companies from lifting oil in the Kirkuk fields.

I do not know whether Minister Ali al-Hussein fully understood the memorandum, though I did explain it to him, but after a pause he suddenly exclaimed 'Dr Chalabi, you are a genius, but for heaven's sake, do not raise these issues because "those guys",' by which he meant other Nasserite politicians and the military, 'will interpret this position as being too lenient towards the companies. They want to appear as tough-line politicians confronting the companies and pursuing "national interests",' which, he admitted, were not measured by the country's economic gain so much as by their own political gain. Thus warned, I returned to my office, shaking my head in wonder and pondering over the question of what kind of government would ask the oil companies to increase production yet place obstacles in their path against the attainment of any agreement, and remove any incentive for the companies to expand production.

Here again was the oil nationalism that lay at the core of irrational policies and ran counter to Iraq's own economic interests; in other words, to the detriment of Iraq's oil and to the advantage of the other producers. In OPEC's Annual Statistical Bulletins, which indicate the cumulative production data of each member country, one can see that from the very start of Saudi Arabia's production in 1937 until 2009 its cumulative oil production has been about four times that of Iraq, despite the fact that Iraqi production began in 1927, ten years before Saudi Arabia's.

In the late 1960s the international oil industry began to change with the gradual enlargement of a global free market, beyond the control of the companies. It was in these new market conditions that Iraq became the first major OPEC country to nationalise its oil, in June 1972, when the Iraqi government under Saddam Hussein took over the IPC oil operations. Saddam pioneered the nationalisation measure to enhance his esteem and political stature in the Arab world. It was a gesture echoing that of Gamal Abdel Nasser's nationalisation of the Suez Canal Company, which had been jointly owned by the British and French.

Even before Saddam was in charge, the nationalisation of Iraq's oil had been considered a top priority by the Ba'ath Party at the time of its *coup d'état* of 17 July 1968, when it overthrew the regime of Abdul Rahman A'ariff (brother of former President Abdul Salam A'ariff). It was General Amash, the then 'no. 2' in the new Ba'ath regime, who told me personally about the intention of the Ba'ath ruling party to nationalise oil. This was in 1971, when I accompanied him to Algeria to hear about the experiences of that country with its oil after it had nationalised a group of small American companies as a reprisal for American support of Israel in the Six Day War in June 1967. While in Algeria, General Amash told me that he clearly saw Iraq's nationalisation of its own oil as inevitable. Soon Amash was removed from his post, which Saddam then took over.

On the eve of 1 June 1972, I was summoned to a meeting of the Revolutionary Command Council, held that evening in the office of Saddam Hussein (as Deputy President) and in the presence of all the members of the Ba'ath Party's Supreme Council. In a majestic manner, with his pipe in his mouth, he declared that the Council of the Revolutionary leadership had decided to nationalise the Iraq Petroleum Company, with the exception of the CFP because of France's more positive attitude towards Arab issues. Saddam then addressed the oil minister and myself, asking us to prepare a draft law to this effect. He finally asked if we had any questions, at which point I raised my hand and said that we had all been waiting for this historic decision but that I had to raise a question of a legal nature. Iraq had concluded a concession agreement with the IPC as a holding company, with no contractual relation with the individual shareholders – the British, American, Dutch and French companies – that owned it. While nationalisation was within the state's jurisdiction, according to international law, the announcement of any discriminatory measure favouring one partner for political reasons could create legal problems that might undermine the nationalisation measure. I then gave an outline of a legal case that had been raised against the Libyan government as a result of discrimination against a British partner in joint venture with Americans.

I was running a huge risk in opposing Saddam, even though it was appropriate to warn of this legal risk, but to my relief he asked me what I would suggest as an alternative. My reply was that the IPC group should be totally nationalised, without any exception. Iraq could later make a side arrangement with the French company, by which the latter could lift its share of the IPC oil in accordance with terms that would not involve the nationalisation of CFP's share. This could be arranged by a special contract or joint venture on the part of INOC and CFP. To my surprise he replied, 'Make a draft of two versions of the law formalising the nationalisation of the IPC: one as you suggest and the other as I have stated.' Then, to my equal surprise, his final decision was to go with my own suggestion.

The Foreign Minister, Abdul Baqui Murtadha, an influential, leading Ba'ath Party member, came forward and congratulated me, saying that I must be a man of some considerable courage as others would not have dared argue! A decision was then taken to sign a ten-year contract with the French company according to my proposal, and to appoint me as chief negotiator with the company's representative, Roland de Montagu (a man of social stature, who later died prematurely of cancer). During our negotiations, de Montagu commented wryly that I was a tough negotiator, verging on parsimony in my determination 'to squeeze the last cent' for my government!

With the nationalisation of the IPC a new problem emerged over the transit fees for Iraqi oil being transported from the north to Banias, Syria, and to Tripoli in Lebanon. When Kirkuk oil was first exported in 1934, the transit pipeline went through the city of Haifa in Palestine, which was at the time under a British mandate. The problem of transit fees did not exist at that time for the Iraqi government because its revenue was based on volume (gold shillings per tonne). But a new pipeline had been constructed that involved switching the export terminal from Haifa to the Port of Banias and to Tripoli, because the city of Haifa had by then become part of the state of Israel, which the Arab League had decided to boycott.

With the inclusion of the 50–50 profit-sharing agreement, in accordance with the 1952 Agreement, the government share was calculated at 50 per cent of the posted price, less half the production cost. Posted prices were set in the Eastern Mediterranean, to which Iraq has no access. This meant that the government's per-barrel revenue now had to be based on the port of Banias, minus the transit fees paid to Syria and Lebanon, which were paid by the companies. In order to avoid the problem of Syria's per-barrel share, the Iraqi government requested a fixed price for the calculation of the Iraqi government's net per-barrel revenue.

After the government's nationalisation of the IPC, Syria nationalised its port pipeline. This measure brought to the fore the negotiations with Syria over the transit fee, during which Syria adopted a tough stance, and in which I myself participated under the leading delegation of Dr Fakhri Kaddouri, who was at that time a prominent member of the Ba'ath Party and Chairman of its Economic Bureau.

The Syrians requested a doubling of the fees extracted from the companies at the time, i.e. the $0.40 per barrel would become $0.80. Their argument was that, prior to nationalisation, Iraq was getting 50 per cent of the profit which after nationalisation would be doubled, and that Syria should be treated in the same way with a doubling of transit fees. The Syrians were unaware that Iraq's 50 per cent was a tax ratio, although it was referred to as 'profit', and that the real market price of a nationalised barrel of oil did not mean twice the amount of the government's actual revenue. At the time, the *posted price* in the Gulf for export oil (which was based on Saudi 'Ras Tanura') was $1.80 per barrel, the government share of which did not exceed $1.00 per barrel; whereas the *real price* did not exceed $1.30 per barrel. I tried to explain this point to the Syrians by reminding them that Syria had the advantage of geographical location, with their port having nearer access to Europe and the USA, and that the value of their geographical advantage should be measured by tanker-transport costs from the Gulf area to Banias, which at the time ought not to exceed $0.40 per barrel.

The Syrian delegation's 'no. 2' responded to my explanation with the comment that he had been teaching economics at the university for the past 20 years but had never heard such obfuscating nonsense. For the sake of concluding the agreement, I ignored his insult, knowing that what I had recommended was simple common sense for anyone with a modicum of knowledge of the oil industry.

With the amount of mediation involved on the part of some of the Arab personalities, there was much delay before the agreement was at last signed for Syria's transit fee not to exceed $0.41 per barrel, much along the lines of what I had already explained to the Syrian 'professor of economics'. This experience led Iraq to implement a project that had been planned by the former IPC (before it was nationalised) involving the construction of a two-way pipeline carrying oil from the north to the southern oil export system, so that Iraq would have the flexibility of exporting Kirkuk oil through the new pipeline to and from the Gulf. This was given the name 'Strategic Pipeline'.

The oil nationalisation measure of June 1972 was confined to the IPC, at that time leaving both the BPC and MPC *un*nationalised. Later, at a meeting in Beirut, OPEC discussed the merits of mediating between the Iraqi government and the oil companies, and it was decided that the mediator should be the oil consultant Dr Nadim Pachachi, who was a former Iraqi oil minister and former Secretary General of OPEC. Negotiations with these companies aimed at reaching a settlement on two counts: both the issue of paying reparations to the companies as compensation for the nationalisation, as well as the government's claims against the companies. The Iraqi delegation was headed by Abdul Baqui Murtadha, the foreign minister. The outstanding issues took a long time to debate and finalise, but an expert committee, which I myself headed, estimated that the government's claims for what was owed by the companies stood at £140m, and that this sum included the government's share of the oil lifted by the companies during the second quarter of 1972. For their part, the companies claimed from the government a certain quantity of oil as compensation for IPC assets, while the remaining shareholders in Basra offered a package that included an increase of Basra oil exports.

I was then asked to attend a meeting at the Presidential Palace, held by President Ahmed Hassan al-Bakr together with Saddam Hussein and all the Ba'ath leadership. I was called in by the oil minister to explain the package offered by the companies in

settlement of all the issues, including that of government participation. I made use of a blackboard to demonstrate the financial
advantages of the package, and my long and involved explanation took some time. With nationalisation of the IPC in mind, the
idea of government participation did not appeal to the politicians.
President al-Bakr was not impressed when I outlined the financial
gain and revenues to be derived from the package. As our expenditure capacity was restricted, he kept reiterating to me, 'We just
need money in an amount that we can spend! But what you are
saying is like offering a man more water than he can drink, or
forcing someone to drink a jug of water when he is not thirsty!'
I was puzzled to hear a head of state arguing *against* incoming
revenues at a time when Iraq was launching ambitious development projects.

Another item on offer from the companies was the expansion of
the loading capacity of the existing deepwater terminal, the Khor
al-Amaia, constructed by them in the 1950s. This was for the purpose of INOC oil exports, against a small fee per barrel, instead
of constructing a new terminal for the INOC, which the Iraqi government was considering at that time. I explained that the companies' proposal was economically more advantageous for Iraq than
INOC's construction of an expensive new terminal. At this President
al-Bakr grew impatient and gave me a stern warning never to imagine they would ever abandon the plan for a 'national' deepwater
terminal. The latter was constructed and named al-Bakr after him.
After Saddam's regime was deposed in 2003, it was renamed the
al-Basra terminal.

Finally, the matter was taken up by a small political group,
including the oil minister, and a deal was struck by which the government's claim concerning the £140m was increased to £141m, as
the government maintained that the previous amount did not cover
minor accounting and financial claims. This amount was then paid
to the government. Against the amount claimed by the companies
as compensation for their nationalised assets it was agreed that payment in a quantity of crude oil would be made, the price of which at
the time was $2.50 per barrel and was to be delivered in instalments.
The companies stood to gain from this deal as this crude price, prevailing at the time, then shot up to $12 per barrel only five months
later, with the price shock of December 1973.

In the course of my long presentation, I noticed Saddam was following it with keen interest and posing perceptive, intelligent questions, in contrast to the others who remained indifferent and silent. In these earlier days of the Ba'ath regime, and certainly on the eve of nationalisation, my experience of Saddam was that he was alert, sharp and eager to learn. In his capacity as Deputy President, Saddam always showed a marked appreciation for those who worked hard, irrespective of their religious affiliation or of whether they were Ba'athist party members. Considering my non-membership of his Ba'ath Party, Saddam was remarkably supportive of my ideas and proposals, and even of me personally – that is, until my departure from Iraq in October 1976. It was Saddam who had promoted me from my post of Director General of Oil Affairs to the post of Undersecretary of Oil, a prominent position in a political regime that normally reserved such positions for its ruling Ba'ath elite.

But even in this more enlightened phase of his rule, there were incidents that revealed his volatile disposition. A year after the 1972 nationalisation, Saddam began to allege that I had opposed the nationalisation measure, claiming that I expressed concern that the per-barrel income for nationalised oil would be less than under the concessionary system. He repeated this false assertion at a meeting at which I was present, saying that the government had decided to nationalise 'despite Dr Chalabi's opposition', to which he then added: 'Nevertheless, in view of Dr Chalabi's good intentions and hard work, he is to be promoted to the post of Undersecretary of Oil.'

This often repeated allegation from Saddam was a complete fabrication, as the only reservation I ever expressed concerned the legal ramifications of making an exception for the French company in the oil nationalisation measure. The legal advice I had offered Saddam and my proposal for a more appropriate course of action was adopted by him and implemented as his own ideas. I can only conclude that what lay behind his accusation was his desire to take full credit for the nationalisation measure.

The unpredictability and increasingly tyrannical nature of Saddam's regime was by now already becoming apparent, and so I was not in a mood to deny publicly what he asserted. I kept silent, as it was far too dangerous even to raise the matter in private. Yet, notwithstanding the proliferation of the regime's brutality, during his term as Deputy President, Saddam's innate intelligence never escaped me, nor his ability to calculate with deadly accuracy and even foresee outcomes. This was why I was bewildered by – and at a loss to explain – the paradox of his stupidity in engaging in two disastrous wars that wrecked his country's economy.

The agreement with the BPC was short-lived because of the Yom Kippur or Arab-Israeli War of 6–26 October 1973 (involving Israel against Egypt and Syria). Because the USA and the Netherlands strongly supported Israel, the Iraqi government decided to nationalise the American and Dutch shares of the company, together with the 5 per cent Gulbekian share: a total of 43 per cent of the companies' shares.

On the eve of this second nationalisation measure, I was at my brother's home in the north of Baghdad, when the telephone rang after 10 o'clock at night. It was the National Assembly (Saddam Hussein's office base) asking me to attend a meeting in his office immediately and advising that a car would fetch me from my brother's house. How they knew I was at my brother's place or knew his telephone number still remains a mystery, and it says much for the astonishing efficiency of Saddam's intelligence apparatus. I was hesitant and rather afraid, not only because at the time Baghdad was gripped in terror of a psychopathic serial killer on the prowl, called 'the axe-man' (who entered houses and slaughtered his victims with an axe, after sessions of torture), but also, and more likely, it could have been a trap set for me by Saddam's henchmen; and so before I left, I checked with my colleagues, Dr Abdul al-Anbari and Mr Mufid Mirza, who to my relief told me that they, too, had received the same telephone call. Thus reassured, I took the car at around 11 p.m. that night.

On arrival, I noticed the Oil Minister Sa'doun Hammadi, his face, as usual, pale and morose. We all dutifully trooped into the office of Saddam Hussein, who then informed us of the decision (of the Revolutionary Commanding Council of the Ba'ath Party) to nationalise the American and Dutch interests in the BPC in retaliation for their support of Israel. He asked us to prepare a draft law to be announced first thing in the morning. Accompanied by Minister Hammadi, we left his office for the Ministry of Oil, where we discovered that there were legal and technical problems to be resolved before the law could be promulgated, in order to avoid any disputes later with the oil companies. This meant we were obliged to work much later into the night than Hammadi had anticipated. At 2 a.m. he asked me to see him in his office at the Ministry, where he complained angrily that our delay was indicative of 'inefficiency'. At this I explained to him the legal issues that we had to resolve to avoid any dispute with the companies later on. With him was Adnan Hamdani, a surprisingly gentle Ba'athist, who at that time was very close to Saddam (before the latter had him assassinated), and who suggested that Minister Hammadi could go home and that he, Hamdani, would stay instead while we finished the work. It was 4 a.m. when we finalised the draft law, which Hamdani then took to Saddam, and which was announced on Baghdad Radio in the first news bulletin that morning.

Nearly two years later, in June 1975, the remaining shares of BP, CFP and the British part of Dutch Shell were also nationalised. This put an end to the oil concessions in Iraq. It was by mutual agreement that the government took over the remaining foreign investments, including the contract of the French company Entreprise de Recherches et d'Activités Pétrolières (ERAP)[4], which was involved in the development of the Abu Ghraib oilfield. In accordance with Law 97 of 1967, all former foreign oil investments were now allocated exclusively to INOC.

The government presented these oil nationalisation measures with considerable triumphal fanfare, celebrating the event as a victorious confrontation with the West, but the reality was that these measures enjoyed a degree of acquiescence from the oil companies. Subsequent events, towards the end of the concession system, indicated a change in the companies' policies. I recall while attending an oil conference organised in Kuwait by the Arab League in March 1970, Professor Edith Penrose commenting to me that it would be in the companies' interests to shift from oil concession ownership to being 'mere lifters of crude oil' from OPEC's NOCs. From that date forward she predicted a radical change in their position and this became evident with the companies' negative stance during the Vienna negotiations in early October 1973, at which OPEC tried to amend the 1971 Tehran Agreement (see pp. 101–102).

The shift in the companies' position had already manifested itself two years earlier in Iraq, where, from early 1971, the intransigence of the companies (the IPC) towards the government's demands for increased production had led to Iraq's oil being nationalised in 1972. The companies had shown a surprising indifference to the nationalisation measure which, had they wished to, they could easily have averted by offering to co-operate with the government over the matter of increasing production levels. Instead, the IPC group seemed to regard nationalisation as a fait accompli, towards which they even appeared to push the Iraqi government.

Each time negotiations in Baghdad with the IPC sought to resolve the ongoing problem of Iraq's low production level, the company negotiators failed to come forward with any proposals towards attaining a mutual understanding – in particular the old cynic Geoffrey Stockwell, who headed the IPC team, and whose colonial air of condescension, bordering on detachment, I found very provoking. Stockwell's obduracy seemed calculated to steer the Iraqi government into nationalising oil. This is exactly what Saddam Hussein was waiting for. As pointed out earlier, he saw in a heroic act of nationalisation an opportunity to achieve prominence, leadership and popularity throughout the Arab world. Saddam was emulating Nasser when he nationalised the Anglo-French Suez Canal Company in 1956. But by 1972, times had changed, the concept of nationalisation was acceptable, and news of Iraq's nationalisation was quite well received by the oil companies as a fait accompli. Saddam seemed unaware that they were not bothered by it.

Later, after the event, Minister Hammadi several times asked me why the companies had seemed so unnaturally obdurate in their refusal to increase production, when they were clearly aware that it would provoke the nationalisation measure. He, no doubt, hoped that my thoughts would coincide with, and confirm, his own deductions. Yet I dared not reveal my suspicion that the companies had obliquely encouraged the nationalisation measure. Expressing such an opinion would have diminished Saddam's great sense of triumph, and this would have posed a real danger for me, as Saddam (regardless of appearing to be well-disposed towards me) never hesitated in physically eliminating anyone who harboured doubts about the wisdom of his actions.

While Saddam and Iraq celebrated the nationalisation victory, history was unfolding with the final demise of the oil concession system among other OPEC Gulf member countries, who were now negotiating bilaterally with the companies to implement OPEC's landmark Resolution 90 of June 1968, beginning with the principle of government participation in the oil concessions. Saudi Arabia's Oil Minister, Sheikh Ahmed Zaki Yamani, was authorised to negotiate with the oil companies so that the agreement reached could form the basis for other OPEC states to follow suit.

To this end, Sheikh Yamani, in 1972, entered into very intricate negotiations with the shareholders of Aramco, some sessions of which took place in his private house in Beit Merri, Lebanon, as well as in Saudi Arabia. Negotiations reached a successful conclusion with a draft agreement between the government of Saudi Arabia and the Aramco partners, by which the government share would start at 25 per cent of the oil concession, to increase until it reached 51 per cent after a number of years. The agreement contained a complex mechanism for marketing the government share of crude in such a way as to avoid upsetting the companies' obligations to their long-term contracts, and thus provided for a necessary period of transition. For this purpose, the draft agreement stipulated that the companies could *buy back* the government share of crude oil in gradually diminishing amounts; it also provided an additional mechanism that enabled the government's crude oil share not to flood the oil market with sudden large quantities that could adversely affect price stability. This oil became known as 'phase-in oil'. This provision allowed the producing countries' NOCs to enter the world market and gradually acquire a strong position, while at the same time it secured price stability.

In my opinion, this draft agreement negotiated by Sheikh Yamani provided a historic opportunity for OPEC to create an atmosphere of close co-operation between their NOCs and the IOCs. This would have achieved far greater market stability, involving an effective participation of the host countries' NOCs in investment, production and marketing plans, and promoting a degree of collaboration between NOCs and IOCs that would have properly integrated the producing countries within the international oil industry.

More importantly, Yamani's remarkable draft agreement would have given the major oil companies an incentive to keep their investments in the low-cost oil areas of the Gulf and the Middle East generally. Instead, the state takeover of the industry would sever the relationship between host countries and IOCs, a severance that only served to motivate the IOCs into investing in new high-cost areas outside OPEC. This new oil would aggressively enter the market to the detriment of the market shares of the major Middle East producing countries.

I remember a meeting held in Kuwait, under the chairmanship of Sheikh Yamani and technical representatives from the Arab Gulf countries, at which I headed a relatively large Iraqi delegation of six people, including my two colleagues, Abdul al-Anbari and Mufid Mirza. Beforehand, I had meticulously studied the draft agreement handed to us by Sheikh Yamani, and I expressed my opinion, and that of the others, that this agreement would be of great benefit to the oil-producing nations because co-operation between their own NOCs and the major IOCs would maintain upstream horizontal integration and thus strengthen OPEC's own national companies. I expressed these ideas without having been informed of my government's attitude. Saddam's agenda of political priorities featured complete nationalisation at the top. For the Iraqi delegates this involved some risk, but fortunately there was no reaction or 'fallout' from this.

Regrettably, Sheikh Yamani's drafted agreement for NOC–IOC co-operation did not take off because of mounting political pressure in the Middle East for outright state ownership, whether through legislation, as in Iraq's case, or through negotiations with the companies.

At first, the Kuwaiti parliament did adopt the Participation Agreement, with the proviso that the state's share must be 60 per cent of the oil concession and be acquired immediately, instead of through the gradual increase proposed in the original drafts. This initial decision was purely political as Kuwait did not wish to appear dilatory following on from Iraq's nationalisation; but late in 1975 the Kuwaiti government's negotiations with the oil companies changed to an outright bid for state acquisition of the Kuwaiti Petroleum Company, after paying indemnities to the former concessionaires. This latter arrangement was also made by Qatar and,

after long involved negotiations with the oil companies, finally
Saudi Arabia adopted the Kuwaiti model.

Iran was an exception in choosing not to adopt this Participation
Agreement. This was because, after Mosaddegh's nationalisation
measure (which proved abortive), an agreement was reached with
the major oil companies whereby the National Iranian Oil Company
(NIOC) would from a legal standpoint own the oil, and in this
way the new post-Mosaddegh government avoided appearing too
intent on repealing the Nationalisation Act in entirety. Instead, an
agreement was reached for the creation of an international consortium that would operate on behalf of the NIOC and provide the
government with the same financial arrangements relating to oil
concessions that prevailed in the area. With this the Iranian government took control of its oil industry, in which the new consortium
became an operator against fees, lifting Iranian crude oil with certain discounts.

The only country in the Gulf region to benefit from adopting the
participation principle was Abu Dhabi, which wisely maintained
the interest of the oil companies, getting 60 per cent of the oil concession, while leaving the companies with 40 percent. Subsequent
events showed that in, doing so, Abu Dhabi was the main benefi-
ciary in the area, as its production and markets have always shown
a healthy growth. Full state ownership by the host countries in
the Gulf, whether by demagogic means, as in the case of Iraq, or
through negotiation with the companies, was one of the major turning points in the international oil industry that would come to play
a very negative role in containing the industry in the Gulf, giving
instead an advantage to new oil investments outside the Gulf.

None of these steps that heralded the demise of the concession
system were taken on a sound, rational or economic footing, but
were instead based on some kind of political outbidding, spurred
by Iraq's nationalisation and, prior to that, by Algeria's measures.
In hindsight, what happened in Iraq – the protracted negotiations
with the oil companies followed by the latter's casual surrender
to nationalisation – was a development that favoured the companies in that they shifted their role from oil industry investors in the
producing countries to lifters of crude oil. Besides Edith Penrose's
in-depth analysis, other Western oil theoreticians in the early 1970s

were already recommending this shift before it actually happened. All these developments converged to put an end to the concession system, so that the state's role changed from tax-collector to 'seller' of crude oil.

The only problem was that the system of vertical and horizontal integration became dismantled by state ownership of oil, thus opening the door to price instability. This happens when a government, having nationalised its oil, neglects investment in downstream operations. There are a few exceptions, such as Venezuela and to a lesser extent Kuwait, but on the whole state ownership has failed to devise any system of co-operation among other NOCs for the sake of securing even a modicum of the vertical and horizontal integration that existed during the concessions era.

Notwithstanding the obvious advantage of abundant, low-cost oil, state control has shrunk the market share of the oil-rich Gulf countries and isolated them from the strong growth prevalent outside the Gulf, where oil is scarce and very expensive to produce. Relative to the expansion of oil investments enjoyed elsewhere, OPEC's oil industry, affected by its own oil price policies, stagnated, its market share was frittered away. This shows how the political slogans that campaigned for full state ownership of oil served only to boost the major oil companies' investment plans outside OPEC.

From the first, this radical shift prompted the newly empowered OPEC to abandon its whole raison d'être of securing price stability and instead to lay the first foundations for huge fluctuations in world oil prices that would backfire on the organisation. It is ironic that the era of 'Third World' political demagogues coincided with the West's interest in a new structure for the oil industry, as the coalescence of these two trajectories dramatically transformed the industry to the detriment of OPEC (above all its Gulf member states with two-thirds of the world's oil reserves) and to the advantage of countries with a relatively limited oil reserve base, operated at a very high cost, as in the case of the North Sea and Alaska.

In the final analysis, we shall see how state ownership along with OPEC price policies revolutionised the energy industry: by encouraging the IOCs into new oil areas where their investments were made viable by the high price regime, at the same time making investments in alternative energy sources equally viable, all at the expense of OPEC's – and above all the Gulf's – share in the world energy market. At the same time OPEC's role in meeting world oil requirements would systematically weaken.

5

The Shah and OPEC's oil price frenzy

By mid-1973 the prices of oil products in the main consuming centres were rising significantly. After netting back the crude oil price with costs for handling, refining and transportation, we reached a free-on-board (F.O.B.) price in the Gulf that was well in excess of the official price of the $3 per barrel stated in the Tehran Agreement of February 1971. This meant that the government's per-barrel share, according to that agreement, was equivalent to considerably less than two-thirds of the netback value of crude. In other words, the companies were reaping windfalls from the new prices of products without sharing them with the host governments. This fact signalled the need for the Tehran-agreed price to be increased at a commensurate rate so as to realign the profit-sharing basis, prior to any increase in the market price.

At that time I was Director General of Oil Affairs in Iraq, responsible for OPEC affairs, and was working with a limited number of young technicians with whom I had begun to study the situation. My mounting interest in the oil market and price developments, together with the active role I had played in the Tehran negotiations of February 1971, led me to hold continuous meetings with these staff members in order to observe the significance of price movements of oil products in Rotterdam and on the east coast of the United States, and their impact on the price of crude.

All this culminated with a study that I presented to Minister Hammadi, in which it was shown that the companies' profits, relative to the Tehran Agreement of February 1971, were exceeding the profit-sharing arrangements. In that same report it was recommended that Iraq's Oil Minister (Hammadi) arrange for this issue to be raised at OPEC's ordinary meeting of 28 June 1973, in Vienna, and for the Tehran-agreed prices to be re-examined in the light of

changed market conditions. My report recommended that to keep
the governments' per-barrel shares in balance with the new prices
of products, the official price should be more than $5 per barrel.
Minister Hammadi accordingly raised the topic at the OPEC meeting, asking the Conference Chairman to permit me to explain it.
It caused not only surprise but some consternation, as my report
recommended an increase of 70 per cent on the posted price of the
1971 Tehran Agreement.

The moment I finished my presentation to the ministers, the
Iranian Oil Minister, Dr Jamshid Amouzegar, rebuked me (rather
than my minister) denouncing my proposal as scandalous, putting
OPEC's credibility at stake in not honouring its signature to the
Tehran Agreement or its obligation to provide stability in the world
market: 'The ink with which the Tehran Agreement was signed
has not yet dried and yet you want to breach that agreement!' he
thundered.

At this, my Minister Hammadi calmly proposed forming a
technical working party, selected from various OPEC countries,
to examine the situation and come forward with various recommendations. This the majority of ministers present supported. The
working party, in fact, came up with more or less the same proposals as those I had already put forward on the Iraqi minister's behalf.
It was then agreed that an extraordinary meeting of the OPEC conference should be held to examine the issue. Held in Vienna on
16 September 1973, it concluded that the same member countries
bordering the Gulf (the signatories of the 1971 Tehran Agreement)
must renegotiate the Tehran-set price with the oil companies.

This key meeting was to take place on 12 October in the
Intercontinental Hotel in Vienna, and was significant not only for
its aim of revising the Tehran deal on the oil price but also because
it marked the remarkable transition of Iran. For in that little intervening month, Iran changed its tune from Minister Amouzegar's
fierce avowal of adherence to the Tehran Agreement (when he had
attacked me for my paper proposing even a moderate revision of it)
to an antithesis of now eagerly embracing the prospect of a massive
increase in the oil price.

Clearly OPEC had a good reason to want to reopen these negotiations with the companies, as it had become necessary to revise
upward the oil price, given prevailing market prices that far

exceeded the earlier Tehran-agreed price, which was left lagging behind. Also additional windfalls gained by the companies ought to have been shared with the producers. Had the companies showed any willingness to budge at all on these issues, we could have reached some agreement, but they were adamant in their refusal not to yield one inch. I shall describe their curious tactics presently, but first I must explain Iran's sudden zeal in single-mindedly pursuing the maximum possible increase in the price.

Evidently what lay behind Iran's sudden volte-face was the Shah's posturing as the West's 'policeman' in the Gulf. This role, encouraged by the USA, demanded far higher oil revenues in the interests of keeping the Shah 'armed to the teeth'. When oil prices were low, he had always pressed the oil companies to increase production and thus maximise income from oil exports, with which to sustain the purchase of imported armaments. This priority had, in fact, driven Iranian oil production to an excess of over 6 mbpd, which was damaging the country's oil fields. At this point, I heard from Iranian technicians who were keen to moderate production so as to conform with sound petroleum practice and preserve the oil fields. According to them, Iran's oil production should remain within a range of around 4 mbpd.

With this needed restraint on Iran's production, it became clear that if export volumes could not increase revenues, then the only way to do so was by advocating extremely high oil prices. Perceiving that the USA did not object to this tactic (an interesting point I shall return to later), the Shah took this as his cue to espouse a zealous campaign to maximise the oil price. This was how Iran transformed overnight into an OPEC hawk, more hawkish even than Algeria or Libya. From that moment onwards, and in all subsequent developments, Iran's role in agitating for extraordinarily high prices became very marked in driving OPEC's decision-making process.

As for OPEC's meeting on 12 October 1973, the story of how our dialogue with the oil companies broke down is a complicated and curious one. The meeting began with Sheikh Yamani leading the OPEC Gulf members' team and George Piercy, President of Exxon, representing the oil companies. The Gulf delegates were all in agreement, now that Iran was on board, that our aim was to demand a 100 per cent increase in the Tehran Agreement's oil price, and that negotiations with the companies must allow for a 'bottom line' increase of 70 per cent.

To our astonishment, the companies were disinclined to negotiate and did not even present any counter-proposals as they had done in both Tehran (in February 1971) and in the later Geneva I and II Agreements of 1971 and 1972. They held that a price increase of the magnitude we proposed would have far-reaching ramifications for the world economy, and for this they were not prepared to take any responsibility.

Having arrived in Vienna (from Baghdad) in advance of Minister Hammadi, I was representing him at the meeting with the companies, with the understanding that when negotiations reached a critical phase Hammadi would then join the OPEC delegates. On the eve of Hammadi's departure from Baghdad to Vienna, my hotel room telephone rang and Sheikh Yamani was on the line enlightening me about the abortive negotiations with the companies, and how, as they had reached a stalemate, there was no point in Hammadi coming to Vienna. But it was already late in the evening and with the time difference it was impossible to contact the Minister before his arrival at Baghdad airport. After much effort and with just two hours to spare, I managed to reach the airport control tower with a message for Hammadi to cancel his trip to Vienna as negotiations had been called off, details of which I would report to him on my return. I was relieved to hear that the message was relayed to him in time and he returned home.

The next day, a number of OPEC ministers met in Sheikh Yamani's large suite in the Intercontinental Hotel in Vienna, where, in the absence of my minister, I represented Iraq. While Sheikh Yamani was explaining the situation his telephone rang, and he went to answer it. After a while he returned to inform us that George Piercy had called to say that the companies' position was that they 'could do nothing'. Given Piercy's air of resignation, both Sheikh Yamani and the Iranian minister agreed that we were facing a strangely definitive juncture from where, to break the deadlock, the only way forward was to hold a meeting without the companies and take a unilateral decision. The companies' obduracy in refusing to concur with or even negotiate over OPEC's proposed increase to the Tehran price – which, set in February 1971, was, by mid-1973, clearly lagging behind market prices – left us with only one option: that OPEC would for the first time fix the price of its oil independently of the oil companies' participation. As OPEC's Secretary General, the Algerian, Abdul Rahman Khene, was not present, I was required to draft and read the ministerial communiqué to an enormous number of press people. It was decided that OPEC would hold a further meeting in Kuwait, a few days later on 16 October in order unilaterally to formalise its decision henceforth to set the price of oil independently of the oil companies.

Meanwhile, there was a problem getting to Kuwait from Vienna for the meeting. With the Arab-Israeli war raging, the Arab Middle East had been declared a no-fly-zone, and all European airlines to the Middle East had been cancelled, leaving me stranded. To my relief, Anis Attar, the efficient OPEC administrator arranged an Air India flight from Geneva to Kuwait, flying through Iranian air space. It was my first flight aboard a Boeing 747 with its upper floor for first class passengers, where, despite my anxieties for the future, I momentarily relaxed in a state of elation and wonder. I was apprehensive about the outcome of the meeting because, while I deemed it unjust that the oil-producing countries continued to submit to the price of their own oil being set by the companies and not by themselves, I could also visualise the risks if somehow OPEC were to mismanage the intricacies of the old, stable system which, with the producers taking over the pricing and destiny of their own oil, would irrevocably cease.

These worries stemmed from my experience of the Tehran negotiations in early 1971, which had shown me that OPEC countries lacked not only the expertise but also an understanding of their oil industry operations. Unilateral pricing decisions could have grave consequences. In my state of apprehension over the forthcoming meeting in Kuwait, I found myself drinking one glass after another of French cognac. On arrival at Kuwait's Sheraton Hotel, I looked forward to recuperating in my room but was informed that the Kuwaiti Oil Minister, Abdul Rahman al-Ateeqi, was waiting for me to brief him about our Vienna meeting. Somehow I managed to switch to a demeanour of alert sobriety and went to greet the Kuwaiti minister.

When I briefed him on the outcome of the Vienna meeting, his response was that it was God's choice, and as such it would be a good one. Though lacking any formal education, this man was most intelligent and courteous, and he had a humorous turn of phrase that eased the tension in meetings. He lamented the move from Geneva to Vienna of OPEC's Secretariat and headquarters, extolling the virtues of Geneva as 'more beautiful and inspiring greater happiness' than Vienna which, with its gloomy skies, bore 'no resemblance to what we used to hear from Asmahan' – a famous Arab diva, who sang of 'nights of pleasure in Vienna... its breeze comes from Paradise'. On one occasion, his mock-wistful tones prompted the Iranian Minister, Jamshid Amouzegar, seated beside me, to mutter a quiet aside that his rapturous yearning for Geneva arose from his having a girlfriend there. Geneva had, since 1961, been the location for OPEC's Secretariat, but the canton of Geneva had refused to grant the status of diplomatic immunity because it deemed OPEC to be a trade association, rather than an inter-governmental organisation. Meanwhile, the charismatic and moderately left-of-centre Herr Bruno Kreisky, who was then Austria's Foreign Minister (later becoming Chancellor, 1970–83), was far-sighted in promoting the international status of Vienna by attracting international organisations to the capital; and in July 1965 the Conference authorised the OPEC Secretariat to sign a 'host agreement', which granted diplomatic immunity to all OPEC officials by virtue of being an international, inter-governmental organisation.

Returning to the subject of OPEC's memorable meeting of 16 October 1973, held at the Sheraton Hotel in Kuwait, as my Minister Hammadi failed to arrive in time for it, I represented Iraq. This Kuwaiti meeting was marked by Iran's Minister Amouzegar, to our continued bemusement, arguing fervently for extremely high price levels. Despite the reasons explained earlier for his dramatic change of mind (after his vociferous objection to my recommendations for *any* upward revision of the 1971 Tehran price), we were still mystified by his sudden zealous pursuit of maximum prices.

OPEC's wresting from the oil companies total command of oil-pricing decisions was theoretically in line with the principle of its Resolution 90 of 1968, whereby the state has sovereignty regarding the unalienable right to its own natural resources, as 'reaffirmed by the General Assembly of the United Nations, most notably in its Resolution 2158 of November 25, 1966'. Yet, despite the meeting's legitimate reference to Resolution 90 as a basis for the OPEC's rightful decision to set the price of its own oil henceforth, no one was quite prepared for the drastic decision to increase the oil price by 70 per cent. It was declared that the official posted price should be based on actual market prices in the Gulf, as well as in other areas, taking into account quality and geographical location differentials (i.e. the value differences among various crudes). In this way the market price would determine the level of the official posted price, while maintaining the same relationship between the two prices as existed in 1971. In other words, this set first the market price and then computed an 'official posted price' in accordance with the concession agreement. In this way, the government's final 'take' per barrel would be equal to the market price. As the market price was $3.65 per barrel, the posted price would be set at around $5.11 per barrel.

OPEC's 'Kuwaiti decision' also made reference to the Geneva Agreements I and II for a price correction in accordance with the dollar exchange rate variations relative to other major world currencies (the dollar being the unit for denominating the value of oil and of payments); also that, in the event of companies refusing to take crude according to these arrangements, the producer countries would make their crude available on the world market on the basis of $3.65 Arab light F.O.B. at Ras Tanura. In keeping with these arrangements, the posted price, on the basis of government take, would be calculated at 1.4 times the market price. (When Minister Hammadi finally arrived at the Kuwait Sheraton meeting, I reported this remarkable outcome, to which his sole response was the word 'good'. He tended to be taciturn until, with his great parsimony of words, he would pronounce 'no' if he was not happy, or 'good' if the outcome was auspicious).

The outcome of the Kuwait decision of 16 October 1973 would be of critical importance, the moment of truth for OPEC and a definitive, historic turning point, as it represented a radical change in policy direction and heralded a dramatic transformation of the world oil industry and of the entire energy structure. Yet I felt ambivalent about these new policy directions. On the one hand, I saw the Kuwait decision simply as the upshot of a process that began with the report I had presented (on Iraq's behalf) recommending a revision of the earlier Tehran-set prices; and I was pleased and proud that the oil-producing countries had regained their legitimate rights, and that OPEC's Resolution 90 of 1968 had become a reality, at a time when people had dismissed it as a 'pipedream'.

On the other hand, I was plagued by vague misgivings about what it might all lead to, knowing as I did the various pressures that OPEC was subject to: conflicting policies and interests, based on short-term political expediency and not on sound economic criteria in the world trade of primary commodities. Subsequently events were to prove that my sense of incipient foreboding – about a state of affairs that resembled a dream too good to be real – presaged future problems for OPEC.

I had first felt this presentiment during our negotiations in Vienna a few days earlier (12 October), when the companies had shown apathy during our attempts to negotiate, in sharp contrast with the earlier Tehran and Geneva negotiations, at which the companies had been serious and willingly engaged in pursuing mutually acceptable solutions. But at the recent Vienna meeting they had offered no counter-proposal to OPEC's demands and conveyed a strange unwillingness to reach *any* form of agreement – as if opting out of any responsibility for the price increases and at the same time not resisting OPEC's wish to go ahead with them. The comments from George Piercy of Exxon were ambiguous, and when he telephoned Sheikh Yamani in his suite, as mentioned earlier, his non-committal declaration that the companies 'could do nothing' expressed an air of both resignation and 'blind-eye' encouragement, amounting to an oblique support for OPEC's unilateral responsibility for raising the oil price – far preferable to having the companies' collusion overtly exposed. This ensured that the blame would fall entirely on OPEC, while the companies would appear irreproachable, though the reality was that the latter would stand to gain as the direct beneficiaries of the new order.

In hindsight, this convoluted conduct of the companies was the first indicator we had of their new investment plans for high-cost oil, outside the traditional low-cost oil regions of the Middle East, as will be discussed at length later. For me, the Vienna experience with these oil companies echoed the ambivalent conduct of the IPC shareholders earlier in Iraq in 1972 (see pp. 71–98), when a similar ploy of oblique obduracy, in the face of reasonable demands for increased production, seemed calculated to push the Iraqi government into nationalising its oil industry.

It was during the course of that memorable OPEC meeting of 16 October, at the Kuwait Sheraton, that the Iranian Minister Amouzegar suddenly announced that a special meeting would take place the next day, the full significance of which I was unable to grasp at the time. He also said with some prescience: 'You will see how oil prices will soar when the Arab ministers meet to discuss oil as a means of applying political pressure in this war with Israel.' Clearly his words indicated some prior knowledge of an Arab oil embargo, an action that would lead to a quadrupling of the Tehran-set price. Later, I understood from Sheikh Ali Al Sabah that, following an instruction from Kuwait's Minister Ateeqi, he had informed Amouzegar of the Gulf countries' intention to cut oil production as a gesture of solidarity and support for Egypt in the Yom Kippur or Arab-Israeli War.

The very next day, with nervous anticipation I attended the momentous meeting of 17 October 1973 – which had nothing to do with OPEC, as it was held by oil ministers as members of OAPEC, and took place at the latter organisation's Kuwait head-quarters (where its Secretary General, Dr Ali Attiqa of Libya, had recently taken up his post). At this phase in the Arab-Israeli War, the Egyptian army's success in crossing the Suez Canal and destroying the legendary Israeli Barleve defence line had exposed as myth the then prevailing belief in the invincibility of the Israeli army, and it had surprised the whole world. At this, Henry Kissinger, holding simultaneously the twin posts of Secretary of State and National Security Advisor, had begun an active pro-Israeli policy in creating an aerial bridge for armaments to Israel. These new incursions in the Middle East inflamed the Arabs, who called upon Arab heads of state to take action against the supporters of Israel, in particular the USA and the Netherlands.

Even before the war, there had been mounting political pressure from activists in the Arab world (chiefly Egyptians, Syrians and Palestinians) to use their oil as a weapon in a conflict that was rated as a battle for survival. This geopolitical pressure resulted in a group of experts (partly under the auspices of the Arab League in Cairo) writing a report about the importance of oil in the world power balance. There followed a great wave of political demagogy, which availed itself of the slogan 'oil as a weapon' in the war with Israel. The Egyptians adopted this tactic in persuading King Faisal of Saudi Arabia to support an oil embargo against the USA and the Netherlands. This spurred the Arab oil producers, at their meeting on 17 October, to undertake successive production cuts, along with an oil embargo against the latter two countries. This fuelled even more the spectacular oil price surge.

Well before that fateful oil embargo meeting in Kuwait on 17 October, earlier that same year, Iraq's Ministry of Foreign Affairs had sent a confidential letter to the Iraqi Oil Minister, seeking his opinion concerning a proposal to cut Arab oil production as a means of applying political pressure. The Minister gave me the letter to comment on, and I wrote a personal report in which I was clearly against the idea of a production cut as a weapon against Israel and its supporters. My main argument was that cutting the Arab oil exports would lead to our losing world markets to the benefit of other producers. I argued at the same time that oil should be dealt with purely on economic terms as a commodity, in accordance with the OPEC statute, and not as a political issue.

My Minister Hammadi was not in favour of the oil embargo, but, as usual very cautious about his future whenever sensitive issues were at stake, did not want to commit himself to being either for or against it. He therefore asked me to send my report in my own name with a letter to the Ministry of Foreign Affairs, which I did.

Hammadi was among the first founding members of the Ba'ath party of Iraq and a follower of Michèle Aflaq, the founding philosopher of the party. For Hammadi, Arab unity was a cult, even if it was to be achieved by force, and yet on any occasion demanding his clarification of the ministry's position in front of higher authorities he was always able to avoid direct involvement. He invariably asked me to speak for him as I was the 'technical man' responsible for OPEC affairs. Thus divesting himself of liability, Hammadi avoided the risk of overt opinion over issues that might jeopardise his future. In this way he survived Saddam's 'Stalinist' regime, which eliminated entire senior ranks of respected Ba'ath veterans. For this reason, in spite of his earlier good reputation, in the end few could take Hammadi seriously. Until the fall of Baghdad in April 2003, he occupied an ineffectual position as Speaker of the National Assembly.

I never did find out what happened to the report I prepared for him. Having sent it to the Foreign Minister it posed for me a considerable risk in a country that considers the Palestinian issue a primary one. Fortunately for me, the Iraqi Government – i.e. Saddam Hussein – had another reason to oppose the proposed cuts in oil production, arguing that cutting Arab oil exports would be harmful worldwide, including to those countries well disposed towards Iraq, and would above all harm developing countries, which at the time tended to be anti-Israel. Saddam was also in favour of using oil as a weapon, but with the more specific target of injuring the USA and Netherlands by nationalising the Arab oil investments of these two nations – and not by imposing an embargo on oil exports generally. The reality was that Saddam, as the architect of the nationalisation of Iraqi oil, could cast Saudi Arabia and Kuwait in the mould of 'protectors of American interests'.

Iraq, therefore, maintained an official position that if the Arabs wanted to punish America and the Netherlands for helping or arming Israel in its war against an Arab nation, why then punish the whole world? Iraq's abstention from the oil embargo decision while nationalising instead the American and Dutch interests in the BPC, was seen as the 'right argument'; though, in truth, it was simply the 'right wording' for a self-aggrandising image with which to bolster Saddam's standing.

Bearing in mind that Iraq (as pointed out in the preceding chapter) had already nationalised the IPC in June 1972, there were two remaining affiliates – the MPC and the BPC, both of which had remained 'un-nationalised' until the agreement of 1 March 1973, whereby the company shareholders relinquished the MPC to the government. Although the BPC, owned by the same shareholders, continued to operate, later that year, entirely as a result of America's involvement in Israel's war and Iraqi policy vis-à-vis the Arab oil embargo, Saddam's government went ahead and nationalised the American share, owned by Exxon and Mobil, as well as the Dutch interests – which represented 40 per cent of Dutch Shell's share, amounting to 23.75 per cent. This resulted in about 33 per cent of the BPC being nationalised.

With the drama unfolding at the oil embargo meeting of 17 October 1973, where the issue of oil being used as a 'weapon' was being debated by all the Arab oil ministers, I was obliged to represent Iraq, standing in for my Minister Hammadi, who had not arrived. The pleasant Kuwaiti Minister Ateeqi, chairing the meeting, proposed that we begin without waiting any longer for Dr Hammadi, but Sheikh Yamani intervened suggesting that we should wait longer to avoid annoying the Iraqi minister. Soon Chairman Ateeqi insisted that we had waited long enough and, though Yamani intervened yet again, he called the meeting to order. A few minutes later Minister Hammadi arrived. Finding the meeting already in progress, he was furious, accusing the delegates of having started the meeting with the purpose of 'passing resolutions in [his] absence'. Ironically he accused Sheikh Yamani of being behind the idea. After a moment's pause, Yamani, in a very quiet, composed manner announced: 'In my life I have two predicaments with the Iraqis: my Iraqi wife makes my life hell at home, and the other is Dr Hammadi! It was I who tried many times to delay the meeting until Dr Hammadi's arrival, as I knew that starting the decision process without him would infuriate him. What is my reward? I am now the culprit. These are my calamities with the Iraqis! What can I do?' Everyone roared with laughter including, eventually, Hammadi, who normally never laughed at anything.

Then, with great bravado, Hammadi launched into a theatrical oration, as if addressing a vast multitude: 'What do you want to do?' he thundered. 'Do you want to punish America for its aggressive act of providing an aerial bridge of weaponry to Israel, or do you want to punish the whole world? After all, what fault is it of the poor Third World countries?' Even his more temperate tones were deafening: 'Once you cut production, prices on the world market will spiral out of control. If you want to punish America, nationalise its oil concessions in your countries, just as we have done.' While he continued in this vein, other Gulf ministers were noticeably quiet, evidently not prepared to advocate Dr Hammadi's recommendations. I doubt if the man literally meant what he was proposing, he was just conveying his government's position, presenting Iraq as a keen supporter of the Arab cause; but because Iraq was ahead of its time in having already nationalised its oil, he rather cleverly showed up the other Gulf countries as having their oil industry too much under US control, regardless of their embargo plan. Nor do I even believe that Hammadi was cognisant of the full impact and market implications of the embargo. The Arab ministers, largely ignoring Hammadi, went ahead with their decision to impose an oil embargo on the USA and the Netherlands, and to reduce production in stages: at first by 10 per cent, and then by 15 per cent. Iraq, meanwhile, did not join them, and more than keeping its production intact even took advantage of the situation to increase it.

The world oil market was jolted by the shock of this decision, and this would later have enormous repercussions on the Gulf's oil. Market prices saw huge increases that left the whole world aghast: from $3.65 – prior to the Arab oil ministers' decision – market prices exceeded $12 per barrel. In fact the Iranian National Oil Company had put an amount of oil from outside the consortium into international auction. Japanese companies in need of this oil were ready to pay $18 per barrel.

That auspicious year, 1973, with the Arab-Israeli conflict a constant anxiety, the oil market grew evermore jittery with grim scenarios depicting the 'fallout' from the Arab oil embargo. It was in these very tense conditions that, as 1973 drew to a close, the oil ministers of the OPEC countries bordering the Gulf decided to meet in Tehran, in late December 1973, to discuss what to do about the oil price. Ministers of other member countries of OPEC, namely Algeria, Indonesia, Libya, Nigeria and Venezuela, attended as observers.

This OPEC meeting in Tehran, held on 23 December 1973, was characterised by a mood of exhilaration at the prospect of massive revenues from the price increases and, as was becoming usual, it was the Iranians who were most fervent. Iran's Dr Amouzegar was elected chairman of this meeting, while their delegation was headed by the President of the Iranian National Oil Company, Riza Fal'ah, whom I had met earlier, in 1969, when in Tehran to discuss the Economics Intelligence Unit's report on co-operation among OPEC's NOCs. Riza Fal'ah struck me as extremely rich, hosting as he did an extravagant reception and dinner for all the delegates at his home (more a palace than a house, its floors covered in vast, precious Persian carpets and a stage-like structure where musicians and singers performed).

During this Tehran meeting, Riza Fal'ah stood out as the most outspoken critic of the notion of oil being sold cheaply. He described oil in a new language, unheard of outside journals of ecology: 'Oil is a depletable resource...a "noble commodity" that should not be burnt up to generate energy, but conserved only for advanced technology, as in the petrochemical industry.' He went on to say that there must be a certain rationale about pricing oil. Although the market was now offering $17 to $18 per barrel, he wanted to establish the price structure on a more economically solid basis. His theory was that the official selling price of oil, at a time when the concession system was still operative, must be such as to generate a net government take of $7 per barrel. To justify this, he gave us a long lecture on how a barrel of crude oil should in a typical refinery be fractured into products, alongside which the cost of alternatives to each of these products should be assessed. Fuel oil, for example, could be replaced by coal or natural gas, the cost of which was low, whereas gasoline, he argued, was irreplaceable, unless synthetic oil was manufactured from coal at a very high cost. For the value of a barrel, he maintained, there should be a 'weighted combination of the alternative cost for each product'. His conclusion was that the value for each barrel of crude oil in the Gulf with its distilled product was extracted by adding up the value of the alternative of each product. This was how he had arrived at $7 per barrel as the net government revenue per barrel. According to the then prevailing fiscal relationship pertaining to the concession system, only a posted price of $11.65 per barrel could yield the required government per barrel take.

With this, the Iranians dominated the entire meeting. It continued to puzzle us that Iran's position in setting the price was still so extreme, given that the suggested posted price was already four times the price of the 1971 Tehran Agreement (which prevailed until a few months prior to this meeting).

Contrary to the experience of the Tehran negotiations of 1971, when it was the Iraqi delegates who were the 'leading lights', at this December meeting in 1973 the Iraqi delegation reacted collectively like a lost soul, with no sense of direction. Minister Hammadi asked me what policy Iraq ought to adopt, given its abundant oil resources. My answer remained consistent: that higher prices would weaken demand for OPEC oil and drive investments to alternative sources. He recoiled from having to think about this, and disliking my argument, he went with the others in setting a price increase of 140 per cent over the prices that had been set in Kuwait only two months earlier on 16 October. Thus the Tehran decision of December 1973 represented an increase of 140 per cent on the initial price set by the

Tehran Agreement of February 1971. This astonishing price level and its mechanism became operative as of January 1974.

The shockwaves this quadrupling of oil prices caused throughout the world were enormous. Oil prices had soared in just a few months from around $2.50 per barrel in mid-1973 to almost $12 per barrel. This colossal increase over such a short time span had instant repercussions that would herald a new era of dramatic changes in world energy. Shaken to the core, the industrialised countries, so reliant on oil, ushered in restrictive measures to control its consumption, especially in the USA, where gasoline prices were causing extremely long queues. The soaring costs of oil import bills affected the whole world economy, which fell into recession after soaring inflation rates had risen to unheard of levels. The world media, especially in the West, accused OPEC of hijacking the world economy, and blame was, of course, attributed to 'those Bedouins', the oil-rich Arab Sheikhs. Yet, as already mentioned, and as will be seen later, the real beneficiaries would be the oil companies, more than 'the Bedouins'.

A great wave of publications, studies, commissioned reports and government recommendations emerged, all talking of a world oil shortage caused by OPEC. Much fantasy was published about world demand for OPEC oil increasing to a degree that the supply capacity could never match the demand and the world would inevitably suffer a disastrous oil crunch. These predictions and forecasts proved false as they failed to account for any modifications on the part of consuming nations.

There still remained one major unanswered question: *why* had Iran so swiftly changed its argument for these higher oil prices? Apart from the Shah's rearmament plans, could the Shah have made this sudden shift in the knowledge of a change in the USA's approach towards higher prices? It is, after all, well documented that the Shah was America's protégé and enjoyed the support of the West in general, so much so that following the British withdrawal from the Gulf in 1971, the Shah did not have to wait long to occupy militarily – with the tacit blessing of Britain and the USA – the three islands near the mouth of the Hormuz Strait which belonged to Shahrja, the United Arab Emirate. Being the indulged protégé or 'spoilt child' of the West, especially of the USA, on whom Iran was dependent as a recipient of political as well as military support, it was hardly conceivable that the Shah would become so hawkish over oil prices against American strategic interests, *unless* he could count on the USA for a degree of tacit agreement.

Evidently (then as now) the USA was eager, after the 1973 price shocks, to invest in new oil supplies to reduce dependence on Middle East oil. This was made explicit by the then head of Oil Affairs at the State Department, James Akins, in an article entitled 'The Oil Crisis: This Time the Wolf is Here',[1] published in 1973 in the quarterly magazine *Foreign Affairs*, in which he advocated the necessity for higher prices. Besides having been the US Ambassador in Saudi Arabia, Akins had previously defended Libya's case for higher prices. In several public speeches, Sheikh Yamani asserted that when he, as King Faisal's envoy to Tehran, had met the Shah to discuss with him the need to moderate OPEC's stance on oil prices, his 'Imperial Majesty' had told him that the USA was far from deterring OPEC's higher prices. He suggested that he (Yamani) should meet Henry Kissinger to ascertain the new American attitude to high prices. A discussion of this crucial shift in the structure of the international oil industry vis-à-vis higher prices will be resumed in Chapter 14.

The fact that the oil companies, as well as financial institutions in the West, evidently benefitted from the sharp oil price increases, reminded me again of my sense of unease, incipient when the oil companies practically pushed OPEC into taking responsibility for oil-pricing and adopting a high-price regime. This was a calculated move on the part of the companies to secure huge profits, with which to invest in high-cost oil-producing regions. At the same time, one might argue, vast amounts of petrodollars were recycled back to the West. The increase in petrodollars was, in fact, staggering. For example, in 1972, before the oil price shocks, the total value of OPEC's oil exports, i.e. gross revenues, was in the order of US $25.6 million; but by 1975, these revenues had jumped to $111 million, and five years later, by 1980, they stood at $299,129 million. More recently, in 2008, OPEC's gross revenues peaked at over $1 trillion (USD$1,006,850,000). Inevitably, however, exorbitant prices are trailed by a consumer backlash, as will be discussed.

Over the same period, the financial performance (as shown in the annual reports) of two major oil companies, BP and Royal Dutch Shell, indicated very clearly how the oil companies' profits increased dramatically with the oil price shock. In 1972, these two companies' net profits amounted to £70 million and £206 million respectively. By 1976, they had jumped to £344 million and £1.2 billion respectively.

Initially one was unable to comprehend all the intricacies of the policy shifts that had led to the great price shocks, but one thing became immediately apparent: the energy policies of the industrialised countries aimed at reducing their dependence on OPEC oil by diversifying their oil supply sources and diversifying their energy mix by shifting to alternatives, particularly (during that period) natural gas and nuclear power. This diversification could never have been achieved without higher oil prices.

The ambivalence I had felt during those momentous meetings of October 1973 soon began to define itself. The assumption by the oil-producing nations of full responsibility for pricing their own oil resources was akin to a young man's dream of rightful sovereignty, and in this I felt proud, just as I had at Mosaddegh's bold nationalisation of Iran's oil, which generated an idealism and nationalistic sentiment among my generation at that time. Indeed, we were dismayed when General Zahidi staged a CIA-backed coup, restoring Iran's Shah from his exile. Yet now it was the economist in me that harboured a dread of unforeseen consequences from these radical changes and their future impact on Iraq's rich oil deposits.

The oil price frenzy, triggered by the Shah, spread like a disease among all the delegates and ministers, irrespective of the impact on world demand and consequently on the rank OPEC oil would occupy, especially the Gulf area with its colossal abundance of oil reserves. Unaware of the consequences in store for their respective shares in the world energy market, OPEC countries, for now, thought only of massive revenues pouring into their coffers, without knowing how to spend them.

The sole OPEC Minister cognisant of the eventual backlash was Sheikh Yamani, who was systematically opposed to further price increases because of their negative impact on world demand for oil, especially Gulf oil. The rest, though, were living under an illusion that the increase in world demand for their oil would continue as before, at the same rate as in the early 1970s with petrodollars pouring in on them like rain. Aware of this fallacy, Yamani saw that further increases after the 1973 price shock would drastically reduce world dependence on OPEC oil, with the oil-rich Gulf particularly affected. Needless to say, for the OPEC hawks such evident logic was inadmissible, and their disquiet grew to dismay when the world's media became fascinated by Yamani and focused on his wise views and sound economics. On every occasion great throngs of journalists and news agencies gravitated towards him, so that he had to battle his way into hotel venues, and at the Intercontinental Hotel in Geneva he had to enter from the rear door, by agreement with the helpful hotel manager, Herr Schott. Led by Algeria and Iran, the hawks were opposed to Yamani's voice of moderation just as they were indifferent to his logic.

Notwithstanding the negative aspects of the 1973 price shock, such as unprecedented inflation rates and adverse effects on OPEC's market share, high prices were to some degree ineluctable, given the compelling reasons behind them for the producers (and to some degree the consumers). Before the first price shock, oil consumption in industrialised countries had been growing at unsustainably high rates, reaching as much as 7 and 8 per cent per annum in Western Europe. This meant that the consumption of resources was doubling over eight or ten years. Neither sound nor tenable, these consumption rates were environmentally damaging and would have led to a disastrously rapid depletion in world reserves, affecting even the Middle East's rich reserves, which remained the main source of supply for world consumption outside the Soviet bloc. The world's proven reserves in 1972 amounted to 673 bn/B enough to sustain production rates at that time for a mere 31 years, while Middle East reserves amounted to 355 bn/B enough to sustain production rates for 54 years. Reducing the rate of consumption became therefore a *sine qua non*.

The 1973 oil price shock signalled a change in energy trends, a necessary abatement of excessive rates of depletion of the reserve base. Yet OPEC delegates and theoreticians spoke of these issues with great exaggeration and with a bravado that paved the way for the next disastrous price shock, in 1979.

6

Of some OPEC 'paper powers'

For the industrialised countries, whose rapid economic growth in the 1950s and 1960s had been nurtured by cheap imported oil, the shock of OPEC's price hikes was traumatic, and as much psychological as economic and political. The West's media played a considerable role in the trauma, dramatising the dire effects of price increases on family budgets, national economies and inflation, while the West's governments rushed to implement severe restrictions on oil consumption and vehicle speed limits. They were for the first time jolted into 'energy conservation', key words for a future world that would be dominated by oil politics. The public emphasis on how to save oil was particularly marked in Western Europe, where a plethora of campaigns urged populations to combat excessive fuel consumption, whether commercial or domestic, such as the over-heating of houses during the winter period. In Austria, where we met frequently, one saw electrically operated trams bearing the slogan in red and white *'Mit uns fahren, energie sparen'* ('Travelling with us is saving energy').

In Washington, in 1974, Henry Kissinger convened a meeting, which eventually spawned the International Energy Agency (IEA). This meeting involved all the Organisation for Economic Co-operation and Development (OECD) countries, except France – which did not formally elect to be a member, though it followed the IEA's recommended procedures and policies for cutbacks on oil consumption, increasing the production of oil from outside OPEC and investing in alternative energy sources, such as nuclear power and natural gas. During this period, OPEC personnel were seen almost as aliens from another planet, and aroused suspicion as well as curiosity. The Arab oil ministers, whose decision on successive production cuts lay behind the first price shock, in an attempt to appease a hostile world, agreed that two oil ministers (namely, the moderate Sheikh Yamani of Saudi Arabia and Belaid Abdesselam of Algeria) should tour the consumer countries to allay anxieties, not just as a PR campaign but as a genuine attempt to elucidate OPEC's position.

Because of his tours in the USA and Europe, Sheikh Yamani became for the West OPEC's incontestable star. Everyone, from oil expert to the man in the street, knew of his reputation as an indispensable dove among OPEC hawks. I remember once, when in Toronto, asking the hotel to provide me with a rented, chauffeur-driven car so that I could see the Niagara Falls. When the driver asked me where I worked and I replied that I was at OPEC in Vienna, he said, 'Ah, so you must have met Sheikh Yamani!' I nodded smiling, having seen Sheikh Yamani on the cover of the current issue of *Newsweek*, and the driver went on to remark, 'What a nice man, more moderate than the others!'

With the exception of the academic or specialist press, Western media for the most part appeared to forget, or to ignore, the enormous gain in profits landing in the lap of the oil companies as a result of the price shocks. Their attention was focused entirely on the Arabs, especially the 'Bedouins', who had so suddenly abandoned camels for Rolls Royce automobiles and private jets. There were mixed feelings among the public: a rueful or grudging admiration for OPEC's emergence as a 'power' to be reckoned with, mingled with dread for its pricing policies. I recall once in Vienna, after one of the OPEC meetings, sitting in a bar, which had a dancehall, and around me there were people with whom I chatted, but as soon as they knew I was from an OPEC country, one of the girls shouted, 'How about giving me a few barrels of oil? I'd be so very grateful!' Suddenly oil was treated like precious gemstones. As a commodity it became known as 'black gold'.

Apart from a handful of the more judicious OPEC representatives, most were in a constant state of intoxication, figuratively speaking. They felt exhilarated, imagining themselves reborn with command over the entire world economy. This heady power, derived from their great oil-wealth, heightened dramatically their sense of self-aggrandizement, especially in view of the very wide media coverage that pursued them at OPEC meetings.

On many occasions the attendees (accredited to the OPEC Secretariat), consisting of journalists, TV reporters and observers from oil companies, numbered between 400 and 500. The sense of opulent splendour and grandeur of some OPEC ministers was in some cases reflected in the very curt manner shown towards earnest reporters or company representatives, many of whom tended to stampede in their eagerness to get a statement from this minister or that. I recall at one of the conferences held in Vienna, the OPEC Secretariat hosted a large reception in one of Vienna's historic palaces, called the Palais Palevicenni for the OPEC delegates, and for which invitations were extended also to observers, journalists and company people. It happened that one of the invitees was Senator Baur, the then President of the Austrian oil company OMV, who, because of the need to buy Libyan oil, asked if I could introduce him to the (late) Libyan oil minister, Izidin Al Mabrouk. Having always enjoyed very good relations with this distinguished OMV chairman, I agreed to this with alacrity.

We waited for some time for the Libya's Oil Minister Al Mabrouk to arrive. When he did, he was at first courteous enough to respond to my greeting, at which point I signalled to Senator Baur to join us. 'Excellency,' I began, 'I would like to introduce to you the President of the OMV, Senator Bauer, who would like to talk to you about Libyan oil supplies to Austria,' At this the tall Oil Minister turned to Santor Bauer, his manner instantly aloof and even irritable, while he disdainfully peered down at him as if at some strange species of animal. As if no introduction had taken place, he abruptly averted his head towards me to enquire about matters concerning the OPEC meeting, ignoring the Senator as if the man was invisible or subhuman. Throughout that evening I felt very ashamed and acutely embarrassed by this deliberately humiliating behaviour – made even more disgraceful by the fact that the recipient was a highly respected and cultured figure. Senator Bauer was, of course, deeply offended. I remember well the fury of this same minister at a conference when the idea was raised of contacting the IEA for the purpose of exchanging information. He lambasted us with the threat that if we made contact with the IEA he would boycott OPEC, adding, 'It is they who need us and not we who need them. In any event, I shall never ever sit with them.' This man (who later died of cancer) had no idea that such extremist attitudes and 'policies', which had become a feature of some 'paper kings', would only serve the new consumers' agency in achieving its objectives, as will be seen. Ironically, many years later OPEC's relationship with the IEA noticeably strengthened.

Breathtaking instances of discourtesy left me musing over how the sudden acquisition of a new and vacuous power complex can reduce *some* (not all) to such rudeness and vanity. On the occasion of an Extraordinary Meeting held by OPEC in Geneva, when I arrived with Minister Hammadi, at the airport, a journalist came forward to greet him but the minister refrained from even acknowledgement, let alone reciprocating, the greeting. The journalist then queried certain matters for discussion, and finally Hammadi berated him in a brusque, offensive manner, telling him to leave him alone as he was tired and not prepared to answer any questions. It left me more taken aback than the journalist was.

A more outlandish individual was the Qatari minister, Abdul Aziz al-Thani (who was later to be replaced by the charismatic Abdullah Al Attiya). The son of the former Emir, al-Thani was a very elegant young man, a handsome Arab with 'desert features' – wide black eyes and a small black beard. In my capacity as Deputy and Acting Secretary General of OPEC, I would meet the ministers at the airport, and whenever this Qatari minister's private jet landed and the doors opened, a large accompaniment of photographers and media people would pour out of the plane ahead of the minister. All took their positions in readiness for the young prince to disembark, which he then did – slowly and elegantly for the benefit of the TV cameras and photographers surrounding him to take shots of him while he adopted extravagant airs and gestures as if he were a movie star. His sole interest in OPEC's conferences was to attend the opening session because of the presence of all the international press and TV reporters in the conference hall, there to listen to the conference chairman's speech, prepared for him by the Secretariat. One would invariably see this minister perched resplendently in his chair and sporting a very elegant tie. After his speech the conference chairman would call the meeting to order and open the first session, at which point the reporters and photographers would disappear – and this Qatari minister would likewise vanish, withdrawing to his suite only to return in time to join the last session when, once again, the cameras were present. For this reason journalists nicknamed him 'Lifo', or 'Last in, first out'. He was very well known for his soirées, to which he would invite some of his intimate friends, but he had no idea of what was going on, and would become instantly confused and incoherent if drawn into any discussion.

Such conduct, however, was very rare as most OPEC people were, by contrast, diligent and contributed well to the conferences. Sheikh Yamani, for example, was a great achiever and a leading light at OPEC conferences. He always communicated with cogency, wisdom and wit, and at the same time was unfailingly courteous and patient with everyone, including journalists. This endeared him to all. After the main press conference (at which the Secretariat reads the resolutions), ministers then hold individual press conferences, and whenever Sheikh Yamani held his he had a huge following and it was unthinkable for any media not to be there participating. This also applied to the Kuwaiti minister, whom I admired very much, Sheikh Ali Khalifa al-Sabah, an admirably sharp-minded, highly professional and capable individual. Like Sheikh Yamani, he was among the very few OPEC ministers who knew what the real problems with the technical details entailed.

The great interest the Western media showed Yamani aroused as much vitriol from the OPEC hawks as did Yamani's objection to their insistence on further oil price increases – aware, as he was, that world dependence on OPEC oil was already in decline. At times, their provocative, gratuitously offensive remarks reached a pitch that was intolerable – as during the OPEC meeting in Bali, Indonesia (late May 1976), when the then Iraqi oil minister, Ta'eh Abdul Karim, accused Sheikh Yamani of implementing US oil policies, with their propensity for 'plundering the wealth of other nations'. Yamani arose and left the conference room with the other delegates from Saudi Arabia. The session was suspended in order to make the necessary mediations and obtain an apology from the Iraqi minister, with whom I pleaded to save the meeting; but he reacted irritably until, at Yamani's insistence and at the intervention of other ministers, he uttered a few words of apology for the effrontery of his hostile slur, which Yamani accepted, and the session resumed. The appointment of the acrimonious Minister Ta'eh Abdul Karim had been entirely political, as he had no knowledge of economics or, a fortiori, oil economics. In contrast to Sa'doun Hammadi (whom he replaced), anything beyond Karim's comprehension he dismissed as a 'conspiracy by the agents of imperialism', which explains his hostility towards both Sheikh Yamani and myself.

For about 20 months I had the ordeal of working under Karim, who had been a primary school English teacher, yet seemed unable to construe or understand a single line of English. No matter how brief, even a telex would have to be translated into Arabic for him. His strange manner seemed to reflect a social complex, possibly connected with his religious background from the west of Iraq: a sect that has its origin in the Ismaeli creed. Because of its arcane rituals, this sect tended to be frowned upon by other Muslims.

Early in 1975, on the day of Karim's appointment, I was in Abu Dhabi representing Minister Hammadi at a meeting of Gulf oil ministers to determine new percentages for royalties and tax to be imposed on the oil companies, in accordance with the concession system. This was important for Iraq, for whose oil (nationalised in 1972) these old ratios were no longer relevant. It was therefore decided, at this Gulf meeting, to increase the royalty to 20 per cent of the posted price, a substantial increase from its original 12.5 per cent. The meeting also decided on an increase in tax to 80 per cent, from its previous 65 per cent and its original 55 per cent. This I was in favour of at that stage, as increasing the tax-paid cost for the oil companies would bolster the world market price, since oil companies would be unable to sell oil at a price below the new higher tax-paid cost incurred by them. This meant that the companies would be forced to lower their discounts to buyers.

On my return to Baghdad, I wrote a report on this Abu Dhabi meeting for the new minister, Karim, and to illustrate the difference in the tax-paid cost, I resorted to a simple arithmetical equation indicating the difference between the old and new system and its impact on the market price, from which nationalised Iraqi oil stood to benefit. It was the simplest of equations to show that the higher the royalty and tax, the higher the government's take per barrel, and the higher the tax-paid cost, all of which would result in consolidating OPEC prices in the world market. When Minister Karim saw my report he called me into his office and asked in cantankerous tones what the 'weird mathematical equations' meant. 'I keep puzzling over them to the point where I dream of them and that I'll never understand them.' He said that my equations now convinced him that the oil companies' manoeuvres aimed to translate

oil affairs into enigmatic formulae that no ordinary man can understand. He imputed to me some arcane motive in employing the
same tactic! Implicit in his remark was the same accusation he had
levelled at Yamani: that I was collaborating with the oil companies;
but this time it was simply because I presented something with a
complexity that was beyond his comprehension. I couldn't believe
my ears. I did my best to reassure him and allay his anxieties by
explaining it very slowly, all over again. I'll never know whether
in the end he finally grasped it or not, but this banal experience,
combined with the political turbulence that began to take place
from mid-1975, only served to drive me away from Iraq. I cite this
particular incident only to demonstrate the level of intellect that
sometimes permeated a top ministerial post, and hence my alarm
at the possibility of major OPEC decisions being influenced by such
people.

A remarkable feature of these OPEC meetings was the extent
of influence and power exerted by small oil producers within the
organisation. This I found rather disturbing as well as incompre-
hensible. Notwithstanding Algeria's very small 1.5 per cent share
in total OPEC reserves (in marked contrast to the 82 per cent held
by the Gulf countries) and small production capacity, which did not
exceed 3.5 per cent of OPEC's total, Algeria was nevertheless able
to exert a great degree of political pressure to serve its own national
interests. Algeria's President Boumidien would unilaterally confer
with kings and heads of state in the Gulf with the aim of persuasion into seeking higher prices. Algeria's influence was thus reinforced by what became the general tenor (evident within OPEC) of
favouring higher oil prices as the quickest means of accumulating
revenue.

The Algerians, in this way – and at that time – could exploit
their country's position as one of the most prominent leaders of
the Non-Alignment movement of the Third World, and could push
for decisions that would directly benefit them. Algeria's media
also played a prominent role in blackmailing the Gulf countries
and their political regimes. If any issue arose that was contrary to
Algeria's own interests, the Algerian press, in particular the powerful newspaper, *El Moujahid*, would attack the Gulf members.
It is hardly surprising, therefore, that at OPEC conferences, the
Algerian delegation was able to project an extraordinary degree

of self-importance, assuming a position of power equal to that of many Gulf ministers, whose countries were sitting on far greater oil reserves than Algeria's – and, in the case of Saudi Arabia, *thirty times* as much.

By the mid-1970s Algeria saw itself as OPEC's de facto 'leader' and at OPEC meetings was able to extract concessions and agreements to its advantage, to which other powerful OPEC members acquiesced, resigned to the prevailing pursuit of ever higher prices that came to dominate the 'collective' thinking of OPEC. Few in the 1970s were aware of the impact that higher prices would have: in denting not only world demand but also the place that OPEC's oil would occupy in the world market, irrespective of the Gulf's prolific oil reserves.

A major reason behind Algeria's prominence, and the forceful punching above its own weight in directing OPEC policy decisions, is the fact that, despite limited oil reserves, Algeria's reserves of natural gas are very significant; and given the link between oil and gas prices, higher oil prices serve a dual advantage for Algeria: increasing its per-barrel income without affecting its market share, while at the same time pushing up the price of its natural gas exports to Europe.

In common with most OPEC members, Algeria has pressing financial needs. High oil prices boost the state revenues available for meeting increasing expenditure requirements for a burgeoning nation, especially in the 1970s, in the aftermath of Algeria's long war of liberation from French colonial rule. Algeria was also ambitious to have a dominant role among developing countries, and for this reason was the first to nationalise the independent oil companies that worked alongside Sonatrach, the national oil company. Algeria could claim to be the first to experience the successful marketing of nationalised oil, and this gave the country a certain kudos within OPEC.

When Algeria organised an OPEC Summit Conference, held during 4–6 March 1975 in Algiers, extensive studies, designed to serve Algeria's interests, were undertaken by outside consultants. Iraq was very keen to attend this summit, not so much because of oil affairs but more on account of Algeria's role in mediating between Iraq and Iran to find a solution for the disputed border, the River Shat al Arab, which is the confluence of the Tigris and Euphrates, where they meet and run down to the Gulf. For a long time this dispute blighted the relationship between the two countries.

When Iraq's oil ministry received the Algerian summit documents, I suggested forming a committee under my chairmanship consisting of bright members like Dr Abdul Amir al-Anbari, who would later hold several key ambassadorial posts during the Saddam regime, and Riadh al-Debuni, a brilliant petroleum engineer (who regrettably died prematurely).

When I began reading the Algerian summit papers, I found they expressed notions about oil-pricing that had nothing to do with even the most rudimentary economics. It was recommended that every possible means be utilised for escalating oil prices to the highest levels, irrespective of the impact on OPEC oil and energy markets. At the time, the cost of finding, developing and producing a barrel of oil in the Gulf did not exceed one US dollar, and I could see that the Algerian proposal for such a massive increase in prices would unquestionably encourage investments in high-cost oil regions outside OPEC, and would, of course, lead to a fall in the world's need for OPEC oil, affecting in particular the Gulf.

In no time at all the higher oil prices gave the companies fabulous profits with which to invest in new areas, non-OPEC oil competitors and eventually in alternatives to oil itself. This trend indicates that for countries like Iraq, Saudi Arabia and Kuwait, with their abundant oil reserves, OPEC's high-price policy would prove self-defeating in the long run.

Thus the committee's recommendations, under my chairmanship, argued that Iraq would be better advised not to adopt such high-pricing proposals and instead co-ordinate with oil-rich OPEC members like Saudi Arabia and Kuwait. However, given the useless advice of Minister Ta'eh Karim, the Saddam government deemed our committee report to be 'reactionary' and instead instructed us to side with Algeria.

Prior to the Algiers Summit of March, a committee was convened at OPEC's Vienna headquarters for the purpose of preparing recommendations and a draft for the Summit's conclusions and statements. This group comprised high-level delegates from all member countries, and as soon as they were all assembled, Sid Ahmed Guzali, who was at the time President of Sonatrach, suggested that they elect me to be the chairman of OPEC's Preparatory Working

Group and to be its spokesman during the OPEC Conference that would follow (on 27 February 1975) a few days before the Algiers Summit.

I felt reluctant to chair such a meeting or be its spokesman, mainly because I did not agree with the rationale expressed in the documentation. What made me even more hesitant in taking up the group's chairmanship was that, at the time, the other Iraqi delegates had been delayed and the only one present was the representative from the Central Bank of Iraq, Subhi Frankul, into whose domain, as a (central) banker, oil affairs simply did not fall, notwithstanding his professional competence. However, because of the agreement of all concerned with Guzali's proposition, I realised that if I opted to decline from chairing the group, it would cause embarrassment all round, and so I accepted.

During the course of our deliberations, I half-suspected that the Algerians, in proposing my chairmanship of this group, assumed that I would feel obliged to comply with all the recommendations in their documents, little realising that I would dismay them with my frank warnings about the impact of high oil prices on world demand and on OPEC oil.

Our group was very large, composed of all the member countries' representatives from their respective ministries of Foreign Affairs, Oil and Finance. Several delegates (besides the Algerians) occupied similarly high positions in their respective governments, such as Omar Muntassir of Libya, a prominent government representative.

We conducted several strenuous but tedious sessions (some lasting well into the night) to cover every aspect of a possible vision for a long-term OPEC policy. The Gulf countries, notwithstanding that they sit on the bulk of the world's oil reserves, predictably allowed themselves to be led by the Algerians and yielded to their demands. This continued to puzzle me. I believe it was because no one produced an alternative strategy – that is, apart from myself, the only one among the delegates who ever discussed the long-term effects of those policies embodied in the declaratory statement. They may not have studied carefully the real significance of the principles embodied in it but the group agreed on a draft of what was termed 'OPEC's Solemn Declaration' for the heads of state to sign.

As the world's foreseeable shift to energy sources outside OPEC was not, at this stage, perceived by OPEC people as feasible, and thus nowhere visible on their 'radar', one could argue that a trait of arrogance that pervaded OPEC circles during this era was attributable to an illusion that the world would always depend on their oil and that consumers could do absolutely nothing to reduce this dependence.

What strengthened such illusions, and the exaggerated self-confidence that went with them, were the many forecasts by oil companies' governments, by academic institutions and even by cultural institutions such as the Club of Rome, all predicting a very grim picture of imminent oil shortages from the scarcity of supplies. These forecasts, which proved to be totally false, predicted that the demand for oil would continue, unmitigated, at the same immoderately high rates, while production capacity would become increasingly limited and ineluctably fail to meet future oil requirements.

None in OPEC could imagine that the order would be reversed: that the demand for OPEC oil would dwindle to far less than their production capacity. OPEC people were ecstatic in their conviction that a shortage of oil was imminent. Under the illusion that oil would soon dry up in much of the Gulf region, they began talking of eventual ghost-towns in OPEC countries, convinced that people would have to abandon their towns. Some OPEC spokesmen preached that Arab oil should be guarded as a noble resource, to be left in the ground – either for future generations or for no one at all.

They evidently failed to realise that in urging this they were facilitating Kissinger's strategy, which heralded the US policy of reducing dependence on OPEC, especially Gulf, oil. This policy began with the formation of the US Department of Energy's (DOE), which was founded in 1977 as a direct result of OPEC's policies and the energy crisis. DOE policies were successful in achieving their goals, entirely thanks to OPEC's inversion of economic logic, turning it upside down in a way that served its competitors.

Meanwhile, in Western Europe and Japan, tough policies promoting efficient fuel utilisation resulted in oil consumption being decoupled from GDP growth or economic growth. In 2008 and 2009 oil consumption was 7 mbpd less than in 1975, whereas the value of their national wealth (GDP) had grown by a factor of over two.

After the Vienna meeting of 27 February, which adopted the recommendations of our Preparatory Working Group, Mr Frankul and I returned to Baghdad. I was met by the Minister Ta'eh Abdul Karim and reported to him what had happened. His immediate comment was that the committee's election of me as its chairman can only have meant a 'conspiracy' to prevent Iraq's voice being heard. Mercifully, Frankul was quick to intervene: 'On the contrary, Excellency, Dr Chalabi acquitted himself very efficiently in chairing the meeting and in expressing Iraq's views at the same time.' Frankul went over the top, declaring 'Chalabi should have a statue erected for his performance!' Minister Karim remained obdurate and unconvinced. His petulant swipes, as always, seemed to reflect a grudge, the reason for which eluded me, beyond realising that perhaps he just felt 'out of depth', having (through no fault of his own) little or no grasp of the basics of the oil industry, which may have left him feeling bitter.

In that session with the minister, I told him that the contents of the Declaratory Statement were not in Iraq's long-term interests because of Iraq's vast oil potential – for which it was paramount that demand for OPEC oil be sustained and augmented if Iraq was to benefit, and that prices should not encourage alternatives to OPEC oil or alternative energy sources. I explained how this statement would give oil prices such a boost that they would promote investments away from OPEC oil, and that, on this basis, Iraq should not agree to such a surge in oil prices. With his air of patronising condescension he replied: 'You economists who have studied in the West always have reactionary theories. Nothing of what you are saying is true because OPEC production continues to grow.' But he was ignorant of the fact that the fall in demand for OPEC oil would take time before it actually showed. According to accepted oil industry practices at the time, it would take at least six or seven years, after the discovery of oil, before additional capacity came on stream. This long lead-time tended to confuse OPEC people, complacent in their misconception that it was possible to increase prices without causing a decline in world demand for OPEC oil.

As the duration of that 1975 Summit in Algiers was two days (4–6 March), each of the delegation chiefs stayed in his own separate guesthouse, while other delegates were placed in hotels and guesthouses belonging to the government. For any onlooker, including myself, the famous heads of state arriving in procession, one after the other, with great solemnity, provided quite a spectacle. I was especially struck by the arrival of the Shah of Iran with Iraq's President Saddam Hussein and, sitting between them, President Boumidien of Algeria. A crowd of photographers and television people assembled to take pictures of the three heads of state and interview them. I remember clearly that when a journalist approached Saddam about the meeting and asked him what he thought, Saddam replied 'Yes, this is a great event in the history of the Third World non-aligned countries, because OPEC countries have been successful in wresting the sovereignty of their own resources from those bloodsuckers.' He meant, of course, the West. The Shah, by contrast, was far more discreet, placing emphasis on the summit being simply 'the greatest event so far in OPEC's history'.

At the time, the conflict between Iraq and Iran was building up, with Iran helping the Kurdish insurgents against the central government in Iraq. As already mentioned in this chapter, there had been a long dispute between the two countries concerning their borders, especially the River Shat al-Arab which separates the two countries. According to the treaties concluded in the 1930s, the entire River Shat al-Arab was under Iraqi sovereignty. The Shah raised the issue that the border between Iraq and Iran should not be the Iranian foreshore but that, applying the Tahlweg principle, the border should be within the riverbed itself. In other words, the Shah wanted to share the sovereignty of the river instead of its being exclusively under Iraq's domain.

To exert pressure on Iraq, the Kurdish chief, Barzani, was encouraged to involve himself in guerrilla warfare against the Iraqi army. This exhausted the country's financial and military resources to the point where Saddam, with his sharp instinct for commanding control, thought a compromise could be reached with the Shah in order to avoid the Kurdish danger to his regime. The deal was actually brokered by the US – by Henry Kissinger, of Richard Nixon's administration. According to this compromise, Iraq accepted the Iranian argument of the Tahlweg principle as the demarcation line of their borders, with the proviso that Iran undertake not to help Iraq's Kurdish insurgents occupy the area. One observes just how cynical politics can be. The Americans had initially encouraged the Kurdish chief, Mustafa Barzani, to rebel against and destabilise the Iraqi government, and yet it was the Americans who now let Barzani down. He became a political exile in the USA (where he later died).

Meanwhile, many Iraqi specialists in international law thought that Saddam's move was legally unjustified and baseless, and that Iraq should have submitted the case to the International Court of Justice in the Hague. One of these lawyers, who had the post of ambassador in the foreign ministry and was in the Iraqi delegation, looked exceedingly gloomy about Iraq's acceptance of the Iranian argument. Although he had been careful to confide his opinion only among intimates, he was punished by Saddam in a most bizarre way: not only with dismissal but also by the special issue of a presidential decree to strip the man of his PhD degree, which he had obtained in Paris, and by the downgrading of his pension.

Just before the Algerian Summit meeting was convened (for 4–5 March 1975), OPEC's Tri-Ministerial Conference was held in Vienna on 27 February. This involved the member states' foreign ministers, as well as their ministers of finance and oil, and it was agreed that the chairman would be the then Algeria's Minister for Foreign Affairs, Abdelaziz Bouteflika. My job was to report to the tri-ministerial meeting about our Preparatory Working Group's progress in Vienna, over which I had presided. As spokesman of the working group, and – as it happened – the only one technically qualified to speak, I found it difficult reporting to oil ministers who knew so little about oil, let alone about the technical operations of their industry. Afterwards, Iraq's Minister of Finance, the late Dr al-Kaisi, a friend of mine, asked me why I was 'making enemies' for myself. Baffled, I asked him what he meant. He explained that by performing 'so well' for the benefit of the ministers I had 'succeeded in dwarfing' my own minister, and so cultivating an enemy in him. This made me laugh. It would take very little effort for anyone to outshine Karim, but at last his grudge was now explained.

With this I grew wiser. In the closing session of the ministerial meetings, the Algerian Foreign Affairs Minister, Bouteflika, impressed by my presentations, suggested that I report to the heads of state meeting, to which everyone agreed except the Iranian Minister Amouzegar, who commented that although he appreciated very much Chalabi's work, it was not appropriate for the heads of state to listen to anyone other than the chairman of our meeting, that is to say Algeria's Minister for Foreign Affairs Abdelaziz Bouteflika. When a colleague of mine remarked that the Iranian minister had deprived me of the privilege, with my new wisdom I replied, 'On the contrary, I have no desire to show off in front of these heads of state, as this would only give me problems back in Baghdad!'

After the closure of the Tri-Ministerial OPEC conference, the summit of heads of state was convened under President Boumidien's chairmanship, the whole outcome of which was tailored according to the Algerian mode of thought. With a unanimous vote the Conference adopted the draft Solemn Declaration that had been prepared by the working group under my chairmanship in Vienna. The Tri-Ministerial Conference's endorsement of it meant that at the Algiers Summit any change would be very difficult to make.

A curious feature of OPEC's pricing policies is the concept of basing oil-pricing on an assumption, articulated in OPEC's Declaration, of an impending scarcity of oil in the very near future; therefore, the price of oil had to be based on the premise of strict conservation of petroleum reserves. This meant putting a limit on production with the aim of conserving oil reserves for as long a period as possible. Later developments proved that this kind of thinking was out of touch with the reality that OPEC's proven reserves are the least depleted in the world, especially in the Gulf, and that the notion of guarding reserves proved to be a fallacy. The current depletion rate of Gulf oil reserves is 1.5 per cent per annum, compared with 16 per cent in the North Sea and 11 per cent in the USA.

OPEC's Declaration also emphasised the availability, utilisation and cost of alternative sources of energy, implying, as a criterion for pricing oil, the principle of putting the oil price at parity with the cost of producing a barrel of synthetic oil from coal, which at that time was extremely high. What was fallacious about this Declaration was its referral to certain criteria for the pricing of petroleum, among which were 'the terms of transfer of goods and technology for the development of OPEC member countries'. I remember Dr Hammadi asking me in Algiers, 'How can one define the "terms of the transfer of technology"?' I replied that I did not know, and he then commented that it was 'nonsense'. Even so Iraq adopted that Solemn Declaration, based on this 'nonsense'. Nonsense or not, the Algerians used this document to bolster their own arguments within OPEC, calling for ever higher prices. OPEC, of course, did not follow this ultimately because subsequent events overtook the Algerian declaration; but, had the heads of state of the Gulf countries been aware of all the implications of the Declaration, they would not have signed the document.

Furthermore, Algeria snatched OPEC's brilliance for its own propaganda in calling for a new economic order within the UN. This was the theme of the UN Conference held in 1975, at which Algerian President Boumidien was the main speaker and called for a new world economic order to support third-world development. After long sessions, in which I participated, nothing of any real substance emerged in the final document agreed upon by the participating countries, yet this UN Conference strengthened Algeria's image in the 1970s as OPEC's 'de facto' leader.

Of particular interest at that summit meeting were the confidential talks held by Saddam Hussein with the Shah of Iran, from which emerged an international agreement between the two countries about the definition of frontiers, as explained earlier. I remember once I was called by Saddam Hussein to his guesthouse. It seemed that some of his doctors, with whom I was acquainted, had suggested to him that instead of having an Algerian as interpreter in his talks with the Shah, Saddam should 'ask Chalabi to interpret for you, as he speaks French.' I do not know what prompted them to suggest such a dangerous role for me, which obviously I would have been powerless to decline, or even consent to! Mercifully Saddam told me to 'wait here until 10 p.m., and if by then you have not been summoned by me, then you can join your hotel.' It was a great relief for me to be returning to my hotel just after 10 p.m., because these were extremely confidential talks, and there were already rumours that Iraqi interpreters for Saddam had disappeared mysteriously following highly secretive talks. There was even a story, told by the Syrians in the days when they were Saddam's arch foe, that the real interpreter for Saddam's talks with the Shah was Boumidien himself, who knew too much to be allowed to survive. The story, which has never been proven, was that the mysterious, unknown illness that killed Boumidien was the result of poisoning by Iraqi intelligence operations in Algeria. True or false, this story is based on a certain wisdom gained from Mafia gangsters who liquidate anybody who knows too much – rather in the manner of the

Hitchcock film of *The Man Who Knew Too Much*, of which I found myself constantly reminded.

After the OPEC summit, the Algerian Foreign Affairs Minister, Bouteflika, held a press conference at which he announced the agreement between the Shah and Saddam Hussein. While he was speaking in French I was standing with some of Saddam's closest aides, who then asked me to translate what Bouteflika was saying. To my surprise they knew nothing about the agreement, and reacted as if they had for the first time discovered the existence of this provision within the agreement; though, of course, none of them would have dared raise a finger against it. Later we shall see how Saddam in September 1980 tore up that same agreement at the outbreak of Iraq's war with Iran, which lasted eight years.

When the summit conference was over, it was decided the next day that we would return to Baghdad by the special presidential plane. It so happened that I had became afflicted with a painful back and was unable to walk or even pack my luggage. Some friends helped me, and I went in another car with my friend, Abdul Amir Anbari, beside me. Meanwhile, Saddam, while walking among a large entourage of security and high-level people, glanced at me sitting in the car and he approached me asking, 'What is wrong with you, Mr Fadhil?' I explained that I was unable to move as I had a problem with my back. To my amazement he showed instant concern about me and urged the entourage in the plane to 'do something to help Dr Chalabi!' It is still very difficult to believe that this man was ever capable of kindly concern, but this could be the case if he felt you were useful to him and posed no threat.

OPEC's other 'phenomenal' feature was Libya, which, like Algeria, was a minor producer that routinely dominated OPEC's major producers. Libya, however, could stake its claim to being the source of the 'new winds' that were blowing through OPEC by 1970, as success with its demands from the oil companies had bestowed on the Libyans a certain cachet, a prestige that they exploited to convey the impression that it was *they* who afforded OPEC its immense bargaining power. Libya conferred on itself a historical right of leadership of OPEC, in the same mould as Algeria. Although relatively higher than Algerian oil reserves, those of Libya are still modest compared with the Gulf's. Its reserves in 1980 stood at 23 bn/B, or

2.8 per cent of OPEC's total; while its production amounted to 2 per cent of OPEC's total. Yet Libya, like Algeria, was able to exert political pressure over the larger Gulf producers. It was rumoured that Colonel Gaddafi used to speak by telephone with many heads of state, persuading them all to agree with Libya's demand for higher prices.

7

OPEC terrorised by the Jackal:
the Carlos affair

OPEC's ordinary meeting of December 1975, in Vienna, focused on a long and fruitless discussion of the problem of value differentials for various OPEC crudes, which reflect differences in their quality and geographical location. Having taken over the pricing of oil from the IOCs two years earlier, in October 1973, OPEC developed a bizarre, non-economic, fixed-price system for Saudi Arabian light crude, 34API Gulf, as a reference price, on the basis of which other OPEC crudes were to be priced, again at fixed levels. By the same token, a higher-quality crude, light and sulphur-free, such as Algerian Sahara crude (geographically nearer the main consuming centres), had a higher fixed price than Arab Light Gulf crude; while heavy crude, with a high sulphur content, had to be priced at lower levels than Arab Light. This rigid system did not take into account the almost daily changes in the value differences among the various crude oils reacting to market changes.

OPEC's engagement in this pricing system exemplified a certain misunderstanding of the market forces that determine price differentials, never at rigidly fixed levels but as a reaction to changes in supply and demand, given that certain crudes vary almost daily in correlation to availability and requirements. According to OPEC's fixed pricing system, member countries were required to set a fixed price of their crudes at levels acceptable to the organisation. This rigid system led to Iraq being accused (mainly by the Algerians) of not complying with the regulations and offering its oil with hidden discounts with the aim of increasing sales. Iraq categorically dismissed and refused even to acknowledge this accusation.

The conference meeting was scheduled to end on the Saturday evening of 20 December, but because of absurdly prolonged debates between the Iraqi minister, Ta'eh Abdul Karim, and the Algerian minister, Belaid Abdesselam, the meeting dragged on, and it was agreed to reconvene it the following morning. We all duly trooped into the conference room at 10 a.m. that Sunday, 21 December, to listen once more to these fruitless debates, during which Ta'eh was incoherent and his tone needlessly aggressive. When responding to Belaid Abdesselam on a technical matter, to support his argument he even recited verses from the Qur'an and Arabic poetry, which were irrelevant.

As soon as 11.30 struck, I suddenly noticed out of the corner of my eye the entire Libyan delegation quietly leaving the conference room. This egress was instantly observed by me as our Iraqi delegation was seated opposite the Libyans in the conference room of OPEC's old headquarters (in Karl Lueger Ring). The Iranian delegation was grouped to my right, while on my left sat the Kuwaiti delegation, alongside which were the Libyans, a positioning that brought them round to face the Iraqis.

Though only vaguely glimpsed by me while discussions were in progress, the careful timing of the Libyans' departure became imprinted in my memory, because only a few minutes later there came a deafening clatter of machine guns and the explosion of a grenade, outside the conference room, followed by unusual movements and noises.

We were then even more startled when an armed, masked young man suddenly stormed into our conference room. Gun in hand, he shouted threats in broken English, commanding us to lie down beneath the tables. He then yelled, 'Anyone who moves will be shot!' The clatter of bullets continued outside. No one had a clue what was happening, hidden as we were under our tables, trembling for fear that death was imminent. In the expectation of finding our short lives tragically curtailed, I began whispering verses from the Qur'an. Time passed very slowly, every minute seeming like an hour while we remained in a state of stunned uncertainty. Suddenly the machine gun clatter ceased and there was a long silence, before a peremptory voice bellowed, 'Who is Yamani?' Sheikh Yamani had to stand up from beneath the table, and I heard him reply, 'Yes, sir, I am Yamani.' After a brief pause, the voice commanded him to stand in a particular corner of the room. Unable to see a thing from beneath our tables, after another minute or so we heard the voice resume its hostile questioning: 'Which one is Amouzegar?' The Iranian minister likewise rose to attention and identified himself. He was commanded to join Yamani in the same corner. Already suspecting the involvement of the dreaded Carlos 'the Jackal', we all awaited our fate in fear and trepidation. As footsteps approached each of the tables, one of the Iranian delegates beside me began snorting from sheer terror, which rather unnerved me. Each of us in turn was asked very curtly 'and where are you from?' and one had to reveal one's identity by standing up. I heard the same voice ordering the other Iranian delegates to stand in the same corner where their minister had gone.

Then my turn came, and hearing the same order I stood up and was surprised to see not a fearsome face but a pleasant-looking young fellow in his late twenties or early thirties, sporting elegant boots and a long leather overcoat in the latest fashion. He had hazel eyes and light brown hair that was evidently dyed. As soon as I answered him with my name and my country, Iraq, he smiled briefly and said, 'You are a friend, not an enemy. Go to that corner over there,' which was in the opposite direction from Yamani's and Amouzegar's corner. With his bullying, forceful air of command and recognisable swagger of revolutionary leader, it was no surprise to learn, moments later, that this was indeed Carlos.

Before introducing himself, he continued his preliminary exercise of herding us like sheep into four groups, the first of which he identified as 'the reactionary' group, comprising Iran, Saudi Arabia, the UAE and Qatar. The second was the 'progressives': Algeria, Iraq and Libya. The third group was the 'non-aligned or neutral' delegates – Venezuela, Ecuador, Indonesia, Gabon and Nigeria; and the fourth group consisted of OPEC Secretariat staff, including the Secretary General, the Nigerian Chief Feide. Carlos then began a rhetorical baiting: 'And what shall I do with the Kuwaiti delegation, which is half-reactionary and half-progressive?' After a pause he told the Kuwaitis that they could join 'the progressive lot'. Thus the Kuwaiti delegation, headed by the conservative Mr Kadimi (an affluent businessman from the Gulf), found itself, to its surprise, relegated to being progressive.

At this moment another man arrived, also masked, who appeared to be European. He was holding his stomach as if in great pain from a bullet wound. We later learnt that he was 'Klein', a German from the Baader Meinhof gang. Then a girl (whom we later discovered was also German) entered wearing a leather jacket, the upper sleeve of which was torn. We found out later that when she had first entered OPEC's premises with her machine gun, Ta'eh's chauffeur, who was also his bodyguard, had grabbed her by the shoulder so forcefully that he had ripped her leather jacket, and at his brave attempt to impede her, she had shot him dead at close range. I understood from Minister Ta'eh that this chauffeur had repeatedly expressed a desire to accompany his boss to Vienna as his bodyguard, really just to see something of this lovely city. Later in Baghdad it was with great sadness that I attended the poor man's burial.

Behind the girl, a small young man entered, clutching a grenade in each hand, his face taut from nerves and the intense effort of appearing permanently fierce. Then the one who had first stormed into the room now removed his mask, a Palestinian nicknamed 'Khalid'. Then came the turn of their young leader to reveal himself, and he announced in melodramatic tones that he was Carlos 'the revolutionary, who has caused a lot of headache and fear for Israel and the West. I belong to a group that struggles against imperialism and Zionism. I defend the Palestinian cause and the liberation of Palestine from the Zionists. I also support the revolutionaries of Dhufar in Oman.' Then he returned to his barrage of questions, first finding out who was in charge of the first aid kit, and at this the OPEC administrator came forward. Carlos asked his name and nationality, and he answered, 'Anis Attar. Austrian, of Iraqi origin.' As soon as he brought the first aid kit to Carlos, he found himself rewarded with instant release.

Carlos then resumed his list of demands, the first of which was to have his statement broadcast on Austrian radio in the English, French and German languages. He then recited to us his 'mission statement', which was full of revolutionary bravado. 'The second demand is that we want to have an airplane, fully equipped, provided by the Austrian authorities to take us from here to an airport of our choice. The third is this: my comrade is wounded, and I want something to be done for him immediately.' He was referring to Klein, the German. The Nigerian Minister immediately announced, 'I am a doctor and I may be able to help.' After a brief examination, he said, 'This man needs instant surgery and intensive care.' He was, of course, unable to help without proper medical equipment. Klein then collapsed.

The problem was that it was a Sunday, and no decisions would be taken without the entire Austrian cabinet's approval. As Chancellor Bruno Kreisky was spending his weekend skiing, we had to wait in this very tense atmosphere without having a clue what the attitude of the Austrian Government would be.

What then intensified our ordeal was our anxious observation of the small, eccentric young man sitting on a chair placed on a table in the middle of the room still clutching the two hand grenades, which he could detonate at any given moment. His behaviour throughout was juvenile. Carlos, meanwhile, kept his composure, talking to one group after another. He spoke to the Venezuelan delegation in his native fluent Spanish, and we understood from the Venezuelan minister, the refined and courteous Hermandez Valentin Acosta, that Carlos was indeed a Venezuelan whose real name was Ramirez-Sanchez, alias 'Ilich' (Lenin's famed patronymic) and his father was a well-known lawyer in Caracas, who held extreme left-wing views.

Knowing that on a public holiday any responses would be protracted, we anxiously awaited the arrival of members of the Austrian government. Chancellor Kreisky returned by helicopter to Vienna and held a cabinet meeting to reach a crucial decision. In the evening, the Chargé d'Affaires of the Iraqi Embassy (a Mr Azzawi, whose demeanour was one of a secret agent) came and told us that the Libyan Ambassador was away in Prague, in his capacity as Ambassador there. He added that he had met those responsible, who had confirmed that there would soon be a solution to this crisis. For Carlos the most immediate problem was finding an Austrian doctor who would be prepared to treat his wounded comrade, Klein, on the plane.

Several hours had by now passed without food and the OPEC Secretariat, having already organised for that evening a dinner party for the delegates in the newly inaugurated Hilton Hotel, now arranged for canapés, grilled chicken, fruit, etc. to be brought over from the Hilton so that we could dine while relishing our 'terror'! Some barely ate, dispensing with nourishment as a secondary issue in the tense situation. Yet other delegates, faced, as they were, with the unknown saw this as a last chance to eat, and plunged for survival's sake into the food, with some notion of camel-like storage. I noticed the Kuwaiti minister stuffing his pockets with apples while tucking into a dish of chicken with great gusto. I myself did not care to eat and instead spent my time in a spirit of alleviating the atmosphere by chatting with friends, Dr Abdul Amir Anbari from Iraq and the late Dr Nureddin Farag, the Egyptian oil adviser in the Kuwaiti delegation.

But terror struck us anew when Carlos repeatedly warned that if the Austrians failed to agree to his demands he would blow up the whole building. He began planting explosives around the walls in readiness. He then ratcheted up the air of fear with his aggressive command to the Saudi Oil Undersecretary, Abdul Aziz Al Turki, to sit in the middle of the room and be 'the first target – in case anything went wrong'. This man's courage and composure were exemplary as he sat on the chair. For this I admired him, notwithstanding his strange antagonism towards me in opposing my appointment as Assistant Secretary General of OAPEC on the grounds that he suspected that I was a communist.

After a while Carlos approached our group, adopting a facial expression of mock-regret and pseudoconcern. Irritated by this, I challenged him with a question, asking him what his purpose was in holding us hostage. 'We do all this to create a big noise,' came his simple answer, 'beaucoup de bruit,' he repeated in French. 'And at an international level,' he continued, 'so that the whole world's attention will be focused on the tragedy of the Palestinian people.' He then added, with a sudden pained expression that just earlier he had been forced to kill 'a friend'. When I asked why, he replied, 'It was the Libyan, Yousef Izmerli, and I mistook him for a Saudi. He held my throat and was about to kill me with his gun, so I had no choice but to shoot him. Really, I was so sorry to kill this man from such a progressive country.' Sounding insane, he repeated, 'I didn't know he was a Libyan. He was so strong that he held on to me, and if I had not killed him he would have killed me.'

Carlos proved to be an inveterate liar, as he had actually shot the Libyan, Yousef Izmerli, in the back while he was fleeing the length of a corridor for cover in one of the rooms in our building. It was very upsetting to learn that the pleasant, quiet, young Yousef had been killed in such a cowardly way. After this event, Sheikh Yamani took care of Yousef's family, including his American wife and the education of their children. I recall seeing him once at the end of one of the meetings hugging his children and telling Yousef's wife to rely on him for anything they needed.

The sudden withdrawal of the Libyan delegation from the meeting just before the attack remained a puzzle for me. We were informed later that the Libyan Oil Minister, Azzidin al-Mabrouk, had hidden in the lavatory, the door of which he had locked *before* the attack. This, together with the strange absence from Vienna of the Libyan Ambassador while travelling to Czechoslovakia at the very time that the OPEC conference had been convened, made me feel uneasy about the Libyan role in this dangerous game.

Carlos then asked the head of each delegation to come and talk to him, and so it was that our Minister Ta'eh met Carlos face to face. When he returned I asked him what it was all about. He replied that they were part of the group called Abu Nidal (Wad'i'e Haddad), Palestinian terrorists, 'ridiculous people,' he added, 'because they make no mention in their statement of any appreciation of Iraq's initiative in nationalising its oil in defiance of imperialism.'

After midnight, Azzawi, the Chargé d'Affaires from the Iraqi Embassy in Vienna, returned to advise that Chancellor Kreisky had accepted the ultimatum of conditions given by Carlos and that this statement would be broadcast on Austrian radio in the three languages, as requested. Also there had been success in obtaining an Austrian aircraft and a bus was to be provided to conduct the hostages to the airport. They had found a doctor who was prepared to join the hostages in order to take care of the wounded Klein, the Baader Meinhof terrorist.

At about 4 o'clock in the morning we were told to be prepared to depart for the airport in a bus. This was one of the most dreadful moments: having just escaped death from the possible explosion of OPEC's headquarters, we were now heading for a totally unknown destiny, emerging from one dangerous predicament only to confront another. Before we boarded the bus, Carlos decided to free the OPEC Secretariat staff. I recall that throughout this tense drama, one of the secretaries, an Austrian, Sylvia Smetbrach, had been crying hysterically and trembling with convulsions, so that even Carlos felt pity enough to free her before the others.

Carlos's next decision was to free the ministers and aides of the 'neutral' delegations. This happened at our first stop, which turned out to be the city of Algiers. As for the others, we would have to 'wait and see'. It was in the very early hours in the morning that we began to shuffle towards the bus in an atmosphere of disquiet, our faces showing how overwrought with anxiety and consternation we felt. Carlos then decided that each Minister should choose two aides to be with him in the plane, and to release the others. I remember Minister Kazemi of Kuwait choosing two aides who did not hold important positions, and he asked Carlos to free Sheikh Ali Khalifa al-Sabah, the 'number two' in the ministry, in addition to Dr Nureddin Farag, the oil adviser – both of whom tried to persuade the Kuwaiti Minister Kazemi to let them remain with him in his ordeal, but Kazemi heroically insisted that only he had the authority to make such a choice. The same sacrificial procedure was adopted by the Algerian Minister Belaid Abdesselam who selected the most junior staff members of Sonatrach, and also insisted on freeing Ahmed Guzali, the President of Sonatrach, and Nourdine Ait Laoussine, its marketing man – as, given the worst-case scenario, it was imperative to keep alive those who were vitally important for keeping the oil industry alive.

Meanwhile our Iraqi Oil Minister Ta'eh insisted that both Dr Anbari and I accompany him to share every second of his trauma. I had no choice but to stay with the minister, but Anbari tried to persuade Carlos to free him, without success. On our way out I picked up several bullet cartridges from the floor as a souvenir of this nightmare, in case we had the good fortune to survive.

Then we began to embark one by one onto the bus. My lot was to sit beside Ta'eh, who was next to the window. There were no seats to our rear, yet the small, nervous Palestinian, Yousef, still clutching the hand grenades, managed to squeeze behind us. Because of the jerks made by the bus, his hands touched my head from time to time. I politely asked him in Arabic to take great care: 'Brother, the grenades in your hands are touching my head. Could you kindly stand a little further away?' His face flashed with anger. 'You coward!' he shouted at me, 'you are afraid of the least thing!' and he muttered to himself 'Cowards! Bah!' Surprisingly enough he pulled away from me, much to my relief.

The bus drove us, imprisoned and helpless, along Vienna's streets, covered in snow under a leaden grey sky, and this experience alone was appalling enough. We were in convoy, with the Austrian Minister of the Interior in a car in front, while the security people drove behind us. Pedestrians stared and as we passed all the buildings people watched us through open windows. Aware that it was enough for just one bullet from outside for the whole bus to be blown up and all its passengers killed, we felt greatly perturbed, like helpless prey caught by a fiendish predator. We took the old road to the airport, which was free of traffic, and the Austrian plane awaited us on the tarmac.

When we boarded the aircraft, we found an Iraqi Kurd, Dr Rawanduzi (the brother of a colleague of mine), waiting to accompany us and take care of the wounded German, Klein, who was lying there with an oxygen mask over his mouth. The doctor asked everybody to refrain from smoking because of the oxygen. I sat near fellow-Iraqi Dr Anbari, and not very far behind us, sitting with other Saudi delegates, was Sheikh Yamani, looking very pale. He was suffering with an acute migraine, and yet he was in complete control, showing no sign of panic despite knowing that the kidnappers were holding him and Amouzegar as their primary targets. With him was al-Turki, the Saudi Undersecretary, and Herzallah, a Saudi of Palestinian origin.

Despite our ignorance of our destination (as nobody told us that the plane would land at Algiers airport), the dreary futility and alienation that had overwhelmed me on the bus was now partly dispelled while I found myself and Anbari chatting together as if resigned to the situation as a fait accompli. As soon as we landed in Algiers, we saw lots of people waiting for us, along with the then Algerian Minister for Foreign Affairs, Abdelaziz Bouteflika. Again there was that sound of sudden unusual activity when the so-called neutral countries' delegates (the third group) left the aircraft, which meant that they had been released. Carlos then asked the Algerian oil minister, Belaid Abdesselam, to disembark with his two aides, but he refused to do so, telling Carlos he was in full solidarity with his colleague ministers and would prefer to face danger with them rather than leave the plane and abandon them to an unknown fate. It was an admirable stance on his part, and he showed complete calm and dignity while talking to Carlos.

Then the emergency medical assistance took Klein to a hospital in Algiers, which meant Dr Rawanduzi was able to fly back to Vienna. After two hours or so, we felt the aircraft moving but with no idea where to. After flying for about an hour we landed and were told it was Tripoli, Libya. The aircraft continued to taxi down the runway until it stopped in a spot far from the runway. We remained waiting for the next thing to happen, until nightfall when we were left in total darkness.

During this long wait, Carlos, clearly nervous, paced to and fro. Then suddenly we saw Jalud, Libya's 'number 2', with another person in the aeroplane, asking Carlos to see him in the cockpit, where they stayed a long while. No one had any idea what they were discussing. Suddenly the cockpit door opened tentatively and Jalud appeared, signalling to his Libyan Minister, Azzidin al-Mabrouk, and the other Libyan, to leave the aircraft together with them. It was by then late at night.

At that moment, Carlos ordered the Algerian minister, Belaid Abdesselam to leave the aircraft with the Libyans, but again this minister (who remained aboard the plane the whole time) refused: 'I shall stay with my colleagues,' he said. This infuriated Carlos, who insisted that he must comply with his order, meaning that if Abdesselam persisted in staying with the other hostages he would be killed. So he finally left, while we continued waiting in the aircraft in complete darkness, except for a shaft of moonlight between the clouds. After a long while, Carlos resumed his nervous pacing, now in a state of rage, repeating loudly to himself, 'Those Libyans are not reliable people! I will not co-operate with them any longer!' They were very tense, frightening moments, yet Anbari and I continued to talk quietly together, until Ali Jaidha of Qatar joined us, concerned at our air of casual normality: 'Are you not aware of the danger we are facing? What if this madman loses his nerves? Something terrible could happen.' We both realised that chatting in such a sociable manner seemed incongruous at such a time, but it had alleviated the forlorn hopelessness one felt being isolated, cut off from all communication with the outside world. A sinister silence fell while the hijacked passengers waited anxiously to hear their fate. The long, black night was interrupted only by clouds moving to reveal a half-moon and by the terrorists pacing back and forth to the cockpit like caged animals, muttering darkly all the while.

Seeing Carlos allow a few (non-Libyans) to disembark, an Iraqi friend of the Libyans, Sahirr Yayha, who worked in Abu Dhabi's Oil Ministry, asked Carlos if he could disembark with them. Carlos refused, roughly demanding, 'What has this to do with you, an Iraqi who does not work in Iraq? No, you will stay with us until the end.' Yayha, now alarmed, pleaded, explaining that if he were to land in Baghdad, the Iraqi government would never permit him to leave again. 'This is another reason for you to stay,' retorted Carlos. Poor Sahirr was in a state of utter despair.

We remained stuck like this for another ten hours or more, an even greater ordeal than the earlier phase as hostages in the OPEC Secretariat, where we had been detained for more than 20 hours without sleep. We later learned that the Libyans had promised to provide Carlos with an aircraft of greater range than the Austrian Airlines' DC9, which could not fly the distance from Tripoli to Baghdad, Carlos's destination plan. The nearest airports within its range were Beirut, Damascus and Cairo, or else Ankara, all of which Carlos wished to avoid for security reasons, as he would likely be arrested at any of them. What enraged Carlos was the Libyans' failure to keep their promise, having now told him that they had only one aircraft of long-range capability but that it was reserved for the Libyans' pilgrimage to Mecca, and therefore could not be given to him. Because of this situation, his original plan to land in Baghdad was scuppered.

We later learnt that Carlos had intended to release first the Iraqi delegation in Baghdad, then fly the Iranian and Saudi delegations to Aden in South Yemen, where the political regime was extreme left. It was also said that Carlos's original diabolical plan was to explode the aircraft containing Sheikh Yamani, Amouzegar and their respective aides, as a mark of his disapproval of Saudi Arabia and its amicable relations with the West.

In the tense atmosphere in the aircraft, suddenly Carlos exclaimed loudly, 'There is no hope with these retarded Libyans, and so we must leave.' In an instant, the jet roared into life and we began to move, to our great surprise and admiration for the Austrian pilots who had shown outstanding resilience and courage after waiting interminably and then, yet again, having to fly under duress, all this time without any break, in contravention of international flying regulations. Since leaving Vienna at about 6 a.m., their flying time had already exceeded 24 hours. Such physical and mental resilience told us a lot about man's ability to adapt to extraordinary circumstances when his survival is at stake. What they achieved was an act of heroism.

The winds were so strong that, once airborne, the aircraft was pulled alternately left and right. Forced to fly at a relatively low level, from the window I could see the passing clouds. We later learned that Carlos had ordered the pilots to land in Tunisia but that the authorities there would not permit it.

Among our tribulations was hearing that the plane's fuel was so low that we would have to make an emergency landing at the nearest airport. This turned out to be Algiers, where we had been only 20 hours earlier. Our horrifying trip in total darkness, except for an intermittent faint moonlight, was made worse by the fierce winds that accosted our plane, like a small ship in a raging ocean, and we kept our seatbelts fastened the whole time. Observing the hijackers, I noticed their grim facial expression, one of simultaneous harshness and fatigue, especially that of the young German girl, who had so ruthlessly killed the Iraqi minister's chauffeur and two Austrian policemen.

It was dawn when the aircraft finally landed at Algiers airport, where a throng of people now waited, among whom stood Algeria's Minister for Foreign Affairs, Abdelaziz Bouteflika, in his duffle coat, unshaven and looking exhausted. Carlos left the aircraft, but the two Palestinians stayed with us for about two hours, without giving us any idea of what was going on. Certain negotiations were afoot between Carlos and Bouteflika. The only thing we knew was that someone had brought us a breakfast of croissants and very strong coffee, and this revived my strength. They finally allowed us to disembark.

It was a very strange sensation at this point, as I could not believe after all this that we were finally free and that the whole ordeal, which had lasted about 46 hours, was at last over. Dr Anbari and I now felt in a better frame of mind than many of the others, no doubt because chatting and discussing so much together had cheered us up. Once I was outside the aircraft, I stood and looked all round me to be certain that I was not dreaming.

We were taken to the VIP room at Algiers airport, where I saw Sheikh Yamani and Dr Amouzegar sitting on a sofa with the Algeria's Minister for Foreign Affairs, Abdelaziz Bouteflika seated in between them, while Carlos the Jackal stood by, with a sullen expression of outrage on his face. All the other hostages had been told to sit at some distance from these two ministers and the Jackal. A bus took us to the hotel, which was very modern, newly constructed and uphill, in a quite high location. Each of us went to his own room without any fresh change of underwear or pyjamas or shaving kit, as we had left everything in our Bristol Hotel in Vienna. The Iraqi Chargé d'Affaires undertook to send on our luggage to Baghdad. I had entrusted to his care my two large 11-volume albums of the complete works of Bach. I had wanted to buy the whole collection (which included the best performances of the complete works, including his church music, chamber music and orchestral works). Just imagine: despite all the drama, I found myself worrying about these precious records. Again it showed the lengths to which man can adapt in a dangerous situation. As for Ta'eh, his main preoccupation was ensuring that the Chargé d'Affaires took charge of his very expensive suit, which required some alterations, for which he had given him the receipt while cautioning him: 'Please take care not to forget my suit!'

Once in my hotel room, after taking off my crumpled clothes and having a refreshing shower, I tried to sleep but could not. I arose and got dressed again, feeling the urge to get outside and walk around the city of Algiers (which I knew quite well). I went to the lift and as soon as it came I got in and pressed the button for the *rez de chaussé*. While standing there in my tense mood, noting that the lift was large enough to take over ten people, suddenly the lift stopped between two floors and I was plunged into darkness. I was startled and felt suddenly helpless in confronting this new danger of being trapped alone in a broken-down lift! After two days of no sleep and the delayed shock of being held captive by hijackers, I imagined I was now being systematically hounded to death, momentarily feeling greater fear than when being held hostage. I had survived one adversity only to be subjected to another and could not believe my ill fate! In the dark I groped the walls of the lift in search of buttons, but nothing happened when I pressed them. However, it did not take more than ten minutes of panic before the lift resumed its descent to the *rez de chaussé*. When I finally emerged on the ground floor and saw daylight, I heaved a sigh of relief at my lucky escape from this new peril. I understood later that when I pressed the button it signalled the hotel reception, and the fault was repaired.

I left the hotel and went for a stroll in the morning sun. After changing money for Algerian dinars, I found a barber for a shave, with whom I spoke in French. In those days, any visitor to Algiers who did not speak French felt lost. He asked where I was from. When I told him Iraq, and that I had been released here by terrorists who had hijacked us, with his razor poised in mid-air he exclaimed, 'Thanks be to Allah!' After shaving me, he did not want to take any money, offering his service gratis, because of my ghastly experience as an Iraqi hostage. Of course I insisted on paying this nice man, who showed a sympathy for the Arabs without any knowledge of their language. My next priority was to buy a shirt as I was still in the same one that I had worn for two days. I went back to the hotel and in the lobby there were various ministers and delegates. When they saw me, their faces lit up, and the Gabonese minister, who was lame and walked with a stick, almost dropped his stick in his excitement. Later my Minister, Ta'eh, appeared and he asked me what I had been doing. When I told him, he said that he wanted me to accompany him after our breakfast so that he could learn something of Algeria. Following the Algiers summit some eight months earlier, this was his second visit to the city.

During our promenade through the city, Ta'eh found himself unable to understand anything as of course everyone spoke in French, so I translated everything for him. He said, 'What is this? In an Arab country one cannot speak Arabic?' I explained to him how the Frenchification of Algeria was a result of colonial rule, as Algeria was considered by France to be French territory. I added that, ever since its liberation, there had been an intensive campaign for the revival of Arabic in Algeria. Later, on our return to the hotel, we found a large number of people sitting about and it was very nice, as well as moving, to see people of different nationalities together celebrating the end of their ordeal, the outcome of which was a sense of unity and common purpose. The following year the Venezuelan Minister, Hermandez Acosta, even recommended to their Venezuelan President, Carlos Andrés Pérez, that he should bestow on me the Simon Bolivar decoration to express their high degree of appreciation for my services for OPEC.

We all met up during the lunch period, when I noticed this great solidarity between Arabs and non-Arabs after experiencing the horror of the hijack together. There I met Abdul Azziz al-Turki and Herzallah of Saudi Arabia who were without their Minister Sheikh Yamani. As we had been directed to leave the airport's VIP lounge without knowing the fate of Sheikh Yamani and Amouzegar, we were totally unaware of what had been happening meanwhile. So I immediately asked al-Turki and Herzallah who apprised me of events that were later confirmed to me by Sheikh Yamani himself: while Yamani and Amouzegar had been in the VIP lounge, their ordeal far from over, they had very nearly been assassinated by Carlos and the Palestinian, Khalid. An astute, very observant, quick-witted security guard was able at the last minute to disarm them, and this is how both these ministers had escaped an appalling death.

We waited at our hotel until evening along with the Kuwaiti delegation, who informed us that a special Kuwaiti flight would take us from Algiers. At that moment I thought the Iraqi Government would supply a plane, but nothing of the kind was forthcoming. Later that night, we boarded the Kuwaiti plane at the invitation of the Kuwaiti minister, Kazemi. The Iraqi Government, meanwhile, showed no concern for its delegates, despite the fact that Ta'eh was a member of the Revolutionary Command Council.

When the plane landed at Kuwait airport, a large number of Kuwaiti officials greeted their delegation, including the then Foreign Minister (now Kuwait's Emir) and several other ministers. I was impressed by the warm-hearted, generous welcome of the Kuwaiti government for its Oil Minister Kazemi, the more so given that he was from the minority Shi'i community, regarded by the Kuwaitis as second-class citizens. We were later told that a small aircraft would take us to Baghdad, where we were met (in contrast to the Kuwaitis' generous reception) by two officials, Mr Adnan Hamdani, a powerful figure within Saddam's circles, accompanied by the head of the INOC. I was struck by the fact that only one government official of any importance (Hamdani) had bothered to meet us. Hamdani came from a good family – unlike the majority of Ba'ath politicians, who emanated from a rather low, uneducated, social stratum. I had heard that his father, who was in the business of river transport between Baghdad and Basra, was a good man, though I never met him. My family, of course, were all there to greet me, and it was a very moving moment when my little daughter, Dounia, then four years of age, came running towards me with my other children and hugged me.

Yet a vague lurking suspicion made me feel uneasy at Baghdad airport – as I could sniff the involvement of the Ba'athists in the hijacking affair. It is known that its mastermind was a Palestinian terrorist, Wadi Haddad, who was at the time in Iraq. The whole experience suggested to me that both Libya and Iraq were involved, but this still left me wondering why and whose interests it served. Carlos was true to his name, 'the Jackal', whose boast I had never taken seriously concerning his object of creating a big stir to attract attention to the Palestinian plight. Everything he said during his siege of the OPEC Secretariat was false, reflecting nothing but distortions of the truth. The reality was that the attack was against OPEC itself, at the height of its power. An operation of this kind could only have the effect of strengthening the notion in the West that Arab oil was too politicised and was an unreliable supply source, whether from the standpoint of security of supply or pricing the commodity. But why, I kept asking myself, were the Libyans and Iraqis involved in this kind of terrorism?

Later Sheikh Yamani enlightened me: the Libyan Oil Minister, Azzidin al-Mabrouk, having been let down by his own government and kicked out of the cabinet by Gadaffi, had been appointed as a member of OAPEC's judicial panel. Azzidin al-Mabrouk was dying of cancer, and when he was in Kuwait he saw Sheikh Yamani in his hotel suite, as Yamani used to call him often to enquire about his health and what he could do to help. Before he left the suite he told Yamani with tears in his eyes how nobody cared about his health except Yamani. Yamani described to me how Mabrouk, in his agonised state of mind, told him that he knew everything about the Jackal affair, and he pleaded for Yamani's forgiveness.

However, David Yallop, in his book *To the Ends of the Earth*, argues that the real plot-schemer was Saddam Hussein himself, in collaboration with the Palestinian terrorist, Wadi Haddad. According to Yallop, Saddam bore Yamani a grudge because of his attitude of moderation over the oil price. The author also maintains that Saddam's ambition was to amass more revenue through higher prices in exactly the same way as the Shah of Iran had craftily done in order to build his own arsenal; and that it was Saddam who insisted that Carlos head the operation to alert worldwide attention. In his book Yallop describes Carlos 'storming through the glass doors of OPEC's headquarters in Vienna ... [and he] at the behest of the Libyan ruler, Mohammed Gadaffi' was paid US$20 million as a ransom for the hostages.[1] In any event, both stories – Yamani's and Yallop's – are not contradictory.

Two days after our arrival in Baghdad, we had to go north to Haditha to a great inauguration of the linking of the northern and southern pipelines, called the Strategic Pipeline. This project gave Iraq flexibility in exporting oil from either the north or south, without being blackmailed by any transit country. The pipeline, which had originally been suggested by the IPC during the royalist regime, gave Iraq the possibility of exporting its oil from its northern oilfields via the Gulf terminals and/or from its southern terminals through the East Mediterranean. Saddam decided to go ahead with the project because, following the nationalisation of the IPC, the Syrians gave Iraq a great deal of headache over the transit fee in a way that constituted blackmail. At the time of oil negotiations with Syria and before the inauguration of that pipeline, the Syrians had been intransigent in extracting exaggerated transit fees. The project placed Iraq in a stronger bargaining position by having at that time both the Syrian and Turkish pipelines, together with the Southern Deepwater Terminals.

The idea of the project, therefore, was not instigated by Saddam but by the previous royalist government under King Faysal, but it had not dared to carry it out for fear of Arab reaction. It was only a strong government like that of Saddam that could execute the scheme. During the inauguration, we had to take a military aeroplane with Saddam to Haditha, and throughout the flight I felt uneasy, fearing that something unforeseen was going to happen, as if the experience of the Jackal affair had come to haunt me. I met many high-level people there, one of whom was the Health Minister, Dr Mustafa, who is the uncle of a friend of mine. He shouted loudly to me 'Fadhil, for heaven's sake tell us whether or not Ta'eh proved to be brave!' I replied that he was.

We did not then know what was involved in the deal between Carlos and the Algerians, except that he obtained a lot of money from them. Thereafter, Carlos used to move from one Arab country to another before he was finally arrested and handed over to the French authorities in 1999. However, from the Algerians' point of view, their having rescued and saved the lives of Sheikh Yamani and Amouzegar was such a great achievement as to allow them to put pressure on Saudi Arabia to increase oil prices. In this connection, Sheikh Yamani told me that on one of the occasions when Boumidien was in Saudi Arabia meeting the then King Khaled in order to impose another oil price increase, the King told Boumidien that such matters were decided by his Oil Minister, Yamani, who did not agree, and who sent a memorandum to the cabinet in which he warned that such huge increases in prices did not serve the interests of Saudi Arabia; and when Sheikh Yamani tried to explain his point of view, President Boumidien told him, 'Zaki, you should not forget that it was I who saved your life. Don't make me regret what I have done for you to survive.'

In the summer of 1976, while attending an OPEC meeting in Vienna, I went with a number of colleagues to one of those Viennese wine taverns called *Hueriger*, meaning 'the wine of the year' or 'new wine'. Musicians play popular songs in these taverns, which abound in the tourist area known as Grizinger. It so happened that Chancellor Bruno Kreisky was sitting with his wife at a table, not far from ours, in the *Hueriger*. I went over and greeted him, and introduced myself as an Iraqi survivor from the hijacking by the terrorists. I said to him, 'Mr Chancellor, I myself and all those who were Carlos's hostages are most grateful for your help. Any decision other than the one you made would have been disastrous, and I thank you again. I don't believe any of the hostages will ever forget what you have done to save our lives.' At this he smiled and replied, 'This is what good governments should do.' The answer of a true statesman.

Plate 1   General Abdul al-Karim Qassim (right) conversing with Sheikh Ahmed Zaki Yamani. Qassim staged the '14th July' 1958 republican coup in Iraq, during which King Faisal II and the royal family were shot - as was Qassim later by the Ba'athists, after their coup of 8 February 1963.

Plate 2   The author, seated third from left, with friends (including famous Iraqi artist, Shakar, on his left) celebrating in Paris the two "14 July revolutions": General Abdul al-Karim Qassim's political coup, deposing King Faisal II on 14 July 1958, and France's Bastille Day 14 July 1789. Qassim's republican revolution motivated the author's return to Iraq to re-join the Ministry of the Economy in Baghdad, and initially inspired the Iraqis, but little did they know what was to come.

Plate 3   OPEC Ministerial Conference, Abu Dhabi, 1978.
Source: OPEC.

Plate 4 Dr Chalabi was Permanent Chairman of OPEC's ECB. Here pictured with the then Director of Research for OPEC.

Source: OPEC.

Plate 5   OPEC: Long Term Strategy Committee Meeting in London 1979, chaired by Sheikh Ahmed Zaki Yamani, Oil Minister of Saudi Arabia, who is seated in the centre next to the author on the left, and OPEC Director of Research on the right.

Source: OPEC.

8

The OAPEC intermezzo and my exit from Saddam's regime

In marked contrast to OPEC, which was founded to defend its member countries' vital interests in terms of oil production, pricing and revenues, and whose actions had far-reaching repercussions in the world energy market, the *raison d'être* of OAPEC was purely political and its impact (if any) on world oil was negligible. The idea of major Arab oil-exporting nations coming together constituted a reaction to the Arab politics of the late 1950s and early 1960s, and to the expansionist policies of Egypt, characteristic of that era.

Having toppled the Egyptian monarchy (in 1952) and championed a republican, pan-Arab cause, Gamal Abdel Nasser emerged as the incontestable Arab leader after the Suez crisis of late 1956. He achieved great popularity among the Arab masses through his nationalisation of the Suez Canal. He had challenged the old colonial order, embodied by Anglo-French domination of the Middle East after Germany's defeat and the fall of the Ottoman Empire at the end of the First World War. (Although Nasser had promised compensation to the Anglo-French Suez Canal Company, the annihilation of huge investments was an impediment, even before the abortive military intervention by Britain and France, in collusion with Israel. The latter fiasco later had fateful repercussions, leading eventually to the Six Day War in 1967 because there had been no peace settlement after the 1956 conflict.)

The 'Nasser phenomenon' not only signalled the demise of colonial rule but also heralded the appearance of two distinct political trends in the Arab world: one considered as 'liberated', led by Nasser, and the other 'reactionary and pro-West', exemplified by the Arab–Persian Gulf region. The fact was that after the Suez Crisis, Nasser began to nurture ambitions to bring the whole

Arab world under his tutelage – a 'united states' in the name of Arab unity, though under Egyptian hegemony and Nasser's own personal leadership. He saw the most effective means of inaugurating (if not fulfilling) his aspirations was to demonstrate that Nasser's Egypt, at the peak of the cold war between the United States and the Soviet Union, was a cornerstone of the so-called Non-Alignment movement (which included Nehru of India, Nkrumah of Ghana, Tito of Yugoslavia, Chou En-lai of China and Sukarno of Indonesia). These pillars of Non-Alignment were, by definition, tied neither to the West (North Atlantic Treaty Organisation) nor to the Soviet Union (the Warsaw Pact).

With his non-aligned diplomacy, Nasser engaged in political games with the USA and the USSR to play one superpower off against the other, tactics that gained for him great popularity and iconic status among Arab countries. He countered any Middle East regimes that opposed him by classifying them as stooges of Western imperialism – such as the monarchist regimes in Iraq and Saudi Arabia. Relations deteriorated between Egypt under Nasser and Iran under the Shah, especially when Nasser, with his pan-Arabism, habitually referred to 'the Arabian Gulf' instead of 'the Persian Gulf', which caused great offence to Iran. Egyptian relations with Iran would sour yet more after the Islamic revolution when Ayatollah Khomeini came to power in 1979.

As a prelude to encompassing the whole Arab sphere under his hegemony, he forged a union with Syria and established the United Arab Republic in 1958. This was the beginning of Nasser's habitual meddling in the internal affairs of other Arab nations, in particular Iraq, which at that time was still under the royalist regime and a partner in what was referred to as the 'pro-Western Baghdad Pact'.

It was with great skill that Nasser utilised his propaganda machine, not only for his own personal cult but also with the aim of challenging any Arab country that attempted to distance itself from Egypt. He became obsessed with the idea of controlling the entire Arab world 'from the Ocean to the Gulf': that is to say from Morocco and Mauritania on the Atlantic seaboard to the Arab–Persian Gulf. To bolster these ambitions, Nasser relied on a formidable propaganda machine and the infiltration of inimical Arab countries with the aim of instigating pro-Nasser elements to revolt against their political regimes. This pan-Arab drive, solely under Nasser's control, caused the outbreak of the Lebanese civil war in 1958, and later the tragic involvement of Egypt in the Yemen war; and also led to Nasser's interference in Iraq, where his plan was to destabilise the then monarchical regime.

The Arab League, with its headquarters in Cairo, provided Nasser with a means for achieving his goals. The League's Secretary General and most of its staff tended to be Egyptians. From the late 1950s onwards, the Arab League convened annual petroleum congresses that served as a platform for pro-Nasser politicians and pseudo-experts in oil who sought to bring pressure to bear on the conservative Arab oil-producers, in particular the Gulf. In this way demagogues flourished and were able to agitate Arab public opinion against the larger conservative nations of the Gulf, which with their oil revenues were considered to be 'the rich among the poor' of the Arab world. Under Egypt's influence, the League's highly politicised annual petroleum congresses became a nuisance for the Gulf oil producers, especially given the way in which demagogic figures, like al-Tureki, invariably politicised Arab oil, discussing it purely as a means of destabilising conservative Arab regimes, and never from an economic viewpoint.

The formation of OAPEC could, therefore, be considered a reaction of neutrality amid an ambience of political agitation; above all it was the culmination of an effort to *depoliticise* Arab oil by removing it from the Egyptian stranglehold, exerted through the Arab League. An agreement was reached between two of the Gulf nations – namely Saudi Arabia and Kuwait – who, together with Libya (under King Idris), founded OAPEC, which officially came into existence on 9 January 1968, when an agreement was signed in Beirut (later ratified on September 11 that year) making Kuwait its official headquarters.

OAPEC, as a 'rival' organisation, was established principally on the initiative of Saudi Arabia to bring attention to the claim that Arab oil issues should be left to the major Arab oil-exporting countries. The message was: if you want to discuss oil, this is the venue and platform – and *not* the Arab League, because this new organisation represents real oil power in the Arab world. Iraq was invited to join but, by that time under Nasser's spell, declined as a gesture of solidarity with Egypt. Some strong pro-Nasser politicians in Iraq,

such as Adib al-Jaddir (at the time President of the INOC) believed
that OAPEC's aim was to isolate Egypt.

Iraq's attitude soon changed with the coup of 17 July 1968, as
the new Ba'athist regime considered Iraq's membership of OAPEC
entirely appropriate, especially as the organisation now included
the United Arab Emirates, Algeria, Bahrain and Qatar. Given the
defiant nature of the new Iraqi regime, other OAPEC Gulf members viewed with suspicion Iraq's desire to join, but the Ba'ath government made great efforts to convince them (in particular Saudi
Arabia) of the merits of an Iraqi partnership. Upon its insistence
a compromise was reached by which the organisation was to be
enlarged to include Egypt and Syria, as well as Iraq. Consequently,
OAPEC now encompassed ten Arab oil-producing and oil-exporting
countries.

After Iraq's admission, the Iraqi government appointed me as
its representative on OAPEC's executive board, which met twice a
year to prepare for the biannual Ministerial Conference. It amuses
me to recall how, with each executive board member being granted
an honorarium of about 500 Kuwaiti dinars (then US$1,600), my
own government insisted that I hand over my entire honorarium to
the Iraqi Treasury, this being their condition for my appointment.

Initially OAPEC had no Secretary General. Sheikh Yamani volunteered to deal with matters until they could agree on whom
to appoint. Suhail Sada'wi of Libya was then chosen as full-time
Secretary General, but very little was done to promote the organisation. Prior to this, Sheikh Yamani had offered this post to the Libyan,
Dr Ali Attiga, who – as a minister in the Libyan government under
King Idris –declined, preferring to keep his post. After Gaddafi's
coup d'état in September 1969, Attiga found himself jobless, apart
from a few activities in the field of insurance. The new Libyan government then nominated him, with Sheikh Yamani's full support,
as OAPEC's Secretary General. Also it helped that Iraq's oil minister at the time was Dr Sa'doun Hammadi, with whom Dr Attiga
had formed a friendship (back in 1953) during their student days
at the University of Wisconsin-Madison (where both gained a PhD
degree). Hammadi later worked in Libya and resumed good relations with Attiga, thereafter lending him his support. Attiga had
thus gained the good fortune of approval from both Saudi Arabia
and Iraq – two nations that rarely struck accord on such issues.

It was during one of the Executive Board sessions in Kuwait that Dr Ali-Attiga, who had not been involved in oil affairs, apart from participating in government relations with US oil companies in Libya, offered me the position of his Assistant Secretary General, having acquired the Egyptian geologist, Mahmoud Amin, for another, identical role. At first, I was not interested because OAPEC (unlike OPEC) was not involved in oil-policy decisions. As I was Undersecretary of Oil in Iraq, my acceptance of Dr Attiga's offer would mean demotion, given the limited role of the organisation.

However, I changed my mind when Ta'yeh Abdul Karim became Oil Minister in early 1975, replacing the good Dr Hammadi. I found myself at odds professionally having to work alongside this new minister, whose appointment was purely political[1] and who had absolutely no background in economics. Also, it was at this stage that I became haunted by a sense of foreboding over unnerving political events, rumours of disappearances and 'eliminations'. Saddam Hussein dominated the Ba'ath Revolutionary Command Council as its Vice Chairman, and as Iraq's 'strong man' he was the sole contender for leadership. But by the time of the oil boom of 1973–74 and the huge petrodollar windfalls for the oil-producing nations, in Baghdad there were already signs that the very concept of statehood was being dismantled by Saddam.

In my capacity as Undersecretary of Oil and as a board member of the Central Bank of Iraq, I was an eye-witness to a sinister turn of events, and was aware of when and how the regime under Saddam began systematically to undermine the state administrative and political infrastructure, its regulations and rule of law. After the nationalisation of Iraqi oil, the country's monetary system began to disintegrate. Prior to nationalisation, the country's deposit of foreign currency income had always been transparent: a quarterly cheque had always been paid by the oil companies (the IPC) direct to the Central Bank of Iraq, and the amounts formed the very basis for determining not only the government's budget but also the amount of Iraqi dinars in circulation. The Central Bank used to issue quarterly reports of the exact sum of the foreign currency reserves to cover Iraqi dinars circulated in the market which, the law provided, should have a cover of at least 70 per cent in gold and foreign currency for each Iraqi dinar. Following nationalisation, however, this transparent system gradually eroded and then collapsed.

Under Saddam Hussein, no one had access to or knowledge of the country's oil income. It seems unthinkable that neither Iraq's new Oil Minister Ta'eh (despite being a member of the Revolutionary Command Council) nor I, his Undersecretary, had a clue of how much or even at what price Iraq was producing and selling its oil. Apart from Saddam himself, only his (then) powerful aide, Adnan Hamdani, and to some extent the head of the marketing, Dr Ramzi Salman, knew the facts about oil income and expenditure. A law now forbade (even members of the Revolutionary Command Council) any disclosure of data concerning oil, non-observance of which would incur capital punishment.

This state of affairs was, needless to say, in total breach of the nation's financial and monetary system, the concept of which began to vanish from 1975–76 onwards. The country's central banking system and government budgets were being eroded, as if oil revenues no longer belonged to the country but to Saddam and the Ba'ath party. There were pervasive rumours that Saddam had decided to allocate 5 per cent of oil revenues into a special account outside Iraq in the name of the Ba'ath party and that there were only three people who knew of its exact value: Saddam, his cousin Adnan Khairalla, who was the Minister of Defence (for whom Saddam later allegedly arranged a fatal plane crash) and Adnan Hamdani (whom he later executed for 'treason' after a sham tribunal). Saddam eliminated all those he believed to harbour misgivings about his regime, as he imagined they posed a threat to his megalomaniac rule, whether Ba'athist or not. He and his half-brother, Barzan, who by 1975 had been appointed head of Iraq's secret service, were brutal in the extreme.

In the circumstances it is little wonder my sense of foreboding told me that people like me, who felt at odds with the regime, would soon be 'eliminated'. It was just a matter of time, and for the sake of self-preservation I ought not to linger in the Oil Ministry or, for that matter, in Iraq. When I saw my country suddenly bereft of its proper statehood, my disenchantment increased swiftly. I was not a party man, nor did I permit myself to get involved with the various aspects of party activities. Saddam had sometimes lent me support, but evidently only to benefit from services I could yield in my professional capacity.

With the initial success of oil nationalisation, followed by OPEC's price shocks and the influx of petrodollars, the Iraqi government was soon indulging itself in a false sense of prosperity and economic strength. It is to be recalled here that in a mere five years Iraq's gross revenue from oil exports increased from a maximum of $0.7 billion in 1970 to $8.3 billion in 1975. For the sake of the country's development, one needs wise leadership when it comes to investing such sudden windfalls prudently, but from my many meetings with Saddam, during which I was invariably anxious, I could see the man was primarily driven in one direction: the acquisition of military hardware.

Later, I met Adnan Hamdani while in Paris, and he took me to lunch at the prestigious Hotel George Cinq where he was staying. I asked him for what purpose such a large Iraqi delegation had arrived, to which he replied half-ruefully and half-sardonically, 'We came here to spend billions of dollars buying steel dolls' – an apt euphemism for useless military hardware. Evidently he disagreed with all the excess of military extravagance in the face of much needed expenditure for crucial development. Discreet though he was, the merest whiff of disapproval was enough for this man to pay the penalty with his life after a sham tribunal set up by Saddam Hussein, just after his accession to the Presidency in July 1979.

By the mid-1970s, it had become apparent to me that the regime was taking a very dangerous path, with a dictator so obsessed with entrenching his power and pursuing wild ambitions for expansion. I became convinced that I must, at all costs, leave Iraq before it was too late. What helped spur this objective was my having to contend with the irksome new minister, Ta'eh Abdul Karim, an embodiment of mediocrity that exemplified the professional deterioration in a country otherwise not lacking in professional talent. The discovery that Ta'eh was evidently keen to get rid of me helped fuel my resolve in taking an irrevocable decision to leave Iraq.

In desperation, I spoke to Dr Ali Attiga and informed him that after further consideration I would accept (with gratitude) his earlier offer of Assistant General Secretary of OAPEC, alongside the Egyptian, Mahmoud Amin, an excellent, unassuming geologist. But already it was becoming difficult to leave Iraq, under a political regime that provides no modicum of freedom of choice for any high-level government official. Despite knowing very well that the new oil minister would be glad to see me leave, he himself was powerless to make any decision in that respect. I was only too aware that Saddam alone would decide whether or not to allow me go to OAPEC.

By a stroke of good fortune Ali Attiga came to Baghdad, accompanied by a delegation composed of representatives of various Arab organisations. Attiga then managed to have an audience with Saddam Hussein, who, as usual, began talking of the vital importance of Arab co-operation and the necessity for putting every possible resource towards achieving Arab unity. Attiga later told me how at that moment he seized the opportunity by advocating the need for qualified people to implement any meaningful co-operation, and then adding that in Iraq there is much talent that could contribute to consolidating Arab co-operation in petroleum. Saddam had replied that he would consider his suggestion and nominate the right man to work in OAPEC. I later understood that Saddam decided that either Dr Abdul Amir Anbari or I would be seconded to OAPEC, if either of us showed interest. I immediately let everyone know that I was indeed interested in the post of Assistant Secretary General of OAPEC, and for many it came as a surprise that I seriously contemplated leaving my position as Undersecretary for Oil in the Iraqi Government, just at a time when everyone was avidly interested in Iraqi oil.

Adnan Hamdani, Saddam's close aide, tried to dissuade me, asking how I, holding my a prominent post as Undersecretary for Oil, could seriously contemplate being Dr Ali Attiga's Assistant Secretary General. 'You are needed here, more than there, and besides,' he added, 'it is bad for Iraq's image having someone of your seniority taking up a junior post in Kuwait.' I tried to convince him by telling him that I felt tired and stressed from the difficulty of achieving anything with the new minister, Ta'eh Abdul Karim, for whom Hamdani himself had no respect, and in this matter, luckily for me, he showed sympathy. If truth be told, my clash with the cantankerous Karim was fortunate, as without this supplementary motive, my pretence of serious interest in moving to a light-weight position in Kuwait could have aroused suspicion.

My professed interest in the OAPEC job coincided with Dr Attiga's plan for two assistants, one for Egypt and one for Iraq, the only two countries involved, given that, at the time, both possessed highly qualified people in the oil industry. In this way, Attiga would secure quite a long term as Secretary General. For me

Attiga's intervention – whether in his own interests or not – secured my release from Saddam's Iraq, a propitious move, for which I remained forever thankful.

In the spring of 1976, an OAPEC ministerial meeting was held in Baghdad, during which my nomination as Assistant Secretary General was discussed (at which point I was required to leave the meeting). During the course of the meeting, the Kuwaiti Minister Kazzimi came out and drew me aside to find out what was going on. Did my government want to get rid of me, he asked, or did I seriously seek 'that junior post'? He urged me to tell him the real reason, as only then could he 'adopt the right position' on my behalf, explaining that he could block the decision if I were simply comply-ing unwillingly with my government's position – especially given that the Saudi Oil Undersecretary, Abdul Azziz al-Turki (in Sheikh Yamani's absence), had already objected to the idea on the grounds that he suspected me of harbouring Marxist sympathies. I told the Kuwaiti Minister that I did indeed want to leave Iraq and would be grateful for his help in voting for me. I said I would be more specific about 'the details' later. al-Turki then telephoned Sheikh Yamani, who instructed him to agree, and a decision was taken in my favour.

Many expressed the view that, with my experience in Iraq and in OPEC, my accepting this appointment to OAPEC was an act of imprudence as a career move. An OPEC Gulf minister, Dr Mana Said Utaiba of the UAE, was critical of my decision, and told me I was putting my professional life 'on ice' and wasting good experi-ence in OPEC affairs. This was said on our way to the airport when I was seeing him off (Minister Ta'eh having joined the other OAPEC ministers at a gala held for the Arab delegates). When I told him that I wanted to leave Iraq, he said that had he known he would have welcomed me in the Ministry of Oil in Abu Dhabi, instead of working for OAPEC, which in his opinion forms no real policies of any consequence. I thanked him adding that I was certain the Iraqi Government would never have agreed to second me to Abu Dhabi. Another prominent critic of my decision was the Iranian Minister, Jamshid Amouzegar, who saw me in the Iraqi delegation at an OPEC meeting, held in Bali, Indonesia, in the summer of 1976. He told me of his surprise reading in the press of my appointment with OAPEC, reiterating that my 'natural place is here with OPEC, not with that ineffectual organisation in Kuwait. Your experience with OPEC is so vast that you should be its Secretary General, and I would suggest that you tell your government to nominate you as such and tell them that Iran will lend you its support. It's a great pity that you are moving away from this dynamic area of oil activity into a futile position with an organisation that has nothing to do with oil policies.'

But at this juncture I did not dare follow Amouzegar's advice, and in any case I was certain that Iraq's new Oil Minister Ta'eh would never agree to it. At this stage, the only thing I could do provisionally was to approach the Undersecretary for Foreign Affairs, my friend Abdul Hussein Jamali, and ask him to discuss the matter with my former minister, Dr Hammadi, who was by then the Foreign Minister. Of course, the latter's answer was typical: he did not wish to interfere as this was a matter for the Oil Minister to decide.

Amouzegar's argument was that – instead of OPEC having a Secretary General on the basis of rotation (each staying only one year, later increased to two years, then replaced by another who would prove equally inexperienced and ineffectual, having little knowledge of oil) – it was about time that this position was filled by a real professional, appointed on the basis of merit and not by rotation. He also held that one should abide by the statute which made the provision for filling the post for *three* years.

I had my doubts about the feasibility of this proposal, so finally I dropped the matter. Many people got to hear about this and blamed me for going ahead with my low-ranking position with OAPEC in Kuwait. However, as we say in Iraq, 'A bird in one hand is better than ten birds on a tree', and there was an additional consideration that made me reluctant to pursue Amouzegar's attractive offer: among the Arab Sunni minority in Iraq, there is a widespread belief that the Arab Iraqis of the Shi'a sect (which represents the majority) are pro-Iranian, or even of Persian origin and allegiance. Such a claim is, of course, spurious and politically motivated to justify minority rule over the majority. Nevertheless, given that I myself came from a Shi'a family, Amouzegar's offer to me may have been misconstrued and given a negative twist by Saddam as a political gesture from Shi'i Iran, lending me support with a sectarian motive.[2]

After the resolution was taken and the Iraqi Government agreed to second me to OAPEC in Kuwait, I arrived there in early September 1976, during the month of Ramadan (when most Islamic people are fasting). When I arrived at the office of Dr Ali Attiga, in his absence I saw his Egyptian secretary, with whom I had been well acquainted in my capacity as an OAPEC Executive Board member, but gone was her friendly manner, and instead I discerned an inhospitable, cool distance, as if she did not quite recognise me: 'His Excellency is fasting and has not yet arrived. You can wait for him.' The sudden lack of courtesy and failure to welcome me to my new post was the first signal I had that the organisation's approach would now be different. Iraq is rich in old folk sayings, and we have apt advice for gauging the true disposition of the person one is visiting: it is instantly perceived in the faces of his servants, children and dogs.

Sure enough, when Attiga arrived and I went into his office, I experienced the same icy reception as his Egyptian secretary had shown me, although on a personal level he was quite friendly. After the first two or three months, I realised I was in the wrong place and that I would stagnate intellectually in an organisation that lacked action-oriented policies for Arab oil-exporting countries. Since its inception, it was decided that this new organisation would not discuss matters pertaining to OPEC. Attiga, who used OAPEC to propagate his views as its Secretary General, was observed at various forums circulating his slogan: 'Arab oil should be the least produced in order to conserve it for future generations, and the only way to achieve this is through higher prices. Otherwise Arab oil will be depleted, and Arab oil wells will run dry'. This was a consequence of the false hypothesis prevailing at the time, especially in the mid-1970s, following many wild predictions of imminent oil shortage, which later turned out to be fantasy. Catchphrases like Attiga's were exactly what Western governments seemed to want to hear so as to justify reducing dependence on Arab oil. What is strange is that in spite of the dramatic fall in world demand for oil, together with a sharp increase of oil supplies from outside OPEC, Attiga continued repeating these unrealistic predictions. He was not directly involved in energy trends or the market scene, and resembled many Arab oil thinkers, for whom higher prices had become a cult, a new fervent belief, like a religion. The impact of high prices on the demand for OPEC oil affected particularly Gulf oil, given the continued erosion of the Gulf's market share, which seemed to be overlooked or considered irrelevant in the drive for ever-higher prices.

When, not so long ago, Dr Ali Attiga remarked to me that the West 'keeps its oil underground while continuing to deplete Arab oil', I replied that the numbers showed that exactly the reverse was the case. The depletion rate of Arab Gulf oil was only 1.0 per cent per annum of its reserves, against 15.5 per cent for UK North Sea, 11.1 per cent for Norway's North Sea, and 10.2 per cent for the USA. But he ignored this argument and continued to harp on the same old theme as if a sacred dogma: that higher prices are necessary to conserve Arab oil.

The only positive thing to emerge from OAPEC was the establishment of certain inter-Arab companies in oil shipping, petroleum investments, oil exploration and drilling. Some of them proved successful. Most, if not all, of the inter-Arab companies are dominated by the Gulf region because of its substantial financial capacity. But aside from these projects, OAPEC has no role to play. It is typical of virtually all Arab organisations, especially those under the umbrella of the Arab League, in that it tends to remunerate staff well while serving as a platform for oratorical speeches, a situation that seems to reflect the Arab mentality. During my two years working for OAPEC, I found its activities amounted to little more than such public relations exercises, all performed with a lot of noise. Furthermore, my assignments, as defined by Attiga, were insignificant.

I soon regarded my service for OAPEC as a transitional stepping-stone, rather like starting all over again. Certainly my position there brought greater financial reward but, faced with intellectual stagnation, my aim was to leave as soon as possible. My first endeavour in this direction was to try and rejoin UNCTAD in Geneva (lbeit in a different capacity from my former one).

However, something else happened that made me change my mind. In the beginning of 1978, OPEC decided to enlarge its Secretariat by recruiting new qualified people. In the organisation's original statute there was a post for Deputy Secretary General for a term of three years, subject to renewal. I saw this as a means of continuing my OPEC work. The position had been frozen for a long period because of disputes between Iraq and Iran, at a time when unanimity among OPEC members was required in voting for any decision regarding this post. Each time Iraq nominated someone, Iran would veto and, of course, vice versa. An amendment was made to the statute, according to which agreement for the post of Deputy Secretary General would be obtained if two-thirds of votes were in accord, and provided that three of the founding members approved, i.e. apart from Iraq or Iran, approval from Saudi Arabia or from Kuwait or Venezuela. There was now a move to fill that post, and my name was mentioned by some OPEC governors and even ministers, all of whom knew me from my contributions in my capacity as Iraqi representative at various OPEC meetings. Earlier I mentioned my role in the Algiers Summit, but frequently I had presented the report of the OPEC Economic Commission Board (ECB) to almost all the Ministerial Conferences. According to an OPEC statute, it is the Deputy Secretary General who should chair the ECB *ex officio*, but in the absence of a Deputy the ECB had to elect a chairman, and invariably I was elected to report to the Ministerial Conferences. I was used to performing the task with total objectivity and my inclusive reporting of all views had made me acceptable as a choice. Finally, to my relief, my nomination to the post of Deputy Secretary General of OPEC had the approval of Saddam Hussein. It was perhaps, after all, fortunate that he knew me well from my contributions on oil matters in Iraq.

Less than a year later, in June 1979, Saddam seized power in a violent coup. My acquaintance with this mutating man makes a rather bizarre tale. Although initially Vice Chairman of the Ba'ath Party's Revolutionary Command Council (i.e. second-in-command to President al-Bakr), Saddam was always the real leader, resolute and forceful. Before the IPC was nationalised on 1 June 1972, Saddam made two trips to the Soviet Union with a large delegation. I was at home when the telephone rang in the afternoon, and a voice asked for Chalabi then continued, 'This is Saddam Hussein. I want you to be prepared to accompany me tomorrow to Moscow as a member of the Iraqi delegation.' I told him my name was not on the list. 'It doesn't matter,' he replied, 'just be ready at the airport on time.'

A remarkable facet of the Saddam of those early days (and in sharp contrast to his later malevolence) was his encouragement of Iraqis of various sects and religious persuasions working together in his offices. Although Saddam was a Sunni Muslim, many working for him in oil were recruited from the Shi'a sect or else were Christians, and they never experienced discrimination. The oil people on whom he relied were mostly Shi'a, such as Mr al-Jabbir, President of the INOC, Dr Ramzi Salman, the oil marketing man, Dr Abdul Amir al-Anbari and many others, including myself.

This was in marked contrast to the office of President al-Bakr whose aides were all Sunni and all from Saddam's home town, Tekreet. Every time I entered his office, I would hear Arabic being spoken with a Tekreet accent by everyone there, and it was not always easily intelligible. Needless to say, there were no Shi'a in al-Bakr's office. I mention this point to illustrate that the Saddam I knew then, when he was Vice President, was in many ways at complete odds with the demonised brute that he later became.

His transformation began with his Palace coup in June 1979, when Saddam forced al-Bakr to step down. This was followed by a massacre in which 21 members of the council close to Saddam, including Adnan Hamdani who was by then Saddam's Prime Minister, were executed, all falsely accused by Saddam of co-ordinating a plot with Syria. A strange metamorphosis had transformed him into a fiend. It was only a matter of time before he felt compelled to wage war against Iran, invade Kuwait and lead his country down a path of destruction.

In October 1978, I joined OPEC in Vienna, after extricating myself from the red tape of the Iraqi Government's procedures for secondment, which delayed my departure from Kuwait. My happiness on arrival in Vienna was such that I felt instantly resuscitated and rejuvenated like a fish returned to water after being deprived of it. At that time the Secretary General was Ali al-Jaidah of Qattar, who, when I first joined the Organisation, I found rather cold and distant in his remaining few months before he left OPEC at the end of 1978.

9

Iran's Ayatollah drives the oil market mad

After decades of cheap oil (during the monopoly era of the concessions) in the wake of 1973's oil price shocks the whole world had awoken to a changed reality of exorbitant energy costs, which for the world economy brought concomitant negative effects of rampant inflation. The price shocks were epoch-making, and behind them were compelling political factors (see pp. 99–116). Confronted by American support for Israel in the Yom Kippur war, the Arab Gulf nations had, on 17 October 1973, imposed an oil embargo, the legacy of which would be the now familiar issue of oil supply security. The event brought to the fore for the first time the politicisation of oil, and it raised questions concerning OPEC's ability and readiness to provide for an expanding global demand for oil.

While this intense politicisation of oil as a commodity generated great economic and political uncertainty, the new phenomenon of 'oil shortage' and an 'energy crisis' induced governments worldwide to deploy every means possible to reduce dependence on imported oil, above all from the Gulf countries, irrespective of the two-thirds of world oil reserves in their possession. In 1974, for the first time in American history, an Energy Research and Development Administration (ERDA) was set up to promote the development of new energy programmes (as well as cover nuclear weaponry issues). From this evolved a specific Department of Energy, headed by James Schlesinger, established (on 4 August 1977) by the newly elected President Jimmy Carter, in order to formulate a new US strategy of 'energy independence' accentuating the urgency of reducing dependence on imported oil.

With the decade thus dominated by a mood of pessimism over the future availability of oil, energy institutions and oil companies were in concert forecasting a world of soaring demand for oil in the face of OPEC's diminishing supply capacity. An 'energy crunch' was seen as unavoidable. The CIA leaked a confidential report in the 1970s predicting how much oil would be needed from OPEC countries to satisfy growing demand; but very inflated numbers were used to calculate what the future call on OPEC oil would be, simply to convey the alarmist notion that demand for OPEC oil exceeded *by far* the organisation's production capacity. For example, the report amplified the future volume of production required from Saudi Arabia as being in the order of 16–18 mbpd, and similarly overstated the production volumes needed from other OPEC countries, such as Kuwait and Iraq. Having read the report, I showed it to the amicable, former Kuwaiti oil minister, Abdul Rahaman al-Ateeqi, on one of his visits to OAPEC's headquarters. His comment was that OPEC countries could not possibly reach the described levels of production, adding that the figure given for Kuwait's actual production capacity had been doubled, and that Kuwait could not possibly produce this much.

By this time the Massachusetts Institute of Technology (MIT) had released, in 1977, their voluminous Workshop on Alternative Energy Strategies (WAES) report, the research of more than 20 world experts, under the supervision of Professor Carroll Wilson. Adopting the same 'energy crunch' panic-stricken tone, it forecast that by the end of the 1980s world demand for oil would be so high that it would far surpass OPEC's production capacity; and it recommended a series of measures to reduce oil consumption and shift to other sources of energy. Concerning the coming scarcity of this commodity, the book's Foreword, which bore the real tone of the report, emphasised that 'world oil would run short sooner than most people realised' and that unless appropriate remedies were applied, the demand for petroleum in the non-Communist world would probably overtake supplies between 1985 and 1995. Professor Wilson would later have blushed to see that in 1985 world demand for OPEC oil was only 15 mbpd, not even half of OPEC's production capacity. Yet, because demand for OPEC oil had been as much as 33–34 mbpd when the WAES report was drawn up in the mid-1970s, this convinced most people – despite all its fantasy scenarios, exemplified by its inaccurate prediction that by the end of the 1980s there would be a 15–20 mbpd supply gap as a result of OPEC's failure to meet growing world demand, and its forecast that the oil production required by 1985 from OPEC would range between 40 and 45 mbpd, while OPEC capacity would be unable to exceed 35 mbpd.

When the WAES report was released in 1977, I was with OAPEC in Kuwait. I studied it in great detail, and was highly sceptical about its conclusions, based, as they were, on unrealistic hypotheses that took no account of the effects of steep prices on oil consumption. One could perceive a subtext in such reports that aimed to foster panic as a spur both for reducing oil consumption and for investing in *non-OPEC* energy supplies. Their influence was such that OPEC policy-makers entirely believed their false assumptions, which were in part political, as underlying them was the avowed aim of reducing dependence on OPEC oil, in particular Gulf oil.

Another thing that struck me as strange was the report's assumption that the developing countries' oil consumption would increase very rapidly, creating additional world demand that would impose impossible pressure on supply. At this point, I recall annotating a remark in the margin of the WAES book, questioning the ability of developing countries to afford anything like the huge cost of the enormously increased volumes of oil imports calculated by the report.[1] I was never in any doubt that its conclusions were fallacious, and years later, in the face of a dramatic decline in real demand for OPEC oil, they were indeed proved to be misconceived. Yet people accepted the doom-laden WAES report as reliable because it matched the widespread panic at the time. Anyone who contested or even cast doubt on its grave predictions was looked upon as a maverick or a blind fool.

MIT was not alone in its mistaken assumptions. While I was still with OAPEC in Kuwait, Robert Mabro, Emeritus Fellow of St Antony's College Oxford, came to speak about oil shortage, pulling out various numbers to prove that by 1985 the world would require OPEC to produce over 36–38 mbpd. At the time OPEC's capacity was 33 mbpd, so everyone was impressed with his arguments. I then asked for the floor to comment on his exposé, and I pointed out that his projections assumed that rates of consumption would continue to soar unchecked and that he had failed to take account of government policies in the consuming countries: that their drastic conservation measures, with a lead time, would modify demand significantly enough for the predicted energy gap not to exist. These logical notions, though, were derided by most of the audience, whose judgement was clouded by bias, more than scepticism, as in the case of Dr Ali Attiga (OAPEC's Secretary General) for whom the concept of high oil prices remains a cult.

Forecasts made by WAES and Robert Mabro were soon contiguous with those of the US Energy Department, of Exxon, the IEA and others, all conveying the same theme of an imminent dearth of energy resources and the impossibility of meeting any future growth in world demand for OPEC oil. In 1978 the IEA warned that the call on OPEC oil would exceed 40 mbpd, and Exxon (1978) also predicted 40 mbpd, while the US Congressional Research Service (1977) surmised that demand for OPEC oil would reach around 42.8 mbpd. Others predicted less: the forecast from the EEC (1979) was 38 mbpd; the US DOE (Department of Energy) (1979) estimated between 27.8 and 36 mbpd.

Only a few years later, the absurdity of these invalid projections was apparent. By mid-1985, it was acknowledged that the world required only 15 mbpd of OPEC production, less than half of its capacity. I now felt vindicated for my scepticism over obsessive projections that I knew to be untenable and wholly unscientific as they disallowed any other economic forces – factors such as consumer reactions to exorbitant oil prices, the impact of higher prices in moderating dependence on oil, promoting a diversification of energy sources, and reinforcing the growth in the alternatives of natural gas and nuclear energy. Nowhere were such trends more marked than in Western Europe and Japan, where government policies played a crucial role in reducing oil consumption, relative to GDP growth, through high taxation on refined products.

In Western Europe, for example, the share of *oil* in total energy consumption fell from 62 per cent in 1973 to 45 per cent in 1985. By contrast, the share of *nuclear energy* in total energy consumption rose from 1 to 13 per cent over the same period. To a lesser degree, there was also a marked shift to natural gas, above all in Japan where, during that same period, oil's share lost 20 percentage points in favour of natural gas, nuclear power and coal.

In 1978, in that tense atmosphere of doom over a perceived oil famine, OPEC decided to form a committee to examine options for a long-term strategy. This was in response to an idea that had been conceived by the Saudi Oil Minister, Sheikh Ahmed Zaki Yamani, of setting up a Long Term Strategy Committee (LTSC) to formulate a new angle of OPEC policy based on long-term objectives, instead of being influenced by short-term factors alone. Sheikh Yamani's proposal (made at earlier meetings before I joined OPEC) was for a form of *retreat*, at which representatives could feel suitably relaxed, away from the constraints of formal meetings, in order to discuss OPEC's long-term strategy.

While I was still in Kuwait, awaiting completion of government procedures for my transfer to OPEC's headquarters in Vienna, I was immersed in OPEC work in advance of officially joining its Secretariat in October 1978, and so was already engrossed in the whole energy crisis debate – into which I then became directly involved when I received a telephone call one evening from Dr Francisco Parra of Petróleos de Venezuela SA (PDVSA), who was at that time in charge of that company's London office. Calling from London, he said, 'We are waiting for you.' I asked what for, and he explained that I was a member of OPEC's LTSC chaired by Sheikh Yamani, and that they wanted me at the first meeting. This was being held in the London office of Saudi Arabia's Petromin (later known as Petronal) in Park Lane, where I joined them.

OPEC had decided to form this committee on two levels: firstly, as a Ministerial Committee, composed of ministers from OPEC's five founding members plus Algeria, under the chairmanship of Sheikh Yamani; secondly, also under his chairmanship, a Technical Committee composed of representatives (personally selected by Sheikh Yamani) representing the same six countries, plus OPEC's Secretariat. The late Farouq Hosseini represented Saudi Arabia, Dr Parvis Mina represented Iran, Dr Abdul Amir Anbari Iraq, while the late Dr Nureddin Farrag represented Kuwait, Nordine Ait-Laoussine Algeria and Dr Francisco Parra Venezuela, while I represented the OPEC Secretariat.

When the LTSC began its work, the oil industry was influenced solely by the grim forecasts of continually rising demand against OPEC's insufficient spare capacity. Consequently, at the Committee's first session, its Chairman (Yamani) proposed that the world was heading for an oil shortage, to be succeeded by an oil surplus and then, again, an oil shortage. At this I guessed that the Chairman himself had finally succumbed to the widespread fear among oil companies,

governments, consultants and economic institutions of the loom-
ing energy crisis. Other Committee members, especially Algeria's
Nordine Ait-Laoussine, were devoted to the oil-crunch theory, and
held that such a scenario could only be avoided if OPEC pursued
maximum prices to encourage consumers to reduce consumption.

To begin with I felt I was not in a position to state the opinion
I had formed from my critical reading of the WAES report (having
already dismissed it as mere fantasy). But at subsequent meetings
I acquired greater clarity of mind and my courage strengthened
enough to argue my point – that reserves in the Middle East were
more than adequate to face increasing demand, and that higher
prices would inevitably lead to a decline in growth rates of world
oil consumption, once investments were in place for increasing
production capacity.

Interestingly, fervent disciples of the oil-shortage theory, with
its justification for increasing already very high prices, tended to
be sceptical about nuclear power as an alternative, and they felt
vindicated by the disastrous accident at America's Three Mile
Island nuclear power station in 1976, which left an indelible fear
that nuclear energy was unsafe and too risky to expand. Therefore,
in the eyes of OPEC and the majority of its LTSC representatives –
Algeria, Iran, Venezuela and even Iraq – the world would continue
to depend even more heavily on oil resources. The LTSC then
played a major role in driving technical discussions with the aim of
adopting a high-price regime and even concurred with the environ-
mentalists' standpoint that the consuming nations must legislate
for oil conservation.

I was, by now, a lone figure in defending a simple economic
principle of following a moderate price regime, precisely to avoid
the impact of high prices collapsing the demand for oil, in particular for OPEC oil. To this end I tried to convince the LTSC that
OPEC should adopt a price strategy linked to the 'movement' of oil
demand, so that when demand fell the oil price would correspondingly adjust to a lower level to induce higher consumption; and
conversely, when demand was too strong, prices would increase to
moderate the growth level.

This very concept is derived from 'cartelisation' theory,
whereby cartel members controlling the bulk of a traded commodity follow a price strategy to defend their market interests, rather

than encourage higher-cost suppliers to compete with them for a larger market share. But these simple arguments fell on deaf ears, proposing as they did the policy of maximising *market share*, and thus maximising oil revenues through *export volumes*.

At one of these sessions I finally posed a question based on simple economics: 'Is it reasonable', I asked, 'for any producer or seller of a commodity to discourage buyers from buying his product, and instead encourage them to buy commodities from his competitors? Economics surely requires the producer to encourage buyers to buy more and follow a strategy that would discourage competitors'. My simple query stated the obvious and sounded naïve, and so they burst out laughing, and yet they appeared never to have considered it. I could understand Iran's position because the Shah's policy at that time was to maximise Iran's oil income for large armaments for his role as the West's 'Gulf policeman'. I was also aware of the Algerian representative's position in his campaign to increase revenues through high prices as being of critical importance for Algeria with its limited oil base and hence lower market share. But for other oil-producing countries, the Gulf in particular, the effect of high prices was negative.

Needless to say, the hardliners won the day, and our LTSC work was instilled with the doom-laden belief that, as the world was about to run out of oil, oil production must be curtailed, demand must be curbed and consumers must abandon or at least conserve oil, in order to restore a healthier balance between supply and demand. While OPEC spokesmen addressed the media with grave concern about the impending energy crunch, urging consumer nations to reduce their oil imports, our LTSC busied itself recommending schemes to help developing nations promote their domestic energy resources to reduce oil imports.

Another factor that led me to challenge the pessimism over insufficient oil supplies was a premonition I had, bordering on mistrust, concerning a possible 'conspiracy theory' (the quick suspicion of 'conspiracy theories' being prevalent in the Arab world, though sometimes with justification). I traced my misgivings back to the first price shock of 1973, which had spurred the West into concerted efforts to reduce their dependence on Gulf oil. As far as the West itself was concerned, its expansion of *non*-OPEC oil markets was a realistic reaction to these events, and a policy clearly planned to safeguard its own interests. Nevertheless, a conspiracy theory was compellingly argued for by some, including F. William Engdahl (in a book[2] to be discussed in Chapter 14). This, according to Engdahl, entailed a deliberate fostering of panic over oil shortage to induce the oil consumers to invest in alternative (non-Gulf) supplies as well as in alternative energy sources. The 1973 price hikes made alternatives such as natural gas and nuclear energy viable, as well as promoting investment in high-cost oil areas outside the Gulf, such as the North Sea and Alaska, which hitherto, under a low price regime, had proved economically unviable.

But well before 1973, the concept of investments in oil reserves outside the Gulf was gaining ground. If given moderately high prices (even without the extreme hikes of 1973 and 1979) the oil majors backed by their governments would have found the expediency of investments in the North Sea and Alaska attractive from the standpoint of national security and securing supplies without geopolitical risk, as investments in new oil are not governed solely by economic criteria. Before Iraq nationalised its oil in 1972, such schemes were already germinating, spurred on by OPEC's Declaratory Statement of Petroleum Policies by Member Countries in its Resolution 90 of June 1968 – given that it was this Statement that had first tolled the bell for OPEC member countries to grab full control of their oil operations, while sounding a 'death-knell' for the monopoly hitherto enjoyed by the major oil companies.

Conspiracy theory or not, I was convinced that the LTSC was mistaken and taking a wrong course, because, with vast low-cost oil reserves of Saudi Arabia, Iraq, Iran and Kuwait, investments for increasing production capacity could easily be expanded in the event of robust growth in world oil demand. But my voice was drowned in the clamour of opposition from the other six members. My impression was that Sheikh Yamani alone understood what I was saying but that he had to take into account the majority view. Constrained by my position, officially representing the Secretariat and not being a representative of my country, I found it difficult to express my own objective views openly at these meetings. Even my old friend from Iraq, Dr Abdul Amir al-Anbari, went with the majority. Normally his line of thinking concurred with mine, for example he had supported my argument that high prices were economically unsound for an oil-rich country like Iraq, as they would simply divert investment elsewhere; and, after all, he had agreed with me concerning the Algiers Summit report, in which we had stated that it was not in Iraq's interest for oil prices to be so high. It was al-Anbari who now wrote a chapter in the final report about the need for OPEC to extend financial aid to help developing countries invest in their own domestic energy resources.

The LTSC's final discussions centred on the principle of maintaining a 'floor price', kept constant by indexing it to both world inflation and US dollar exchange rate variations against other currencies, as defined by the Geneva I and II Agreements (described in Chapter 3). Of particular note was a proposal, which gained wide acceptance at the time, for this floor price to be increased through indexation to the GNP of OECD countries, i.e. the oil price would in real terms increase at rates commensurate with the economic growth in the industrialised countries. This would cause a huge price escalation.

When I presented the final report at OPEC's Vienna conference in May 1980, some delegates, in particular Iran, went to extremes in justifying massive annual incremental price increases by linking the oil price in real terms to the GDP growth of OPEC countries, whose economies depend on the oil price. The OPEC conference did not accept Iran's proposal. Evidently certain LTSC members were completely out of touch with economic realities and with the dramatic changes already apparent in the structure of the oil industry as a result of the first price shock.

However, notwithstanding the divergence of views, the LTSC meetings under Sheikh Yamani's chairmanship were pervaded by a pleasantly relaxed ambience, encouraged by the friendly manner in which he conducted discussions with committee members. As some of the committee meetings were held in his country house in Surrey, we would stay overnight at the nearby Pennyhill Park Hotel with its beautiful grounds. Other meetings were conducted at the offices of Petromin in Park Lane, London, or at Ta'if, in Saudi Arabia, where Sheikh Yamani had a house in the high hill area of al-Haddah. What made it a pleasure working with him was his warm personality and his steady, philosophical attitude, also his modesty – notwithstanding his fame as Oil Minister of OPEC's most important member, Saudi Arabia.

Outside people would sometimes come and discuss matters with the committee, including major oil company representatives, such as Mr Peacock of Shell, all of them in agreement over the acute energy crisis. I recall a group arriving directly from the airport, headed by a former US Energy Secretary, to present their case with a series of charts and slides to prove that the energy crunch was imminent. I argued that consumption of fuel oil had already fallen drastically since the price hikes, and that this factor would counter-act, or make more remote, the threat of a severe energy crisis.

On one occasion we had a meeting in London with the European Commission on Energy, whose chief representative took a very forceful approach throughout the meeting. When he touched on whether OPEC's oil production should be commensurate with world demand, I made the simple observation that oil consumption in Europe was already falling and that OPEC production capac-ity was already proving adequate. After the meeting, he issued a strange statement accusing the OPEC delegation of pursuing a pol-icy of 'brinkmanship', and we were later told that his intention was to use the meeting to further the political aims of his own country (Germany) in addressing its economic concerns.

While discussions of the LTSC were in progress, the world was anxiously watching political developments in Iran. The waning power of the Shah; the emergence of a politically powerful move-ment among the clerics led by the mullah, Ayatollah Rouhollah Musavi Khomeini; violent clashes between religious demonstra-tors and government forces, first in Qom and then spreading across the country – all these events would have far-reaching repercussions on the oil industry and the oil market, beginning with the exiled Khomeini's expulsion from Iraq in early October 1978. As it is a tradition among the Muslim Shi'i clergy in Iran to involve themselves in politics and political agitation against rulers whom they consider have usurped power illegitimately, it is to be recorded here that in the early years of the twentieth century, the notion of *mashruteia* (conditionality) was first adopted by Iran's clergy as a means of subjecting their ruler to accountability, with the ruler's exercise of power being conditional upon his obser-vation of the rule of law and respect for civil rights. The Shah's regime had become entrenched following the downfall of the Qajari dynasty, and its impregnability had led to many reprisals against both the father, Rezā Shāh, and the son, Mohammad Rezā Shāh Pahlavi.

In 1963 the prominent mullah, Ayatollah Rouhollah Musavi Khomeini denounced the Shah and led an uprising against him in Qom. No sooner had he served his prison term and been released, he threw himself anew into more political agitation and uprisings, and was imprisoned so frequently that he was finally forced into exile. He chose as his place of refuge the Shi'i holy city of Najaf in Iraq, which housed the Shi'a shrine of the Imam Ali, the Prophet Mohammed's cousin and son-in-law who was buried there. Najaf also represents for the Shi'a Muslims the holy seat of a highly esteemed religious teaching order. During the 14 years he spent there, Khomeini never ceased his politically subversive activities against the Shah. He had many followers inside and outside Iran – chiefly among the Iranian opposition groups, many of whom were political exiles in America. While sheltering in Najaf, Iraq, Khomeini, far from keeping a low profile, ceaselessly recorded cassettes and deployed every means possible to spread his anti-Shah, anti-West, pro-Islamic Republic sentiments. He even invented a new element in the Shi'a creed stipulating that the most senior mullah could legitimately claim to be ruler until the reappearance of the Twelfth Imam, al-Mahdi, who having vanished was, according to the Shi'a creed, destined to reappear one day to rule the world and bestow upon it justice and prosperity.

The secularist Shah was acutely aware of the danger posed by the mullah Khomeini, and following the Algiers agreement of 1975 between the Shah and Saddam, inaugurating a period of 'good relations' between the two countries, the Shah requested the expulsion of Khomeini from Iraq. To this the Iraqi government readily agreed. For the Shah, this would prove to be a fateful error. It was said that Saddam sent his half-brother, Barzan Takriti, who was in charge of the formidable apparatus of Iraqi Intelligence, to visit the Shah and propose that they liquidate the troublesome Khomeini while he was still on Iraqi territory, as the Shah's suggestion of mere expulsion would not deter Khomeini from continuing his attempts at political subversion from afar. But the Shah declined this offer, insisting that they expel him, preferring for humanitarian reasons to avoid bloodshed, and for political reasons to avoid making a martyr of Khomeini.

As Kuwait refused to give Khomeini asylum, he fled to France (where, during the time of the Shah's rule, no entry visa was required by Iranian nationals). He chose for his exile Neauphle-le-Château, a small town on the outskirts of Paris, from where – far from keeping a low profile – he pursued his political agitation without hindrance. Before his arrival in Paris the world had not heard of this hitherto obscure mullah, who suddenly found himself surrounded by pro-revolutionary Iranians and troops of foreign correspondents and TV channels. Overnight Khomeini emerged from obscurity to become the focus of worldwide media attention as a famous religious cleric determined to topple the Shah's regime. Although the Shah was considered their protégé, the Americans were taken by surprise at the extent to which Ayatollah Khomeini appeared to reach out to the whole of Iran as well as Iranian exiles by means of his 'Revolution of the Cassette', all of which Khomeini was able to conduct from his safe base in the Paris suburb of Neauphle-le-Château, where he was shown on television with his entourage, clamouring for the overthrow of the Shah. Khomeini's cassettes, on which he recorded his radical sermons, exhorted all 'faithful' Shi'as to rise up against the Shah. This highly politicised mullah provoked several strikes and protest marches in Iran, especially in the spiritual city of Quom.

By mid-1978, during Khomeini's exile in France, these strikes became widespread among Iran's oil industry workers. This totally disrupted Iran's oil production and led to a cessation of its oil exports, causing a frenzy of price volatility throughout the world oil markets. The shortage of petroleum products in the domestic market also aggravated the situation.

As late as January 1979, in a last-ditch attempt to forestall an Islamic fundamentalist revolution, the Shah appointed a civil member of the opposition, Shahpur Bahktiar, as Prime Minister. Following American advice, the Shah encouraged Bakhtiar's modest concessions towards democracy and pluralism, as well as attempts to curb the fearful Savak security and intelligence apparatus. But whatever was resorted to, the masses continued defiantly with their revolt against the Shah's government. When the Shah's army endeavoured to crush the political uprisings, vast numbers of determined people gave their lives (in scenes of violence that would be mirrored in Tehran 30 years later at the outcome of the

2009 elections). These uprisings, compounded by oil sector strikes, forced the Shah to flee to Cairo where President Sadat gave him an official welcome. But the revolt continued and Bahktiar's government was unable to appease the anti-Shah agitators. The episode finally resolved itself when, on 1 February 1979, Khomeini and his entourage flew back to Tehran in a private Air France jet. When he stepped out of his plane, Khomeini found himself rapturously welcomed by over a million Iranians, celebrating the arrival of their incontestable leader. Meanwhile the Shah left Cairo for the USA, where, with his problems and failing health, he soon died, and was then flown back to Cairo to be buried.

This revolutionary turmoil, which toppled Iran's Shah and created an Islamic republic, completely overtook our LTSC report. Its recommendations were abandoned and never implemented. At the 1980 Vienna conference, alluded to above, at which I had presented the LTSC's final report, no further decision was taken beyond an official recognition and appreciation expressed to Sheikh Yamani for the work done.

Prior to this period, after the first price shock of 1973 until the 1979 Iranian revolution, OPEC had attempted to adopt a judicious approach to oil prices. At its September 1975 conference in Vienna, held 21 months after the Tehran decision to set the posted price at $10.84 per barrel, OPEC increased the official price by 10 per cent to $11.46 per barrel. Later, at the end of 1976 when the conference was held in Doha, Qatar, there was a split over the price. The majority opted for a 10 per cent increase followed by another 5 per cent; whereas Saudi Arabia and the UAE opted for an increase of only 5 per cent. Later, in the summer of 1977, a compromise was reached over a unified increase of 10 per cent, which brought the price to $12.70. OPEC later increased the price by a further 10 per cent for the ensuing year, its aim at the time being to steer a steady course of gradual percentage increases.

But by mid-1978 Iran's political turmoil began to unhinge OPEC's careful pricing system, which now veered into a sharp upward spiral. First the strikes, then the shutdown of Iranian oil fields sent the spot market price soaring to unheard of levels, doubling OPEC's official price. To begin with OPEC had maintained a rational approach in adding a surcharge to its price, intended as a temporary measure, to be removed once market conditions were back to normal. It was left to each country to impose the surcharge or premium, as warranted by the market. But Ayatollah Khomeini's revolution caused chaos on the markets and drove the price into a frenzied spiral and, in a matter of a few months, it reached $40 per barrel. This led to OPEC's official price increase to $18 per barrel *excluding the premiums*, which varied greatly among the types of crude, widening the differential between heavy and light.

The question now arose of how OPEC, overtaken by spiralling market prices, should handle the cascading effect that it was forced to follow. Initially OPEC had good reason to impose 'temporary' market premiums on the basic price (which at that time stood at about $14 per barrel) but this measure was on the understanding, suggested by Sheikh Ali al-Sabah of Kuwait, that, once the oil crisis abated and the interruption of Iranian oil was compensated for by increased production from Saudi Arabia and Iraq, the market price would fall back to its pre-crisis level. However, the hawks – Libya, Algeria and the new Iran – insisted that the (presumed temporary) premiums were not to be relinquished but instead to be incorporated into OPEC's official price. With the widening gap between OPEC prices and spot market prices, a free-for-all market turmoil ensued with producing countries now adding premiums to their prices.

Having been the cause of massive inflation and then recession, the oil market was in turmoil, generating fear in the consuming countries that oil price escalation was set to continue. Saudi Arabia unilaterally increased its price by $6 to bring the price of Arab Light to $24 per barrel.

Then, in mid-December 1979, a very important OPEC conference took place in Caracas, Venezuela, at which the new $24 Saudi price was taken as a base from which to increase the price by a further $4 to around $28 per barrel. I was on my way to Caracas to attend the conference in my capacity as OPEC's Deputy Secretary General, when I was invited (while staying for two days in Paris en route) to participate in a panel organised by French television about OPEC's price hikes. The panel comprised Sheikh Al Sabah (of Kuwait), James Schlesinger, who was then US Secretary of Energy, Francisco Parra (Venezuela), Ali Attiga (OAPEC) and myself. I spoke in French, the others in English with simultaneous translation, and it was a long session with high audience ratings – the oil price being a topic of fundamental importance worldwide. During this TV panel discussion I argued that the industrialised countries should not worry excessively about oil price increases because the expanding production capacity and augmented oil wealth created by OPEC countries' own hugely increased oil revenues would be recycled back to the industrialised countries, further boosting economic growth. I also argued that high oil prices would force industrialised countries to use oil more efficiently and hence reduce consumption and invest in other sources of energy. After the session, while Ali Attiga remained as indifferent as ever to my comments, James Schlesinger approached me and complimented me for raising and handling this important point very well.

While Iran's Islamic Revolution was in full spate, it was decided that OPEC should commemorate at summit level the occasion of the twentieth anniversary of its foundation (in Baghdad on 14 September 1980). For this reason it was agreed that there would be a Tri-Ministerial Meeting in the summer of 1980, involving ministers of foreign affairs, oil and finance – similar to that held in Algiers in 1975. This Tri-Ministerial Meeting took place not at OPEC's Vienna headquarters, too small to accommodate all these delegates, but instead at the Hofburg Imperial Palace, which had won a prestigious design award for architectural creativity. The Saudi delegate was headed by Prince Saud al-Faisal, the Saudi Foreign Minister. He possessed all the traits of a prince with Arabic features: elegance, grace, modesty and a well-modulated tone of voice. I recall on one occasion, while we were in Geneva, I was sitting beside my minister, the taciturn Sa'doun Hammadi. This man, as a rule, never spoke a word of praise nor laughed, he rarely uttered a word, but when Prince al-Faisal, who was at that time Saudi Arabia's Undersecretary for Oil, took his seat nearby, suddenly Hammadi leant towards him and uttered effusively, 'Mr Saud. You are indeed a true prince in form and content.' Such effusive praise from Hammadi was so out of character that we laughed and the Kuwaiti Oil Minister, al-Ateequi, commented, 'How right you are, Dr Hammadi!' The Prince (whom, personally speaking, I like very much) felt acutely embarrassed, beads of perspiration formed on his forehead, but he graciously thanked Hammadi for his kind words.

Throughout the 1980 Tri-Ministerial Meeting in Vienna, it became very clear that the conference planned for 14 September in

Baghdad that same year could not be held because of the tension and severe deterioration in relations between Iran and Iraq. Already by the summer of 1980 their border skirmishes were as frequent as their heated exchanges. The Iranian delegation, addressing the Tri-Ministerial meeting, tersely raised the question as to how the rest of us could even conceive of asking them to attend a summit meeting in Baghdad when the Iraqi air force had attacked an Iranian helicopter, killing high-level personnel; or even propose that the head of state of Iran attend the meeting in this hostile atmosphere of military provocation and aggression. With their mutual accusations, soon Iran and Iraq drifted unavoidably into all-out warfare.

In 1980, in the course of conversation, a friend of mine, Adnan Janabi, spoke to me of his conviction that war with Iran would soon erupt. My reply was (ironically) that I felt that Saddam was too intelligent to embark on such a risk with Iran being such a powerful neighbour and a larger nation than Iraq. 'From the geopolitical angle,' I continued, 'the risk would be that Iran could win the war and become the dominant power in the Gulf, which the West would not accept. And if Saddam loses, it would mean an instant loss of power for him.' Clearly my friend knew better than I did, and when he expressed the opinion that 'Saddam will not win the war, and yet he will not lose power,' he was proved right.

Only a few weeks after this conversation we heard the news of the Iraqi army's invasion of Mohamara, the south of Iran, following which a long and vicious war dragged on for eight years. Iraq survived but at a great detriment to its economy. Despite financial aid from the Gulf countries, especially from Saudi Arabia, Iraq emerged war-torn and with huge external debts, all a result of the rapid militarisation of the economy, with excessive overspending on military hardware.

During the first two weeks of the war, the two deepwater terminals in the south, serving the bulk of Iraq's oil exports, were destroyed. The Iranians attacked the al-Bakr terminal while the Khor al-Amaya terminal was destroyed by the Iraqi airforce because of its occupation by an Iranian battalion. Iraq's oil exports declined from 3.4 mbpd to only 600 tbpd (thousand barrels per day), which was its former, initial capacity before the Turkish pipeline was constructed. At the same time, Hafez al-Assad of Syria closed the Syrian pipeline to the East Mediterranean terminals, with the result that Iraq's exports now fell by 2.8 mbpd, a huge setback to its economy. This loss of oil also aggravated the world oil markets with yet more price volatility.

It was in these circumstances that another OPEC conference was held in mid-December 1980, in Bali, Indonesia, at which the majority of OPEC ministers wanted to raise the official price of OPEC oil to an exorbitant $36 per barrel. Not surprisingly Saudi Arabia's oil minister, Sheikh Yamani, claimed that this was excessive as it would affect demand and the whole world economy. He defended the $32 price but, in spite of his valid argument, he stood alone. Even the intelligent al-Sabah of Kuwait sided with the majority. We ended up having to arrange a two-tiered price system of $32 and $36 per barrel, which gave rise to a technical problem: the OPEC official price was based on Saudi crude Arab Light F.O.B. at 'Ras Tanura', but this now involved two prices for the same crude. To differentiate between the two, al-Sabah proposed qualifying the Arab Light official price by adding the term: '*deemed* Arab Light' at $36; while 'Arab Light *proper*' was to be at $32 per barrel. At the time journalists wrongly attributed to me the decision to qualify Arab Light with the term 'deemed'.

This two-tiered price system inevitably confused the markets. On the one hand, Aramco shareholders were taking Arab Light at $32, whereas the rest sold their oil at $4 higher. This created an incentive for Aramco shareholders to lift increasing quantities of oil, with the result that Saudi Arabia's oil production increased to about 10 mbpd. The two-tiered system was short lived, as a compromise was soon reached to agree on one price of $34 per barrel.

With this agreement announced on 16 December 1980, all delegates left the island of Bali in a buoyant mood, now that the oil price stood at $34 per barrel, more than 12 times the level it was in mid-1973. The Iraqi oil minister, Ta'eh Karim, was in the highest of spirits, as if he personally had achieved a great victory. The Conference also dealt with the question of who should succeed René Ortiz of Ecuador, whose term of office as OPEC's Secretary General was supposed to pass to Gabon, the thirteenth member; but, as the Gabonese candidate proved not to be senior enough, the Conference decided to renew Ortiz's term for a further six months, or until the Gabonese government would present a more qualified candidate. In July of 1981 their new candidate took office, a Dr Marc Nguema, whom I had known while serving UNCTAD in Geneva (where he did little other than fill his country's personnel quota). Marc Nguema noticed that ministers, above all the Gulf ministers, routinely liaised with me as Deputy Secretary General, rather than with him, and to this he objected fiercely. During an OPEC seminar at the Intercontinental in Vienna, Maurice Strong approached me simply to discuss some related news items, and the oversensitive Nguema, in a fit of pique, nearly clouted me and then bellowed at the bewildered Maurice Strong: 'I am the Secretary General...you must speak to me first!' Imbued with a sense of grandeur and self-importance, he wore (it was said) a bullet-proof vest – as if fearing an assault because of the importance of his position.

The hype over oil prices drew a huge crowd of journalists, reporters and company observers to the OPEC Conference in Bali, by which time, in mid-December 1980, the Iran–Iraq war was not only raging but Iran's oil minister, who was at the front, had been captured by the Iraqis. With this news, the Iranian delegation solemnly placed a portrait of their minister on his empty chair! Hostility between Iranians and Iraqis was ignited to fever pitch, and the Indonesian Oil Minister, Subroto, solemnly insisted that all those present at the OPEC meeting must be unarmed. Distracted by their excitement over high oil prices, their enormous oil revenues and now the war, OPEC people paid no attention to the structural transformation happening to the world oil industry that would damage their long-term interests.

10

The backlash: OPEC is cornered

Some months later, after OPEC's disastrous decision in adopting the two-tiered (albeit short-lived) pricing system,[1] Dr Marcello Colitti of Italy's national energy company, ENI, organised a seminar in Rome, in early April 1981. The seminar was presented with a voluminous study, complete with an Interdependence Model proposing a strategy for co-operation between producers and consumers, which in fact ended up being ignored by both. This study had been prepared, over a period of two years, by two groups of economists, one group of which comprised young Arab economists.

At this Rome seminar (attended by many from both OPEC and OAPEC), I presented a paper that caused an uproar among OPEC members, and even jeopardized my position in the organisation. My paper's first premise was that the West was on the threshold of a transition, a structural transformation in the energy industry that would diminish dependence on OPEC oil; and that therefore it was in the interests of OPEC producers to avoid a too rapid transition, which would harm their economies, given their total dependence on oil revenues. My next premise was that the oil price was the factor that would determine the rapidity of this transition, because high prices would act as a spur in hastening a decline in world demand for OPEC oil. The inescapable conclusion, therefore, was that escalating oil prices in real terms would decrease OPEC's share in the world energy market, to the advantage of oil investment outside OPEC and investment in alternative energy sources of natural gas and nuclear energy.

Attending this conference was the Kuwaiti Oil Minister, Sheikh Ali al-Sabah, whom I had shown various charts indicative of the fall in demand already evident in Western Europe as a reaction to steep prices (beginning with fuel oil); and also demonstrating

how OPEC's policy of high prices would harm those Gulf countries with huge reserves, like Saudi Arabia, Iraq and Kuwait. My
point, I explained to him, was to demonstrate that if this trend of
high prices continued, the importance of these OPEC countries in
the world energy balance would be affected. al-Sabah understood
but he wanted to warn me: 'Taking a stand on this matter could
harm your own interests because they don't understand what you
are saying.' It was friendly advice, from one who knew that most
at OPEC were vehemently against my line of argument, especially
Dr Ali-Attiga, Secretary General of OAPEC, who accused me of
wanting 'to deplete so quickly our Arab oil resources, which should
be kept for future generations'. By now OPEC people viewed me
as a complete maverick. For them what I said amounted to heresy,
there being no accommodation for differing viewpoints.

It so happened that the *International Herald Tribune* journalist,
Yousef Ibrahim, was at the conference and wrote a feature published on 14 April 1981, entitled 'OPEC Reportedly Starting to
Worry about Oil Prices', parts of which I shall quote in full because
of the historical importance of my being the first voice within OPEC
ever to dare warn the organisation that its high-price policy would
weaken demand for OPEC oil:

> For the first time in years, the Organisation of Petroleum Exporting
> Countries seems worried that it has pushed oil prices too far too fast.
> This sentiment came through loud and clear last week at a conference
> in Rome on economic co-operation between oil producers and
> consumers.
>
> OPEC leaders'... startling realization [is that] the fast-rising price
> of OPEC oil – a 20-fold increase over the past decade – has forced
> major consumers in the industrialized countries to look for alter-
> natives at a much faster pace than OPEC would like... demand for
> OPEC oil is dropping too fast; the same could happen soon to OPEC
> revenues... 'Substantially higher prices in real terms in the future
> will no doubt accelerate the pace of transition and hence speedily
> reduce OPEC's share of total energy requirements,' warned Fadhil
> al-Chalabi... Deputy Secretary General of OPEC.
>
> His central argument: the industrialized countries can move
> much faster toward finding alternative sources of fuel than OPEC
> members can move toward diversifying away from total dependence
> on oil exports. The surprise was that Mr Chalabi's audience of Arab

oil ministers and senior oil executives was more than ready to hear him out.

The publication of this article had worldwide repercussions, a more pleasant sample of which I experienced later on arrival in Mexico, where I was met by people from Pemex, Mexico's national oil company. Adrian Lajous[2] of Pemex, showed me a Spanish translation of my paper and told me he was so impressed that he had arranged a meeting for me with Mexico's Minister of Oil. By contrast, the Iranian member of the OPEC Board of Governors, H. Sadat, reacted bitterly to the press quotations, and sent a stern telex to the then Secretary General of OPEC, René Ortiz from Ecuador:

> Since the press version of Dr Chalabi's recent speech in Rome gives rise to certain questions, we shall appreciate [it] if you would forward to us full text thereof soonest to enable us submit our views if necessary.
>
> Best regards.
> H. Sadat
> Deputy Minister of Petroleum
> Islamic Republic of Iran

When he received this, Secretary General René Ortiz telephoned me to warn that Sadat was profoundly perturbed and wanted me put before the staff disciplinary committee. I explained to Ortiz that I was only stating the obvious and that it was a question of simple economics: higher prices mean lower demand, and economic reality decrees a certain market price elasticity vis-à-vis demand. However, Ortiz, already irritated by my relations with the Gulf ministers, and feeling that this was an appropriate occasion for weakening my position at the Secretariat, rebuked me for statements contained in my paper on the grounds that they contradicted my prerogative as Deputy Secretary General. I replied that the best thing was to send a copy of my paper to the Iranian Governor to show him that I implied no criticism of OPEC but simply stated a truthful economic fact: that sooner or later the consumers of a commodity will react against higher prices by reducing consumption. The only difference between oil and non-oil commodities is that oil has a greater lead-time. Ortiz obliged me by sending a copy of my paper to the Iranian Governor to clarify my point, but the latter's anger was not in the least mollified, though he could point to no hard evidence that my paper amounted to a critique of OPEC's pricing policy.

Violent reactions emanated from various OPEC quarters, not only from Iran but from the other hawks, Algeria and Libya. When I recounted all this to the Kuwaiti Minister, Sheikh Ali al-Sabah, he reminded me 'Didn't I warn you? I knew they would misinterpret your arguments and turn against you.' What made matters worse at the time was that, in the midst of the Iran–Iraq war, it felt as if the Iranians were taking it out on me as an Iraqi. After this experience I decided that for the sake of avoiding further problems, I would eschew the validity of my economic views and refrain from publishing any more on the matter.

In the summer of that year, 1981, the famous Paul Frankel of Petroleum Economics, who was considered to be the world's foremost petroleum expert, organised a seminar in Vienna, to which he invited many top executives from the oil industry. Frankel himself posed the inevitable question: 'Dr Chalabi, we read something attributed to you about the effects of higher prices on demand.' Fearing that OPEC people would overhear, I became evasive, at which he said, 'I understand...You are a good survivor! You do not want to be as frank as you were in Rome and antagonise your OPEC colleagues.' Later, at a meeting, I had a chance to explain to him the trouble my Rome paper had caused. He showed great sympathy and understanding.

Frankel was inspirational when I was preparing my PhD dissertation on oil in Paris, at a time when, apart from his book *The Essentials of Petroleum*, there was a dearth of available literature on oil. Frankel being renowned as the best authority on the subject, this book had been translated into many languages, and it had given me such an insight into the nature of the oil industry. When his company, Petroleum Economics, later organised an obituary for him, I was invited to say a few words about the influence of his book on my thoughts and ideas concerning oil matters. Frankel also had a very kind nature, exemplified by the concern he showed when I underwent my heart bypass surgery. He not only enquired about me but asked if he could visit me while I was convalescing at home, and I found it typically kind of him to take this trouble.

Not long after the storm caused by my 'controversial' paper, there were marked indications of the fall that I had predicted in oil consumption in the industrial world. It was heartening to feel at least vindicated. The non-Communist world's oil consumption fell from 51.2 mbpd in 1979 to 45 mbpd in 1982. The decline in oil consumption was especially dramatic in Western Europe and Japan, because of tough taxation and conservation measures.

This becomes even more remarkable when observed over a long period: over 36 years, between 1973 and 2009, despite demographic density and sustained GDP growth, the share of oil in total primary energy consumption in Western Europe has fallen from nearly 60 per cent in 1973 to 42 per cent in 2009. Over the same period, the share of natural gas and nuclear energy grew from 11.7 to 37.6 per cent respectively. In the case of Japan, the decline in oil's share in primary energy is even more marked, falling from 77.5 to 46.5 per cent during the same period, despite long periods of sustained economic growth.

Western Europe was the first region to enforce tough conservation measures to rationalise oil consumption. On one occasion in Paris, I met the late André Giraud, the then French minister of industry, who told me of the quest to reduce energy consumption in France, in reaction to the first price shock of 1973. He produced from his pocket a thermometer, carried by many and scrutinised frequently to monitor the temperature, so that whenever it exceeded an optimum 22°C, heating would be switched off. This illustrated the seriousness with which energy conservation was taken in the West.

The most significant development in Western Europe was the sudden shift to alternative sources of energy, above all in power generation. France pioneered a major shift to nuclear energy, doubling its production of that source in a matter of three years, between 1979 and 1982, and increasing production throughout the 1980s, so that the contribution of nuclear energy in power generation soon reached about 80 per cent. Fiscal policies in Europe increased the taxation component in the price paid by the end-consumer, so that the petroleum price became far higher than the crude oil price on the world market. This was another means of inducing consumers to consume less. Meanwhile car manufacturers succeeded in fitting vehicles with more fuel-efficient engines, reducing the amount per mile of gasoline consumed.

OPEC's high prices, as already pointed out, continued to encourage oil companies to invest in high-cost oil areas outside OPEC, such as the North Sea, formerly considered economically unfeasible under a low price regime. New non-OPEC oil began growing rapidly, while there was also a very marked shift to natural gas, with the result that the share of non-oil energy sources (including nuclear power) in the total energy consumption of Western Europe rose from 179.8 tons in 1975 to, in 1985, 2,917 tons of oil equivalent.

All these developments had been impelled by OPEC's high-price policy, which in no time had the effect of backfiring on the organisation, cornering its oil into a scenario of paradoxes: declining oil consumption yet a rapid expansion of oil investments and production *outside OPEC*, displacing world demand for OPEC oil. At the time OPEC had adopted a strange and totally non-economic system of pricing various OPEC crudes relative to the 'marker crude' Arab Light Ras Tanura[3] (Saudi Arabia's port on the Gulf). Ras Tanura was conceived as a 'fixed price', and each member country had to sell its crude below or above this marker-crude price, at levels that allowed for quality differential and advantages in geographical locations. Tedious discussions ensued, in which questions were raised amid fierce exchanges about who was selling oil and at what price. This caused a problem for Iraq, for me in particular, to the extent that a conflict arose between me and the Algerian delegate, Nordine Ait-Laoussine, who accused Iraq of selling oil for less than its fixed price and trying to market oil at a price below its real value.

This was not a sound pricing system, whether for the marker crude or other OPEC crudes, as it was pitted against changing market dynamics, with huge gaps between OPEC prices and spot market prices. Not fully cognisant of varying market conditions, many OPEC people tended to be unaware of the altering value differential. A problem arose in that Algeria, enjoying close proximity to Europe, had a natural, secured European market for its high-quality crude 'Sahara Blend', which is, as already mentioned, light and sulphur-free. This gave Algeria an advantage over the Gulf producers, whose marketing outlets were more problematic, and geographically less advantageous. Many years later, OPEC realised this problem and cancelled the fixed market price and price differentials.

Another inconsistency with OPEC's price system is that OPEC does not always export oil in the form of crude. For example, in the case of Venezuela it is refined products that constitute the bulk of exports, which are exempt from OPEC's pricing, while most member countries, in particular Saudi Arabia and Iraq, are obliged to sell their crude oil according to OPEC's rigid pricing system. Naturally oil producers outside OPEC are free to set their prices according to the market, and thus gain an advantage and a larger market share by undercutting OPEC's price, at the same time providing greater investment incentives for the oil companies' involvement – increasingly at the expense of OPEC oil.

In November 1978 – not long after my nomination as OPEC's Deputy Secretary General – I presented a paper on this very subject, at an OAPEC conference held in Oslo. Explaining that OPEC had a problem in having to contend with the competition from, and advantage gained by, non-OPEC oil being sold at less than OPEC's fixed price, I argued that oil companies working in the North Sea, with their very high profit margins, were able to take advantage of OPEC's fixed price level, which enabled them to relinquish a portion of it in order to sell more oil at the expense of OPEC's market share. The Norwegian representatives from Statoil were particularly interested in my line of argument, and my paper had repercussions in the press. *Petroleum Intelligence Weekly* seized on the theme as an important point that could be raised in negotiations between OPEC and the new producers. But OPEC circles, lost in ecstasy over their new high income levels, were not interested, and gave my paper scarcely any attention (as this was a few years before my more noticeably controversial paper in Rome in 1981).

North Sea crude oil production from both Norway and the UK increased rapidly: from 32 tbpd in 1974 to 2.1 mbpd in 1984 and 3.3 mbpd in 1985. Such a huge leap in production from a limited, high-cost resource base would never have happened without OPEC's pricing policies. Naturally this increasing volume of North Sea oil replaced OPEC oil on the world market. It is interesting to note that Norwegian and UK production continued increasing and reached 3.5 mbpd (in 1990), 5.3 mbpd (in 1995) and 5.7 mbpd (in 2000). However, production from these two countries then began to decline – to 4.4 mbpd in 2005 and 3.3 mbpd in 2009.

Similarly, oil production from other regions (both existing and new, and all beneficiaries of OPEC policy) has gained increasing market share. Production, for example, from Brazil, Canada, Egypt, India, Malaysia, Mexico and Oman increased from 3.3 mbpd in 1975 to 7.4 mbpd in 1985 and kept growing, reaching 9.9 mbpd by 2000 and 10.6mbpd by 2009. Total *non*-OPEC production, excluding the US and Former Soviet Union (FSU), increased from 8.2 mbpd in 1975 to 17.1 mbpd in 1985, 23.1 mbpd in 1995 and 26.3 mbpd in 2005; though it declined to 25.3 mbpd in 2009, owing to dwindling demand caused by global recession. This oil production history is illustrated in the following Figure 10.1.

With this state of affairs, OPEC began to see limitations in its price protection policy. In mid-1982 in Vienna, Sheikh Ali al-Khalifa of Kuwait was the first to put forward the idea of limiting OPEC production to 18 mbpd at a time when its capacity was above 31 mbpd. In the interests of bolstering or defending the price, it was unofficially agreed to apportion this 18 mbpd production level among OPEC countries. This was an incipient forerunner of OPEC's quota system, which impaired its market share even further.

By 1983, increasing downward pressure on the OPEC price, emanating from the low demand for its oil, pushed the organisation

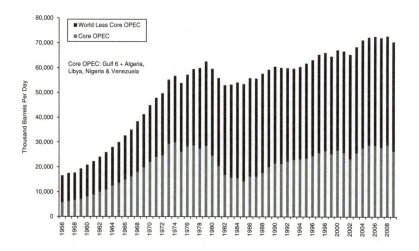

Figure.10.1   Crude oil production history 1956–2009. Core OPEC and the rest of the world

Source: Oil & Gas Journal and CGES.

into convening an Extraordinary Meeting in London in March 1983, at which the OPEC price was reduced to $28 per barrel. At this meeting OPEC officially introduced a quota system as a price defence mechanism, by which OPEC production would swing downwards or upwards according to world market needs for its production: in other words, OPEC would be the residual supplier, or supplier of 'last resort'. This involved consumers buying first non-OPEC oil, then resorting to OPEC oil to fill the gap between non-OPEC oil requisitions and consumer requirements. The OPEC quota would then be decided in the light of this residual supply. The scheme was presented as being, theoretically, applicable both ways: i.e. if non-OPEC oil increased, or conversely if non-OPEC oil decreased, OPEC supplies would correspondingly swing downward or upward in filling the gap. However, OPEC's upward provision to ease a tight market has invariably not been forthcoming.

In determining the overall quota from OPEC, there must always be an estimate of world production outside OPEC, an estimate of net exports of non-centrally planned economies and an estimate of OPEC natural gas liquids (NGL) consumption. The total of these three components would then be deducted from the estimated world demand for oil, and the result should then represent OPEC's total quota, i.e. the maximum OPEC should produce if it is to defend the price.

Within OPEC's residual (or swing) production, Saudi Arabia was designated the role of residual/swing producer (with an amount of 5 mbpd), thus lacking the advantage given most other OPEC members who could all produce their full quotas. The balance would then be subtracted from Saudi Arabia, so that if the call on OPEC oil were less than 18 mbpd, the burden would fall on Saudi Arabia, as the 'downward' swing producer within OPEC production. As 'the swing within the swing' Saudi Arabia suffered a disproportionate loss of production share. The less the call on OPEC, the less the call on Saudi oil.

An economically illogical system, it became incumbent on OPEC alone to carry the burden of price defence, to the advantage of all oil producers outside OPEC. By mid-1985 the call on Saudi oil production had dropped radically from a capacity of 10 mbpd to a drastic 2.5 mbpd, an amount insufficient to produce the associated gas, badly needed for water desalination plants and power generation.

Such a bizarre production and pricing policy, by which other high-cost producers end up as the beneficiaries, was the upshot of an urgency in maximising oil revenues in the short term, dictated by OPEC's small producers with limited reserves – such as Algeria, Libya, Venezuela and Qatar.

The system is contrary to basic economic principles – a *sine qua non* of which allows the producer with abundant reserves and low-cost production the privilege of being the first to set his market share at a competitive price. This then marginalises the market share of other producers with limited higher-cost reserves, who can do no more than react by selling at prices reflecting their higher costs. But OPEC had set up a reverse situation in which higher-cost non-OPEC producers are the first to set their market share, leaving the balance of market requirements for the major (OPEC) producers of low-cost oil output, while the non-OPEC producers gain from OPEC's maximum price levels. This system is contrary to the pricing policy expected of the cartel, which OPEC has been mythically labelled. As will be shown in Chapter 14, OPEC, unlike a cartel, does not competitively set its market share, instead leaving the balance to high-cost producers outside the OPEC group, whose prices are governed by higher costs. A true cartel maximizes revenue through higher export volumes and sets prices for the marginal producer. The difference between the price set for the high production costs of the marginal producer and the cartel's low costs is considered as *economic rent* enjoyed by low-cost producers, a point that will later be elaborated on.

During the early 1980s, when the call on OPEC oil was already falling, I continually held personal discussions with Sheikh Yamani and the Kuwaiti Oil Minister, Sheikh Ali al-Sabah, as to what OPEC could do in order to regain its share of the world market. This sensitive issue was of particular importance to those member countries with large reserves, like Saudi Arabia, Iraq and Kuwait. Iran also had large reserves but was among the OPEC hawks determined to retain the highest possible oil price. Smaller producers (lacking the very long-term potential of the big producers) paid little heed to the issue of market share as they were so keen to maximise the immediate per-barrel income from higher prices, and at the same time they were producing at full capacity, thus benefitting from the system both ways.

To begin with I approached Minister al-Sabah, an extremely intelligent man with a high level of training in economics and very good experience in the oil industry in his own country. He reacted positively and remarked that it was necessary to pursue the matter further.

While chairing the Conference's Economic Commission Board, from which I presented reports to the Ministerial Conference because of my *ex officio* chairmanship, I continued to puzzle over why OPEC should bind itself to a quota system that was fixed as a 'residue' after deducting non-OPEC production, including Soviet Union net exports. My argument was always: *why not fix in the first place what OPEC wants to produce?* The answer I was invariably given was that oil prices would then fall, to which my reply was that with lower prices OPEC would increase revenues from an increased volume of exports, instead of relying on revenues obtained by the per-barrel income of higher prices. The only ones aware of this logic seemed to be Sheikh Yamani and Sheikh al-Sabah.

In 1984, OPEC opened a dialogue with non-OPEC producers, with the aim of securing their co-operation in OPEC's endeavour to defend the price by reducing production. I approached the then chairman of Norway's Statoil (whom I knew from one of the Oxford Energy Seminars) and suggested that he meet with Sheikh Yamani and me to establish some form of dialogue between OPEC and Norway. He welcomed the idea and we both joined Sheikh Yamani in the latter's suite in the Intercontinental, Geneva. To begin with he expressed his concern for price stability and for the burden of price defence not to fall entirely on OPEC. He agreed to discuss the matter with his company and he arranged a meeting in Oslo, where Sheikh Yamani and I met the Norwegian oil minister. The latter, though very courteous, was emphatic that Statoil, as a state-owned company, could take no decision, as the question of restricting Norwegian production would have to be addressed to the Parliament. Yamani and I returned to Geneva, empty handed.

By mid-1985, OPEC meetings were fraught with member countries accusing each other over their respective production shares. Many were deemed to be 'cheating' on their quotas, communicating production numbers to the OPEC secretariat that were perhaps near enough the official quota but at variance with the actual production estimated by the specialist petroleum press, such as the *Middle*

East Economic Survey and *Petroleum Intelligence Weekly*. As member countries were producing at levels higher than the quotas agreed in London in 1983, Saudi Arabia constantly had to adjust with a downwards swing of its own production. In the circumstances, it was decided by Sheikh Yamani that he and I (in my capacity as Acting for the Secretary General) would renew our attempts to persuade non-OPEC producers to share the burden of price defence. To this end, Sheikh Yamani renewed negotiations with Statoil in Norway, then with Malaysia, Egypt, Oman and Mexico among others. I stayed in Jeddah for two days before accompanying Sheikh Yamani in his private jet to Kuala Lumpur. Both Yamani and his charming wife showed such gracious hospitality, and I was presented with an Arab gown, a *distasha* so that I would feel more comfortable for the long flight.

The reception for Sheikh Yamani in Kuala Lumpur was very special, not only because he was Saudi Arabia's oil minister but because of his connections and religious status. Yamani's father was the highly respected imam of the Shafii creed in Mecca. Having travelled from Mecca to Yemen and Indonesia, he was also regarded extremely highly in the region we were visiting. We met the Malaysian oil minister in his office, along with the head of the national oil company, Petronas, and a number of other ministers. After all this, we were informed that Malaysia was unable to cut its production to help OPEC, just as we expected.

I had first visited Kuala Lumpur in mid-1976, when OPEC held a conference in Bali, Indonesia, and my friend Adnan Janabi and I took a few days leave to explore, visiting first Kuala Lumpur, then Hong Kong, Bangkok and Singapore. But on this later occasion of our production mission, Yamani and I were taken to see some beautiful Islamic architectural sites: mosques and seminar venues for young students of Islam. At one of these seminars someone asked Sheikh Yamani if there could be a system of economics specific to Islam. His reply was that economics is global and that there is no exclusively Islamic economics. From an historical standpoint I did not agree, but declined to intervene at the time.[4]

From Kuala Lumpur our itinerary was supposed to take us to Brunei, which I had long wished to visit, but Sheikh Yamani decided against this as no preparations were made for our arrival. Instead we flew to Indonesia's capital, Jakarta, with which I was already acquainted and not much enamoured, and where we met the astute Indonesian minister, Dr Subroto. We then flew to Australia and New Zealand, first landing in Melbourne, where Sheikh Yamani was invited to give a lecture about oil. This was my first visit to Australia, and a dinner was organised at which I found myself seated at the head table with Yamani. While speeches were in progress, an Australian went to the microphone and talked about Arab civilisation and the wisdom of the Arab people. He quoted from Arab literature a well-known saying of Ibin al-Mukafa, describing four categories of men: 'The one who does not know that he does not know [i.e. unaware of his own ignorance] is a stupid fool to be avoided. There is another who does not know but he *is aware* that he does not know, and this is a man in want of enlightenment. There is a third who knows, yet is unaware that he knows. This is a 'sleeper', who must be awoken. The fourth is the one who realises that he knows, a wise man whom you should respect.' I was very impressed by this knowledge of Mukafa so far away in Australia, as even in the Arabic world many do not know of him, especially concerning this gem of wisdom.

The next day we undertook a short trip to the capital, Canberra, where the Prime Minister arranged a special dinner in honour of Sheikh Yamani, to which I was also invited. It was in this city that I saw my first kangaroo, and I was amazed at its marsupial characteristic of pocketing its young, and at its movement by giant leaps and bounds, so unlike other mammals. What impressed me above all was the stunning natural beauty of New Zealand, which we visited after Australia, spending a night in Auckland before flying to the capital, Wellington, where the Prime Minister held a dinner in honour of Sheikh Yamani. I found its scenery entrancing, with the changing colours of its spectacular mountains and skies.

A fascinating part of that long trip was the two-day break that Sheikh Yamani decided we should take in the French island colony of Tahiti, called by its natives 'Bora Bora'. When the French Governor greeted us on arrival, I asked whether there was a possibility of visiting the tomb of Paul Gauguin, the great French impressionist (whose magnificent canvasses of Tahiti I had admired since my youth, and who left his family in Paris to paint his most memorable works of genius in these parts, sadly dying of syphilis there at the early age of only 50). The Governor informed me that it was a two-hour drive by car and thus some five hours for the round trip, which our time constraints ruled out. Nevertheless, I was content to find myself accommodated in a small wooden cabin on the seashore, with a terrace from where one could observe the changing colours of the ocean and surrounding scenery.

From there we headed for Mexico, where the oil minister showed a welcome readiness to co-operate with OPEC yet gave no final commitment to reduce production. From Mexico City we went to Cancun on the Atlantic coast. 'Cancun' is a native Amerindian word meaning 'snake-pit', a misnomer for such a beautiful place, and it was unfortunate that I missed the opportunity of seeing more of it as, having caught a cold, I had to confine myself to my room for two days, during which time Yamani and his wife went aboard the government yacht for a fishing trip.

After our return to Geneva, we subsequently headed off to Egypt for similar discussions with the oil minister, Abdel-Hadi Kandeel, who installed us in the aristocratic Mina House Hotel with its wide terraces overlooking the Sphinx and the Pyramids. I enjoyed immensely one particular evening on the hotel terrace listening to a talented Egyptian singer, born blind yet singing various famous songs beautifully. Although we were given amiable words of support at our meetings in Cairo, yet again we secured no firm commitment to reduce production. During our discussions I asked the Egyptian minister how Egyptian oil was priced, he replied that this was always according to the market. Though I conceded that unlike OPEC members he was not held to a fixed price, I suggested that Egypt could follow the OPEC system. At this, the minister declared that it would restrict Egyptian oil exports, and then rather deftly added that it would be 'unthinkable for Egypt to operate in competition with OPEC' and that 'this was not the purpose for which the organisation was created'. I then reminded him that he was benefitting from OPEC's pricing and production mechanism, while having the freedom to sell Egyptian oil without restriction and at a lower price than OPEC's. Having made my point and having achieved nothing, we departed.

I accompanied Sheikh Yamani once again to Norway, where the former oil minister was now a professor of economics at Oslo University. He showed some understanding of OPEC's problem in shouldering the burden of price defence alone and that this could be avoided if there were proper production management for the sake of price stability. He assured us he would present the case to the Norwegian government and parliament with a recommendation that Norway join a price-defence scheme in solidarity with OPEC. But this undertaking proved fruitless, and once again our hopes were dashed. In retrospect the entire mission had turned into an expensive tourist excursion, with our plans reaching no fruition beyond pleasantries and well-intentioned expressions of commitment and goodwill that amounted to nothing but hot air.

In a last-ditch attempt to induce non-OPEC oil countries to make cuts in their production, OPEC began inviting their representatives as observers. They attended closed ministerial-level meetings and discussions without taking any measures to help OPEC maintain the price. The Egyptian minister, Abdel-Hadi Kandeel, attended our Geneva Conference as an observer, afterwards declaring to the press that it was not in Egypt's interest to reduce production 'not even by a single barrel of oil'; while the Oman minister addressed OPEC delegates with an amusing remark, to the effect that 'you complain that we increase our oil production, instead of cutting it back as you do, but in the first place it is your fault for raising the oil price so high that you encourage oil companies to invest in our oil. This is your fault and you have to bear the consequences'. Despite his brusque manner, he was speaking the plain truth.

By contrast, Mexico's Undersecretary for Oil assured OPEC delegates of his country's readiness to co-operate, because he knew only too well that if OPEC confronted other producers, price wars could ensue, resulting in producers like Mexico having to compete with the Middle East's lower costs.

While our efforts to secure co-operation with other producers had proved abortive, it was in a way inevitable that OPEC, having chosen to be the residual (last-resort) producer, would now be unable to retract from its position as such – with the knowledge among the other oil producers that OPEC's policies would prevail in providing for them a nice price guarantee without their having to share with OPEC the onus of production constraints to defend that price. Their unwillingness to ease OPEC's 'yoke' had made OPEC's pricing system particularly difficult to maintain.

In my capacity as Deputy Secretary General, acting for the Secretary General, I was unable to involve myself too deeply in this issue or bring it to any useful fruition as a topic of discussion because it contradicted the policies of several OPEC members (Iran, Venezuela, Libya and Algeria). Meanwhile Iraq had no role to play because it was at war with Iran and dependent on financial aid from the Gulf producers. As mentioned earlier, the only two people who understood my theoretical stance were Yamani and al-Sabah, to whom I had repeated that OPEC in general – and the Gulf in particular – would, in the final analysis, be the market-share losers to the advantage of non-OPEC producers, and that the system of fixed prices was simply bad economics.

Apart from the perennial problem for Saudi Arabia of being the residual producer within OPEC, carrying, as explained, the heavier burden of restricting Saudi output, while some member countries had an unfair advantage in being able to produce their quotas in full, there were several disparities in the quota system that are discussed in the next chapter. But at this juncture it is important to reiterate the case of Venezuela, the bulk of whose oil exports constitute *refined products*, because these evade the fixed price structure, enabling the country to circumvent any burden-sharing in the price defence scheme. Some other OPEC countries include their oil exports within the system through barter-trade, in which oil exports are counter-traded by imports from the trading partner, so that the system can cover hidden discounts. These countries can likewise evade the fixed price system and produce their quotas in full.

In fact, crude oil that is sold at a fixed price should not represent more than 30 per cent of total OPEC exports. Therefore, if only 30 per cent of total OPEC oil exports is subject to the fixed price system, this means that OPEC's burden of price defence is borne by only a few Gulf countries: Saudi Arabia, Iraq and, to a lesser extent, Kuwait.

All these aspects evince the untenability of a system that inverts the logic of energy economics. A system of last-resort production at a fixed price, requiring OPEC to carry the burden of price defence for both oil *and* non-oil energy (and with only a few Gulf members bearing the brunt of this policy) creates an inherently unstable structure, resembling an inverted pyramid with a fragile, narrow base, always on the verge of collapse.

An upshot of the quota system's inexpedience can be seen in the attempts of member countries to subvert it, by bypassing the rules and exceeding their production quota. With the lack of credibility over 'official' production data communicated by member countries to the Secretariat, compared with the actual 'real' production numbers published in the specialist petroleum press, each minister attempted to play down the disparity. The unworkability of the system led to a proposal (put forward by Minister al-Sabah of Kuwait) to appoint international auditors, and the Conference decided to appoint a Dutch firm of accountants to undertake the task of auditing production in each member country, checking not only export numbers but pumping stations on the ground. A Ministerial Executive Council (MEC) was appointed within OPEC to examine the auditors' reports. As the MEC's secretary, I had to scrutinise the auditors' reports and was expected periodically to present them with my own summary to the Conference and give my personal views. The whole auditing process was extremely expensive and for a period not exceeding one year the cost was over US$3 million. This at least should have been 'the moment of truth', but no final conclusions were reached. This was because the countries attempting to conceal the truth about their actual production and export numbers devised ways of obstructing the auditors' work by withholding or even abstaining from granting them entry visas, or else preventing them from entering the installations in the name of national sovereignty.

With my direct responsibility for the whole exercise, I was subjected to attacks and accusations by those member countries giving false information, and I found it all extremely wearying. During this period I was Acting for the Secretary General in addition to my responsibilities as Deputy Secretary General, which included the supervision of energy research, involving a lot of study, as well as administration and information departments. I was working on average no less than ten hours a day, so that having to write these reports on the auditors' reports was an additional burden. Before convening each Conference (usually held in Geneva) I used to make the trip to Geneva via Zurich, where I would wait with my loyal, efficient assistant, Janet Roberts, for several hours before boarding the connecting Swiss Air flight to Geneva. I would use this waiting time to dictate very detailed auditing reports to Janet, which took at least three hours, so that we would finally arrive in Geneva exhausted, only to find that these auditors' reports were never taken seriously by the ministers. (At one of these sessions, the Algerian minister, always disparaging, even managed to be sarcastic about our choice of 'MEC' as an abbreviation of Ministerial Executive Council – given the French colloquialism, *mec*, denoting 'fellow'!)

11

The short-lived price collapse

The year 1985 was proving increasingly difficult. The continuous decline in OPEC production was now critical, in particular the level of Saudi Arabia's production (see Chapter 15). At the Geneva Conference of 25 July that year, Sheikh Yamani raised the issue of the price structure, OPEC's burden of price defence and Saudi Arabia's consequent fate as the member most penalised by the pricing system. He felt that it was high time OPEC reconsidered its pricing policy and secured a greater share of the world market, instead of leaving non-OPEC producers with the advantage of expanding their production capacity at OPEC's expense.

To my complete surprise, the Geneva Conference that year suddenly agreed that OPEC should declare its determination to acquire and defend a 'fair market share in conformity with its development requirements'.

While I was writing the press communiqué, I realised that those who had agreed to the decision were unaware of the significance of having a higher market share. Setting higher production targets would result in fiercer competition between OPEC and non-OPEC oil because the latter would continue to produce the maximum possible at prices that would now become uncomfortably low, relative to their high degree of investment as sunk capital. This, in the final analysis, would risk an outright price collapse. After the conference I went to see Sheikh Yamani in his suite on the top floor of the Intercontinental Hotel, where the Kuwaiti Oil Minister, Sheikh Ali al-Sabah, was also present. I asked whether they felt those who had agreed to the concept of a higher market share understood the implications, and at this both Yamani and al-Sabah burst out laughing, clearly as amused as I was.

It had been decided to form a committee, chaired by the Venezuelan oil minister, Arturo Grisanti, but it failed to reach any conclusions, especially in determining what was meant by a 'fair share' of the world market, as many delegates still seemed oblivious to the consequences of their decision. Events would soon supersede the committee's deliberations as a result of Saudi Arabia's new market-oriented pricing initiative, which led to the collapse of the quota system.

In my capacity as Acting Secretary General, I was not really qualified to discuss matters pertaining to the essential interests of individual member countries, but during the Geneva Conference, while OPEC was discussing its resolution concerning the market share issue, at least I was able to address all these issues freely with both Yamani and al-Sabah in Yamani's hotel suite. The Saudi Arabian Oil Undersecretary, Abdul Aziz al-Turki, was also present when Yamani asked what I thought about this latest OPEC decision. I replied instantly that at last we had a chance to break free from the shackles of OPEC's rigid production and pricing structure that had for so long penalised Gulf oil, and that unless we ceased to defend a high and, in my opinion, artificial price that effectively corners OPEC but helps the other producers, OPEC would revert to reducing its own production and thus securing markets for non-OPEC producers, at OPEC's expense. Aware of my additional audience, I clarified my case that such policies served only to secure huge windfall profits for the oil companies to reinvest in high-cost North Sea oil, produced at maximum capacity; while OPEC, especially the Gulf, had to retreat into a corner and restrict its production, despite the Gulf having the bulk of world reserves. While talking in this vein, I was aware of the vexed expression on al-Turki's face. He then remarked sternly that the revenues of the OPEC countries would fall as a result of lower oil prices. I politely pointed out that this might happen in only one or two areas; but that, even there, the situation would soon be reversed and Gulf countries would reap huge economic benefits from increased export volumes, which in turn would bolster the price. But while explaining this, I saw al-Turki's expression of displeased scepticism – in contrast to Sheikh Yamani, who was listening with interest. I bid them goodnight and left, feeling greatly relieved at having at least got the matter off my chest.

Also I felt some contentment at having seized the opportunity to express my convictions to the most powerful minister in OPEC, something I had been prevented from doing in the presence of the others, all of whom capitulated to pressure from Iran, Algeria and, above all, the Venezuelan minister, Arturo Grisanti, whose perception of me was as a dangerous instrument in the hands of the Iraqi state. The Iranians, similarly hostile, were unable to do anything because of the support given me by the Gulf ministers.

The hostility of this clique became palpable when my term (which would normally have ended in 1985) came up for renewal for a further three-year extension. The charming Libyan minister, Kamil al-Makkhour, was President of the Conference at that time, and when I discussed the matter with him, he kindly volunteered to write a letter to the Conference recommending that my term be extended. The reaction from Algeria was churlish enough, but the kindly al-Makkhour later informed me that when an Iranian delegate, ali-Shams, saw his letter of recommendation, he visited al-Makkhour in his hotel to protest, complaining that 'Chalabi is considered to be Yamani's stooge.' To this al-Makkhour replied that his recommendation had arisen from his own conviction of my efficiency and performance and he added that 'if Chalabi is seen as Yamani's stooge, then I am also Yamani's stooge.'

Later that year, in September 1985, at a session of Robert Mabro's Oxford Energy Seminar, to which both Sheikh Yamani and I were invited, Yamani made an intervention, the essence of which was that Saudi Arabia could no longer live with the present situation. Indirectly he indicated that his country sought to 'correct' the present quota system, which unfairly penalised it. His comments caused a sensation, exploding as headline news throughout the petroleum press and the general press worldwide, carrying also the assumption of a fait accompli, by which Saudi Arabia had taken steps to depart from the quota system. As the Ministerial Committee (headed by Arturo Grisanti of Venezuela) had in fact implemented nothing at this stage, Saudi Arabia seized the initiative and began selling its own share at market prices, freeing itself from the shackles of the 'fixed price' system of selling crude at a price set at netback levels – in other words, at the price of petroleum products in the main selling areas of Rotterdam, East Coast USA and Singapore, minus the refining and transportation costs to Ras Tanura in the Gulf, determining the f.o.b. price at that point. This, in practice, amounted to abandoning both the quota and fixed-price systems.

With Saudi Arabia's initiative in selling its oil at the netback price, after OPEC's resolution (earlier that year) to acquire a higher market share, a storm erupted with huge repercussions throughout the world oil industry. As soon as this 'new approach' was adopted, demand for OPEC oil increased, in particular oil from Saudi Arabia, whose production now doubled from 3 mbpd in 1985 to 6 mbpd by the summer of 1986. But the problem was that it unleashed a price war with other oil producers following suit. Production became a free-for-all, with each producer, whether within or outside OPEC, abandoning any price commitment. The consequence was, of course, the great oil price collapse in mid-1986 when the price of Arab light crude crashed to $6 per barrel.

This had a dramatic financial impact, affecting not only OPEC but the world oil industry, and in particular the high-cost oil of the USA and the UK. Including Alaska, America's oil-producing states – where financial and economic activities revolve around high-cost oil – were unable to cope with the low prices. Many oil fields had to shut down, especially their 'stripper-wells'. In Texas the extremely low oil price caused a serious economic recession, with oil fields and several banks having to close. For the UK, the price war also impacted negatively on the profitability of North Sea oil operations.

OPEC conferences erupted in tumult, with oil ministers in perpetual fury, especially Algeria, Indonesia and other small suppliers, whose finances depend entirely on oil revenues. I recall Dr Subroto declaring that the President of Indonesia had warned him that if he did nothing to reverse the situation towards a higher price regime, he would lose his job. Meanwhile, al-Sabah and Yamani tried to appease these ministers, explaining that the situation was only temporary, as demand for OPEC oil would increase dramatically and subsequently correct the per-barrel income by increasing the export volume. But any argument involving economic logic was wasted on the combative clique of hawks, Arturo Grisanti of Venezuela, Belkacem Nabi of Algeria and Fawzi Shakshuki of Libya. It served only to entrench their antagonism towards both Sheikh Yamani and me.

While the year 1986 was one of successive crises, it also proved the most hectic year in OPEC's history. Acting for the Secretary General, I was serving, supervising or chairing about 50 meetings.

Besides chairing technical meetings, I chaired the ECB, deliberations for which were arduous and so lengthy that sometimes I was
there until 4 a.m. Chairing these ECB meetings demanded a great
effort on my part to accommodate the conflicting positions of those
who were termed 'experts', whose antithetical viewpoints were
policy driven. These delegates could not approach discussions on
a sound economic basis, but instead presented supply and demand
numbers that would serve the political position of their governments. Those representing the hawks (Iran, Algeria, Libya), in particular the Algerian Yousefi, overstepped by far the boundary for
minimal courtesy. They were extremely hostile, always anticipating my habitual opposition to their bid for maximum prices. One
of the Iranian delegates, a Mr Sepahban, had the patience to read
through all the Secretariat reports and selectively manipulate them
to support his argument that the price of oil should reflect the cost
of extracting synthetic oil from coal, which was extremely expensive: i.e. over US$40 per barrel in 1986.

On a more personal level, difficulties arose in dealing with
certain ECB members, such as the 'heavy-weight' Saudi, Osama
Trabulsi, who, representing as he did OPEC's largest oil producer,
invariably tried to dominate the proceedings. Whenever I presented a discourse not to his liking, he would glare disapprovingly
at me in silence. In my capacity as Chairman I had to listen to every
delegate very carefully, and apart from contradicting each other,
many were difficult to follow. The Algerian delegate would mix
English with French (though this posed no problem for me), while
the pleasant Nigerian, Orolemfemi, whose English baffled me, was
kind enough to praise my chairmanship as well as my (apparently)
articulate reviews of our discussions – though some people joked
about the way I converted his jumbled remarks into some sort of
comprehensible form in the ECB summaries. An interesting incident arose involving a very intelligent Kuwaiti lady, named Siham
Rezouki. She was a little awkward but I used to make considerable
effort to accommodate her. Then, once while she was speaking on
behalf of her delegation, I turned to an aide of mine sitting beside
me and made an unfortunate aside remark: 'What does this woman
want?' without realising that my microphone was still switched on.
This infuriated her and she stormed out of the conference room.
Feeling as mortified as she, I went to her and apologised profusely,

and with great effort succeeded in bringing her back into the meeting. My remark had been uttered in idiomatic Iraqi Arabic, equally comprehensible for a Kuwaiti, and it was the colloquialism used for 'woman' that was offensive for this lady – the very use of which reveals the condescending attitude of Arab men towards women.

That busy year of 1986 saw seven ministerial meetings of the Conference, and, apart from the ECB meetings that preceded each Ministerial Conference, I had to report to the Conference every time. Having the perennial problem of circumventing the Venezuelan and Algerian ministers' animosity, and outwitting their caustic comments, I styled the report (written under my chairmanship) in such a way as to reflect their differing views, leaving these ministers with no valid reason to attack me. Yet their antagonism – because of my economist's views – remained forever palpable. I recall a friend, Dr Felix Rossi from the Venezuelan delegation, telling me how his minister, Arturo Grisanti, had remarked that whenever I presented my reports I was intelligible 'and yet,' Grisanti had added, 'I do not like him.' Besides these difficult meetings, I had to serve four meetings of the Governors' Board, many ministerial committees and also technical meetings.

In retrospect, while writing this memoir, I wonder at my physical and mental resilience, which evidently helped me survive a constant barrage of attack for daring to be rational. But the intense effort to avoid being a constant target took its toll and I was thankful to be able to unwind from the stress when one of the OPEC ministerial conferences was held on the beautiful island of Brioni in Yugoslavia, where the Government's representatives were most hospitable. In between meetings I relaxed by taking long walks, struck by the island's remarkable natural beauty and its gazelles, with their wide black beautiful eyes, wandering through the woods. I was even more struck by the supreme luxury of Marshal Tito's retreat there: as a holiday residence belonging to a Communist president, it far excelled in luxury that of any top Western politician.

Meanwhile, other oil-producing countries were approached – and once again the Norwegian Energy Minister agreed to meet Sheikh Yamani and me, this time on Yamani's yacht in Venice. He expressed great concern about the situation and repeated his resolve that *this time* his government would co-operate with OPEC. But this proved to be yet another time-wasting case of lip service for action that would never happen.

Political repercussions from the free-for-all oil-market situation were soon evident. It was astonishing that the then US President Reagan seemed oblivious of the implications of low prices for the US economy and oil industry that would directly affect the lower 48 states. He was actually crowing with glee that the price of oil had plummeted to $6 per barrel, triumphantly declaring, 'We have succeeded in bringing that infamous cartel OPEC to its knees.' By contrast, Vice President George Bush (Snr), an oil man who felt keenly the bite of low prices and the negative impact on the US oil industry and economy, stepped in to defend the interests of the oil producers in Texas and the other producing states. He flew to Saudi Arabia to meet King Fahd, with whom he agreed that the price should be corrected upwards to $18 per barrel, and he was quoted in the press as emphasising the strategic importance of maintaining $18 as a minimum price per barrel. Prime Minister Margaret Thatcher likewise clamoured for action because of the harmful impact on North Sea operations. Pressure mounted also from other OPEC member countries for King Fahd to agree.

It followed, therefore, that at the next OPEC conference of November 1986, held in Geneva, Sheikh Yamani announced, 'His Majesty, the King of Saudi Arabia, wishes to raise the price to $18 per barrel.' Yamani was deliberately distancing himself by putting the proposal to the Conference not as his own initiative but as an order from the King. The consequence was that Sheikh Yamani had to leave his ministerial post. At this news there was great jubilation on the part of the hawks in OPEC and gratuitously sardonic remarks, such as Grisanti crowing that 'now there would be only one lawyer,' i.e. he, Grisanti (Yamani having trained as a lawyer); while the Algerian Minister, Belkacem Nabi, mockingly lamented how they would miss the delicious dates that Yamani used to bring from his farms in Saudi Arabia. Apart from his dedication and boundless generosity, Sheikh Yamani will in time be granted a place in history recording the extent of his courageous role in adopting for his country a policy that was independent of Western oil interests.

Just prior to OPEC's Geneva conference in 1986, at which Sheikh Yamani was replaced by Hisham Nazir, I called Yamani at his home in Jeddah in an attempt to cheer him with the words that it was

'God's good will that you are now out of this.' I heard his reply in the affirmative as he reflected upon the outcome with some happiness. Meanwhile in Geneva, while I sat in my little suite (which the Intercontinental Hotel's director, Herr Schott, so kindly offered me for the same price as a standard room), I was suddenly pervaded by a sense of serenity and clarity of mind. I was studying my German grammar, something I normally found quite arduous, and yet it became suddenly clear and easy to absorb. The next day Yamani called me from the President Hotel in Geneva (which he had chosen in order to be as far from the Intercontinental and OPEC proceedings as possible). He asked if I would like to join him for lunch. I naturally replied that I would.

It was during our lunch that Yamani revealed his plans. He explained to me that, relieved of his ministerial responsibilities, he had first and foremost two projects in mind: to establish both a centre for Islamic cultural studies and an institute of energy studies, both based in London. At this point he added that he wished me to be the director of the energy studies project. I responded very positively and assured him that I was very happy to accept this offer but that I had issues to resolve with my government, as I was still on secondment from the Ministry of Oil in Baghdad. I feared that Saddam's ruthless regime would view my departure from OPEC very critically and would swiftly turn against me, which would expose my family and me to danger. I asked Yamani if he could agree to give me time to make arrangements that would ensure some degree of safety. He affirmed his understanding and agreement to this. This episode heralded the end of an era which, all in all, I still hold dear.

Wary of approaching the matter of my departure with OPEC carefully, I first talked to the then President of the Conference, who at the time was the charming Nigerian, Rilwanu Lukman, with whom I had always enjoyed a very good working relationship, and who had always been able to rely on me for data and information. I recounted to Lukman the fact of Yamani's proposal, and while expressing my wish to take up his offer I could not help but articulate my dread of causing any trouble with Saddam's government. Lukman asked me how he could help, and so I told him that I would be very grateful if, when my term of office ended in August 1988, he and the Conference would refrain from requesting a renewal of my term. This would then give me a pretext not to return to Iraq. We had to wait a long time for the next OPEC Conference when my case could be examined. When the moment at last came, Lukman was then faced with an unexpected complication with the Iraqi Oil Minister, at that time Issam al-Chalabi (my unrelated namesake). Despite an instruction from the Presidency to obtain for me a renewal of my term with OPEC, Issam al-Chalabi had it in mind to replace me with Ramzi Salman, then head of SOMO, the marketing arm of Iraq's oil ministry. For this reason he did not agree to my sudden withdrawal, wanting instead a partial renewal; and so he insisted that I stay on, not for a full term but long enough for a new Secretary General to be appointed.

At that time, Dr Subroto of Indonesia, who had left the oil ministry to return to university teaching, made some statements in the press to the effect that he was interested in the OPEC Secretary Generalship and wished this position to be based on merit, instead of rotation, and that it should be a three-year term, renewable for a further three years. For the Conference, this seemed an ideal solution to the deadlock over appointing a new Secretary General after Mare Nangwema's term finished; also for the cessation of my own term as Acting Secretary General (from 1983 to 1988). In this way, a compromise was reached: the Conference would appoint Subroto with unanimity and also extend my own term to the end of June 1989.

When I told Lukman that I had hoped to leave the OPEC Secretariat much sooner, he explained the difficulty with my minister, and that it was the best he could do, after discussing it with various ministers including al-Sabah, to whom I had also mentioned my reluctance to accept the protracted departure date.

Soon after this episode, the Saudi Arabian Prince Abdul Aziz bin Salman al-Saud ('number two' to the new Saudi Minister Hisham Nazir) approached me in my office and offered me a job working for them as a consultant. I thanked him and politely declined, explaining the difficult situation with my government. The slightest revelation of Sheikh Yamani's confidential arrangements with me was, of course, unthinkable. He repeatedly affirmed his wish (and his Minister Abou Lo'ai's wish) to offer me this position, explaining that they were very impressed with my performance and knowledge. He then asked me how much I had been earning with OPEC, and what I thought about my employment conditions, implying that they would offer the same or better. For diplomatic reasons I remained evasive. Shortly after this he telephoned me from London to invite me to a meeting at the Dorchester Hotel, where he repeated his offer during an elaborate dinner with superb wine – though he himself does not drink. Again, I remained courteously evasive, unable to reveal my agreement with Yamani, to whom my commitment was final.

After OPEC's return to both the fixed price and the quota system, the new Saudi Oil Minister, Hisham Nazir, contacted me, asking me to visit him in his hotel suite, where he asked for my opinion of OPEC's re-adoption of a fixed price. I explained how this system would always leave Saudi Arabia as the last-resort supplier, whether it liked it or not: i.e. Saudi production would be reduced below quota, while other OPEC members could produce their quotas in full, which disadvantaged Saudi Arabia. Later he asked me to join him in his car so that I could continue elaborating on the economics of this argument, and I clarified the point that basing OPEC prices on the reference price of Arab light crude Ras Tanura in the Gulf induced Saudi Arabia to be more committed to that price in a way that would affect Saudi production levels. His response was that he would now refuse to accept any reduction in Saudi Arabia's quota and that Saudi Arab Light should no longer be used as OPEC's reference price. 'In that case,' I said, 'you have to abandon the concept of the fixed price.' He thanked me for this advice.

The OPEC Conference, therefore, decided that this matter be studied by the Kuwaiti Minister, Sheikh Ali al-Sabah, who was chairing the Committee, which included the ministers of Ecuador and Libya. As it happened, the Ecuadorian minister was unable to travel to Vienna for work-related reasons and so it was agreed that the meeting would be held instead in Quito, Ecuador, in late November 1986. al-Sabah kindly invited me to fly there in his private jet, and I found his companionship most pleasant during this very long flight.

At this November 1986 meeting, held the day after our arrival in Quito, our discussion focused crucially on how to replace the Saudi Arab Light Ras Tanura oil as a reference price at the level of $18 per barrel. The Committee arrived at a strange solution in adopting as a new reference price a basket of several crudes: Sahara Blend from Algeria, Minas crude from Indonesia, Bonny Light crude from Nigeria, Arab Light from Saudi Arabia, a light crude from Dubai, Tia Juana Light from Venezuela and (surprisingly) Isthmus crude from Mexico, although the latter is not an OPEC member.

This unorthodox system of pricing had never existed on the market, and the end result was that the reference price switched to North Sea Brent crude, in relation to which other crudes, including OPEC's, have been priced ever since. This situation has created an eccentric element in the oil industry, involving a transference away from Gulf oil, especially Saudi Arabia's, to the advantage of other crudes in terms of pricing for the world market, especially the futures market, which by then was burgeoning.

At a time when Saudi production was reaching 6 mbpd, the volume of Brent crude on the market amounted to only 0.7 mbpd, and yet the latter became the de facto reference crude. In both the spot market and futures market, Arab light does not exist as a reference price. al-Sabah remained unconvinced but gave in because of political pressure from other ministers. Later he told me that the new reference price had the advantage of giving greater weight to light crudes, attracting a wider differential for heavier crudes relative to light crudes.

12

Quota-system problems: OPEC's disputed reserves fuel 'peak-oil' theory

Leaving behind the traumas of the price collapse of 1986, the Conference decided in 1987 to discuss the adoption of a more rational quota system. As was mentioned, the first attempt at a quota system in 1982 predicated itself on de facto production levels, which then formed the basis for the official quota system adopted in March 1983. Problems soon arose concerning which criteria should be used to establish a more logical national quota distribution. Recalling these discussions, the glaring heterogeneity and conflict of interests were apparent among OPEC member countries, with each vying to accord greater weight to the parameters that best served its own interests, without considering the realities of the industry. Given this state of affairs, finding the perfect quota system was doomed to failure.

These futile discussions – far from helping to resolve the thorny issue of 'cheating' (which could have been assuaged had a logical quota system been agreed on) – later gave rise to curious anomalies concerning member countries' reserves and the authenticity of data submitted to the OPEC Secretariat compared with numbers for reserves published in the specialised press. The assessment of individual OPEC members' reserves was deemed to be critical as the main criterion for allocating each quota. Once the irregularities of OPEC's reserves were exposed, they became instrumental in fomenting a worldwide debate about oil reserves, which has driven discussions back to the old contention that the world has already reached, or will soon reach, peak oil. Doubts were continually raised about the authenticity of the unrealistic data for OPEC's reserves, which seem to have been 'qualified' perhaps for political reasons.

When allocating national quotas, clearly OPEC's chief parameter was the *magnitude* of oil reserves because, in the final analysis, production volume is determined by the life span of the reserves before depletion. This geological reality should be the guide to production and to geographical distribution. Nevertheless, this self-evident parameter was contested or strongly downplayed by member countries with limited reserves (Algeria, Libya, Indonesia[1]) in the realisation that it put them at a disadvantage.

This drove OPEC to take up various additional parameters, often completely irrelevant, such as local oil consumption, oil production costs, degree of dependence on oil exports, external debts, population size, land surface, etc. When discussions turned to the main parameter of oil reserves, strong objections were raised concerning the source of information about these reserves.

Eager to gain a higher quota, member countries with vast oil reserves, like Saudi Arabia, naturally threw their weight behind promoting parameters that involved the size of reserves. Conversely, size parameters were opposed by countries with smaller reserves. For the same reason, there was disagreement when the question was raised whether to measure only currently known recoverable reserves, or whether to include probable ultimate reserves.

More important was establishing the published source of reserve levels. Usually oil reserves of OPEC member countries are taken from numbers published periodically in the *Oil & Gas Journal* and in the *BP Statistical Review*. Many OPEC countries, contesting these sources, went by their own much augmented numbers to communicate the magnitude of their reserves directly to the OPEC Secretariat, but their estimates of reserves were manifestly inflated. For example, according to the *BP Statistical Review*, Abu Dhabi's recoverable reserves in 1985 stood at 31 bn/B, yet only two years later these reserves when communicated to the OPEC Secretariat were shown to be of the order of 92 bn/B, three times the amount recorded by the *Statistical Review*. Saudi Arabia's reserves also increased but to a lesser extent: from 170 bn/B in 1987 to 255 bn/B in 1988; while Venezuela's jumped from 28 bn/B in 1984 to 54 bn/B in 1985. All in all, if we compare numbers in the specialised statistical reviews with those communicated later to the Secretariat, we can see that total OPEC reserves jumped from 478 bn/B in 1983 to 764 bn/B in 1988, an increase of around 70 per cent.

Such disparity between OPEC's new numbers and those recorded previously by the petroleum press, or by secondary sources, was so marked that it caused much speculation about the reliability of OPEC's statistical data on reserves. Some cases could be explained while others could not. In the case of Iraq, for example, discoveries had been made in the 1970s of huge reserves and giant oilfields such as the Majnoon and West Qurna, which had never been publicly announced, and figures for which were long out-of-date because Saddam had prohibited the disclosure of any new additional reserves (under pain of capital punishment), and behind his obsession with secrecy was a fear of exposing the country's economic muscle by divulging the magnitude of its known reserves. Interestingly, when this became the quota-determining parameter, Saddam changed his tune and instructed that accurate data could now be conveyed to OPEC. He saw that this would reap benefits in terms of a higher production quota. Saudi reserves were similarly regarded as genuine, as previous data recorded by the oil companies had underestimated them. At the time, we, in the Secretariat, were given to understand that Abu Dhabi's calculations included probable *ultimate* reserves, not *proven* recoverable reserves alone, but no explanation was ever officially communicated to the Secretariat.

If we were to take *reserves* alone as the most logical, quota-determining parameter – with production shares based on higher reserves entailing far higher quotas – Algeria would end up with only 1.1 per cent of OPEC's total quota, as against 33.5 per cent for Saudi Arabia. Members with low reserves naturally campaigned for alternative criteria, one of which was even the *historical* share of member countries, but this, too, was rejected, as historically both Iraq and Iran had very high shares that would gain for each an unfairly high quota percentage.

Another rather whimsical parameter was demographically based, the logic for proposing it being 'the greater the population, the greater the need for oil revenues'. This, of course, would have favoured the densely populated Indonesia and Nigeria, while penalising sparsely populated countries like Saudi Arabia, Libya, Kuwait and Abu Dhabi. While the demographic factor was being debated, a heated discussion ensued in which the vivacious UAE minister, Dr Otaiba, humorously intervened: 'Gentlemen, what is OPEC? OPEC is the Organisation of Petroleum Exporting Countries. We are exporters of oil, not of populations.' His remark caused much mirth and alleviated the tension. An equally bizarre parameter, insisted upon by Libya, was *land surface*, the 'logic' behind which was that Libya's vast land area required investment in transportation.

With such unrealistic input, our discussions were doomed to failure, and the quota system continued with ever greater disparity, exposed by the actual production levels reported by secondary sources of the petroleum press, which invariably refuted the production levels communicated by member countries to the OPEC Secretariat. With each country trying to assert its own data authenticity, a glaring example that later came to light was evinced by an amusing incident when Venezuela (supposedly in accordance with its quota) reported to the Secretariat numbers purported to be near their official quota, although it was a well-known fact that in 1996 and 1997 Venezuela's real production was 1 mbpd above its quota. The press at the time revealed how the then Venezuelan oil minister, Dr Erwin Arrieta Valera, when his insistence on the authenticity of his official figures was challenged, suddenly retorted, 'Well... nobody but ghosts can report the exact amount of oil actually produced from the oil wells.' A journalist then showed him an official report from Venezuela to the World Bank, in which Venezuelan production numbers were as reported in the press.

With its data thus invalidated by varying degrees of misinformation from its member countries, OPEC was faced with an impasse it could not resolve. When the oil price fell in 1998, finally OPEC decided that details of production and quota levels would in future be passed to secondary sources.

The CGES has undertaken several thorough studies of oil production capacity and also of oil reserves in Iraq, Iran, Saudi Arabia, the UAE and Venezuela. In its joint study[2] with Petrolog, CGES has shown that the published 120 bn/B for Iraq's oil greatly underestimates the country's massive oil potential, which is discussed at greater length below. Meanwhile, Iran has made important discoveries that could bring the country's total reserves up to 130 bn/B. In the case of Venezuela, CGES's joint study with Global Business Consultants shows that the total numbers given for its reserves were the result of Venezuela's addition of very heavy crude oil in the Orinoco belt area, amounting to 15–18 bn/B. The assumed volume of this addition has been contested by experts. A CGES study of Saudi Arabia shows results to be nearer the published 265 bn/B,[3] while another CGES study estimates the magnitude of UAE reserves at 60–70 bn/B.

Revelations concerning OPEC reserves, unearthed during its quota system disputes, have fuelled the peak-oil controversy, given that accuracy over global oil reserves lies at the heart of the current debate of whether or not we have reached peak oil. The peak-oil debate focuses on the Hubbert Curve,[4] but this curve computation can be adapted to any scenario (or bias, if the intention is to reinforce the notion that the world's ultimate recoverable reserves will be exhausted now, or sooner than expected).

Advocates of peak-oil theory contend that the reported magnitude of OPEC's reserves still remains exaggerated and that its true reserves are far less. This supposition arose from earlier confusion over inaccurate numbers given by OPEC's member countries for their reserves in the mid-1980s.

OPEC's reserves have evidently increased since the 1980s and in all probability there is the potential for vast additional reserves. It is interesting to note in Figure 12.1 below that the number of completed wells in OPEC countries has been negligible relative to the rest of the world.

Africa, the Middle East and above all the oil-rich Gulf have vast areas that remain unexplored, or barely explored. Official calculations still underestimate Iraq's oil reserves and are far too conservative to represent anything like the real oil potential of the country. A study undertaken by CGES and Petrolog (referred to above) estimates that the published numbers for Iraq's reserves represent only one-third of the country's real potential. This is because over a period of 83 years, since the discovery of the giant Kirkuk oilfield in 1927 until 2010, the exploration undertaken amounts to only 15 years of mostly sporadic activity. During this 15 year phase, the only two periods of intensive exploratory activity were between 1952 and 1960 (when the giant Rumaila oilfield was discovered) and between 1972 and 1980; and yet just in those few intervening years Iraq was able to add 45 bn/B of new oil reserves. These exploratory efforts then came to a halt with Saddam's wars and the UN sanctions.

In the case of Iran substantial new reserves have recently been discovered during a short burst of exploratory activity, bringing the country's total reserves to 130 bn/B. In Saudi Arabia, exploratory activities began only recently and at this stage no one can predict the real potential of that vast country's reserves.

The impossibility of knowing the full extent of reserves leaves peak-oil theory flawed. The danger is that it leads itself astray because it overlooks, or intentionally ignores, the most elementary factors and trends. Apart from sparse exploratory activity among vast tracts of potentially very oil-rich Gulf areas, there are other aspects, such as the sweeping changes in the world energy market, the far lower rates of world oil-demand growth, especially in the OECD countries where demand has been declining dramatically since the millennium; and now even in the emerging economies the rate of incremental growth in oil demand has been notably weaker since 2006, and especially since 2008's 'third' oil-price shock. This is already marked in China and India, whose governments have also declared a determination to reduce and remove subsidies on petro-leum products and develop alternative energy sources because of global warming concerns. Such developments auger far more moderate rates of depletion of oil reserves.

Peak-oil theory also ignores technological improvements in speeding up the process for adding new reserves and the enhanced recovery techniques used for existing reserves. In fact, estimates for reserves should always be treated in the light of changing technology and science.

Under closer scrutiny the set of assumptions offered by the advocates of peak-oil (many of them concealing a vested interest in high oil prices) fuel unfounded panic that the world is already running out of oil. In this way peak-oil theory ultimately presents itself as another myth.

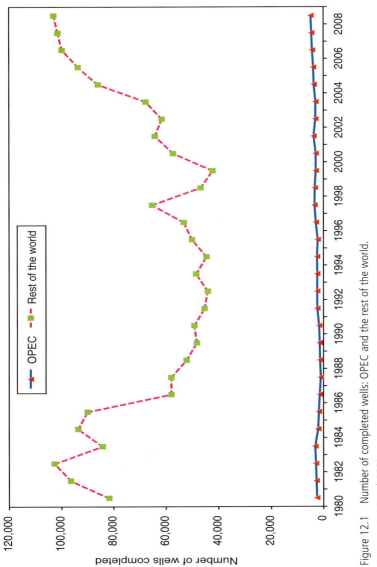

Figure 12.1 Number of completed wells: OPEC and the rest of the world.

Source: OPEC and CGES.

Plate 6   OPEC Conference, Bali, October 1981. Dr Subroto, Oil Minister of Indonesia and at the time President of the OPEC Conference, with the author (right).
Source: OPEC.

Plate 8   OPEC Conference, Geneva, 1986. The author with H.E. Alhaji Rilwanu Lukman, Nigeria's Oil Minister and President of the Conference, standing at the microphone.
Source: OPEC.

Plate 7 Historic OPEC meeting (1985): seated left to right: Mr Ramsey Salman, Marketing Director of Iraq Oil Ministry; Mr Taki Oraibi, Iraq's Oil Minister; Sheikh Ahmed Zaki Yamani, Saudi Arabia's Oil Minister; Dr Mana Said Otaiba, UAE's Oil Minister; Mr Belkacem Nabi, Algeria's Oil Minister; the author (smiling directly at camera); Mr Fawzi, Libya's Oil Minister; Mr Rilwanu Lukman, Nigeria's Oil Minister.

Source: OPEC.

Plate 9   OPEC Conference, Geneva, July 1986. Seated foreground (L to R) are Dr Yousifi, Algeria's Oil Minister, Dr Fadhil Chalabi, Acting Secretary General, Arturo Grisanti, Venezuela's Oil Minister, and seated on the right, the Iranian, Ecuadorian and Libyan ministers.

Source OPEC.

Plate 10   OPEC Vienna Conference, December 1987. L to R: the author, Acting Secretary General, reads OPEC's resolutions to the Conference and to the press, shown here with H.E. Alhaji Rilwanu Lukman (Nigeria's Oil Minister) during Lukman's Presidency of the OPEC Conference, and the then OPEC Director of Information.

Source: OPEC.

Plate 11 The author in conversation with Dr Mana Said Otaiba, Oil Minister of the United Arab Emirates. *Source:* OPEC.

Plate 12   Fadhil Chalabi's final OPEC 'all Ministers' Conference, 1989, before his departure from Vienna to London.

Source: OPEC.

Plate 13   H.E. Sheikh Ahmed Zaki Yamani (left), former Oil Minister of Saudi Arabia, conversing with Fadhil Chalabi (right) some years after they had both established the London-based think-tank, Centre for Global Energy Studies in August 1989.

13

Meeting OPEC heads of state:
The quest for quota compliance

The new formula of returning to the quota system with a price of $18 per barrel did not work. In 1987 OPEC production continued to fall in varying degrees, and production in Saudi Arabia and Kuwait had to drop for the benefit of Iran.

In June 1987 the OPEC Conference decided to form a ministerial committee with the aim of travelling to member countries to urge their heads of state to abide by their assigned quotas. The committee's delegation, chaired by Lukman in his capacity as Conference President, included Subroto of Indonesia, Arturo Grisanti of Venezuela and myself, in my capacity as Acting for the Secretary General.

Our first trip was to Saudi Arabia, where, having landed in Riyadh, we were met by the Saudi Oil Minister, Hisham Nazir, who informed us that King Fahd was in Jeddah. When we arrived at the palace in Jeddah, after a very long wait, we met King Fahd, who launched into a monologue about the balance of payments predicament faced by OPEC countries, with falling prices for oil exports yet rising costs of importing products from the industrialised countries. Every time Lukman embarked on an explanation of the nature of our mission, the King wished to continue talking of other matters. Finally Lukman was able to elucidate OPEC's concern over the non-adherence to the quota system, a situation that created a surplus in the market and hence falling oil prices. This prompted another discourse on OPEC's economic developmental setbacks caused by the low oil prices against costly imports, but the King now gave us his attention inasmuch as he declared that our mission was indeed germane, and that in terms of quota compliance Saudi Arabia was itself a pioneer. Nodding in agreement, we bowed out of his royal presence. While making our exit from the palace, I felt overwhelmed by its very grandiose architecture, its marble-walled, gigantic design and furnishings, the style of which was oppressive, with all the lavish excess of over-expenditure.

Our next trip, to Qatar, was very different. When we met the Emir of Qatar, his facial expression on first acquaintance suggested a sense of unease and our discussion was initially awkward, but soon his eyes shone with a glow of interest and a pleasant earnestness, and we felt his welcome was genuine. I found him to be an adroit actor as, during the course of our discussions, he gave the impression of knowing nothing and yet was shrewd in his ability to anticipate and outwit. He naturally leapt to his country's defence, claiming that Qatar was not exceeding its quota and in any event is such a small country compared with Saudi Arabia. When we rose to leave I happened to be the last one to exit his office and, after my favourable impression of this Emir, I was then astonished to see his swift change of expression as he turned angrily to his son, the Minister of Oil, Abdul Aziz, brutally scolding him as if a junior school miscreant. I could not hear the topic of his tirade as I was out of earshot, but found the scene disturbing, and his son, the poor minister, observing my expression of surprise, blushed with embarrassment.

We then took the private jet to Kuwait, where later in the evening we would see Minister Sheikh Ali al-Sabah. As we reached the hotel I caught sight of my son Talik, who at the time was working in Kuwait before his departure for Harvard University where he would obtain his MSc in Architectural Design. While Talik and I were happily chatting, Minister al-Sabah approached and greeted us, and then asked me to meet him separately. When I joined him he told me he was rather puzzled by OPEC's mission: 'What do these people want?' he asked, to which I replied that they wished him to abide by the quota, to avoid the excess oil production that was causing the price to fall. 'But don't they realise there's a war raging in this region?' he continued. 'We're living in unusual circumstances, to say the least.' Despite his protest, I had great confidence in al-Sabah, and remained with him discussing the war and OPEC's problems, so that we both went together to meet the Emir the following morning.

Entering the Emir's office I was struck by its simplicity and lack of lavishness, which contrasted refreshingly with the excess I had encountered in the Jeddah palace. There were just a few leather chairs around a medium-sized table, on which lay the Qur'an bound in beautiful leather. Notwithstanding his royal status as a prince, this Palace al-Seef was very simple. At the entrance there was beautiful Arab calligraphy which, with wisdom, declared, 'If it [i.e. power] had endured too long for those before you, it would never have reached you.' This increased the favourable impression I already had of this Emir, who was circumspect, very courteous and listened to what Lukman and the other ministers had to say concerning the problem of non-compliance with OPEC quotas. When the discussion touched on Iraq, he reminded us that here was a country in the middle of a war and that we should not interfere because oil for Iraq was 'now a matter of life or death' and that we could not ask the Iraqis to do anything that was not in their own interests. The interview ended with the promise to look at the quota matter 'in the light of prevailing circumstances'. We then headed for the airport with al-Sabah and his Secretary, Ferid Zabal. When we boarded the aircraft, we noticed beautiful Persian rugs folded in such a way as to show each person's name. The rug that was so generously presented to me was massive, and to this day it still adorns a good part of my salon.

After Kuwait, we landed in Baghdad where instantly I felt very uneasy. As we left the aircraft we were greeted by the Iraqi Oil Minister, who was at that time Issam al-Chalabi, along with other high-ranking officials. Each time I had to travel to Baghdad, my heart would thump with fearful anticipation of the coercion to which I might be subjected to persuade me to work for Saddam's intelligence apparatus. This was what had kept me away for so long, especially when I was alerted to the position of Iraqis whose services were seconded to international organisations abroad, because now if we visited Iraq we risked not being granted permission to leave the country unless we agreed to undertake intelligence work. What worried me in particular was the prospect of being summoned by Sami Hannah who at the time masterminded intelligence at the Iraq Embassy in Vienna. He had tried to approach me when I first joined OPEC in 1979. He was later expelled from

Austria because of his attempt to put an incendiary bomb in the Iranian Embassy there.

Prior to my departure from Vienna to Baghdad at the start of the Iran–Iraq war, in September 1980, this man was again obtrusive, harassing me at every opportunity with obliquely intimidating messages whose subtexts were veiled as pleasantries: like his greeting me with 'the Director General sends you his regards', and when I asked to whom he referred his ominous reply was 'Mr Barzan Takriti', Saddam Hussein's notoriously brutal half-brother (later executed in 2008).

My heart missed a beat while I thanked him for this pseudo-complimentary salutation. He continued in a tone barely masking a threat, warning me that the Iraqi government counted on people like me: 'We expect you, as a good Iraqi patriot, to keep us informed with feedback on any material we can use.' At this I reminded him that information on OPEC was sent regularly to the Ministry of Oil in Baghdad and to the Iraqi representatives on the Board of Governors and the Economic Commission Board. 'I don't mean that kind of information,' came his sullen reply. 'We know the Gulf ministers have a high regard for you and so we expect you at the very least to report to us on their policies and plans, and what they say about Iraq.' To his demand that I become an outright spy, I replied with mock-surprise, 'Do you seriously imagine that those ministers are so naïve as to disclose to me confidential matters concerning their countries? They impart *only* information that concerns OPEC matters, and my relations with them concern *only* my performance in my professional capacity at OPEC.' With growing impatience, Sami Hannah reacted angrily: 'We are aware that you know a lot and are reluctant to co-operate with us.'

His sinister retort and equally sinister 'greeting' from Barzan Takriti, and the prospect of causing this half-brother of Saddam Hussein any displeasure, made me tremble inwardly. Because of this incident I did not return to Baghdad for over six years, not until Takriti was replaced as head of the intelligence service, having lost his position following disputes with Saddam. After such a long period of absence, I had to summon enormous courage to participate at a conference held, six years later, in Baghdad, where fortunately nothing transpired as I had feared. I was not, after all, detained by Iraqi Intelligence. In fact, no one demanded anything of me, and to my amazement I departed safe and sound.

Then, with OPEC's 'quota mission' in 1987, once more I found myself in Baghdad. After our arrival, Minister Issam al-Chalabi held a luncheon for us, following which I ventured north of Baghdad to visit my brother and sister, whom I had not seen for many years. Our reunion was made the more poignant by my discovery that my brother had lost his eyesight. Sadly, both he and my sister, who had joined us at his house, died shortly after this family reunion. I am glad that I stayed with them until as late as possible that evening. My brother, Mohammed, my senior by 12 years, had been extremely kind to me in my childhood. There was a car waiting to take me back to where our delegation was staying, and on my departure I even kissed my brother's hand, so moved that I wept for most of the long drive back to the hotel. I asked to be awoken at an early hour, then fell into such a deep slumber that I did not even hear the resounding blast of an Iranian rocket, exploding shortly after dawn in Baghdad.

Nerve-wracking moments followed. Because of the renewed hostilities with Iran, Saddam was unable to receive our delegation until later, and we were told that we would instead meet the Vice President of the Republic, Taha Ramadan al-Jezrawi (later executed in 2008), another evil man whom I remembered only too well. Although al-Jezrawi and I were well acquainted, when we entered his office he welcomed the minister but glanced at me without any apparent recognition. In the past I had felt simultaneous fear and loathing whenever I met him. An army private, who had been unable to complete his studies to train at the military academy, he evidently modelled himself on Saddam, even training his eyes to emit the same ruthless expression characteristic of a psychopath who knows nothing of humanity, and who would not hesitate to kill in cold blood without a flinch of facial muscle.

In the early 1970s (when I was still resident in Iraq), I recall well the pride he took in murdering numerous people when the Ba'ath Party conducted a campaign of terror, having falsely alleged that there was an American conspiracy against the regime. He chaired a notorious tribunal, unjustly sentencing to death more than 40 innocent people. Compelled under torture to confess to a conspiracy, they were even forced to confess openly on television to things they had never done, and al-Jezrawi was nothing short of barbaric in the satisfaction he took from the ensuing carnage. Soon after this heinous crime, I was sitting amid the Iraqi delegation at a Ba'ath government dinner for officials from the Democratic Republic of East Germany, when I heard al-Jezrawi ask the interpreter to tell the East German delegation that they ought to know that they were dealing with a man who had recently executed a large number of Iraqi people. The fact that the former Communist regime of East Germany was recognised by the Ba'ath government was in breach of terms decreed by the western Federal German Republic, according to which any country recognising East Germany would necessarily forfeit diplomatic relations with West Germany.

Now on our OPEC quota mission, while lingering in the office of the same fiendish al-Jezrawi, we were informed that President Saddam Hussain would see our delegation at noon. I hurried to the hotel to take a shower and change before joining the delegation on our way to the presidential palace. After waiting for some time we were ushered into Saddam's office. He was dressed in his military attire, complete with loaded gun in its leather holster adorning his waist. Saddam had never trained at Baghdad's military academy but had bestowed upon himself the rank of Marshal in order to be the supreme commander of the Iraqi army, which he always viewed as a potential source of political rebellion. The first to greet him was Oil Minister Issam al-Chalabi, who, though an engineer by training, was similarly in military attire and, standing in front of the president, he gave a military salute in a rather awkward fashion.

Issam al-Chalabi then introduced to Saddam our delegation, member by member. When my turn came to shake hands with Saddam I noticed that his face had come to resemble a mask more than a human countenance. Saddam gestured to us to sit down, and I half-dreaded that he would ask me to be the interpreter, and was relieved when an official interpreter arrived. We waited courteously for the President to address us, and a whole minute passed in silence before Saddam suddenly launched into a baffling preamble about our Creator and His Creation, the universe, the position of man within it and other mystical matters, all of which was as impenetrable as it was inexpressible for the poor interpreter, whose flow became disconnected in the attempt to translate this incongruous rhetoric into English. It was strangely reminiscent of a Sufi session with the Sufi's heightened mystical experience. But such an arcanely religious outburst from Saddam Hussein was perplexing.

As soon as there was a pause, Lukman politely turned to business and began talking about the general lack of commitment of member countries in complying with their quotas, the consequent downward pressure on the oil price, and on OPEC's credibility. For this reason, he explained, the Conference had decided to visit each member country in turn with the aim of convincing each of the importance of quota compliance. At this Saddam switched in seconds to his politically unyielding self. He declared that, as he was now at war with Iran, 'the bullet or rocket that Iran uses against *me* must be counterbalanced by an Iraqi bullet or rocket. This means that if Iran produces one barrel of oil to buy weaponry, *I* must produce an equivalent barrel of oil for the same purpose. Iraq must produce as much as Iran, not even one barrel of oil less.' Saddam then added resolutely: 'That is something I would never accept, as it would weaken my position.' It was impossible for the OPEC delegation to counter (as nobody dared contradict) Saddam's forceful, uncompromising resolve that any reduction in Iraq's oil production was unthinkable if it risked being less than Iran's. While we were all leaving his office, I was the last in line to shake hands with Saddam and I wished him well in his war with Iran. He looked at me and replied with conviction, 'It is God's will.' He then added, 'You have not changed in all these years. You look the same.' I thanked him. These were my last words with him. After a quick lunch, we boarded our flight for Abu Dhabi, and as our plane prepared its take-off from Baghdad, it was with sheer relief that I found myself once again leaving, by the grace of God, unscathed. I felt all the nightmarish oppression lift from me.

Oil Minister Dr Mana Said Otaiba (who was the head of OPEC's UAE delegation) met us on arrival at Abu Dhabi and took us to his own house – another example of extraordinary lavishness in design and furnishings. In the entrance he had placed a very large and handsome self-portrait, in which he was depicted elegantly sporting a smart Western-style raincoat, belted below the waist as was the fashion in the West at the time. Before the oil era hit Abu Dhabi, Otaiba, in his youth, had been granted a scholarship by the Iraqi government, to pursue his studies for a law degree at

Baghdad University, and also an apartment, which he had shared with another student from the Emirates. But now his oil wealth had bought him a luxurious palace, adorned with magnificent Persian rugs and exorbitant hangings on the walls of vast reception rooms that could seat scores of guests in armchairs with ornate arm-rests. Mana Otaiba suggested that we all move into a 'small cosy room', which turned out to be a palatial study with a huge desk and stairs leading to another level. At the sight of this, the Venezuelan minister, Arturo Grisanti, gave an amused laugh, humorously mocking the Gulf's concept of 'a small cosy room'.

Minister Otaiba enjoyed a very close relationship with the President of the Emirates, Sheikh Za'yed, of whom it was said he was a distant relative through the female line. What they had in common was poetry, written and pronounced in the particular local dialect. Otaiba himself was a well-known poet and every now and then published collections of poetry. As his lyrics were sung by famous singers, his poetry had become renowned throughout the Arab world. Otaiba also held a doctorate from Cairo University (of which he was justly proud, and he would not accept being addressed without his title 'Doctor'). I found him to be a most pleasant man, and to me personally, as he was invariably most supportive every time my term renewal came up for discussion. He showed an appreciation of my work to the extent that he even included my name in one of his poems! This happened during an OPEC Conference in Helsinki (in the summer of 1983). The term of Secretary General Nguema had ended without agreement on a successor, as the system of appointment by alphabetical order was being called into question (as mentioned above). The Iranians insisted on the appointment of an Iranian successor, which other Gulf ministers found unacceptable, and so it was decided to place me in charge as Acting for the Secretary General. To mollify the Iranians, a provision was made that OPEC's Conference President would supervise my work, and fortunately for me this Conference President was Mana Otaiba, to whom I had to refer matters constantly. He expressed in a poem a lament for these 'OPEC headaches', a line of which mentioned 'there is no Secretary General today to look after these problems – only me and my friend Fadhil Chalabi!'

Returning to the present, Mana Otaiba informed us that President Sheikh Za'yed was not in Abu Dhabi but staying at the oasis of al-Ayeen, and that he would arrive later. During that night we joined a party celebrating the marriage of Otaiba's son, Ahmed, at which Sheikh Za'yed himself later arrived wearing sandals. He was a very dynamic person, a Bedouin with an innate intelligence often characteristic of those of the Arabian desert, and whenever he addressed people he would habitually gaze deeply into their eyes. During the course of the celebrations, we met in a special room where Za'yed enquired about the purpose of OPEC's mission, which Mana Otaiba clarified. This led us into discussing the problem Abu Dhabi faced in terms of one emirate yoked to other emirates, the greatest difficulty being Dubai's refusal to concede to any restriction of its oil production. Abu Dhabi, the largest of the Emirates, had to bear most of the burden of the Emirates' budget, and without Dubai's co-operation over oil production cuts, Abu Dhabi for its part was now left with the prospect of being the sole Emirate to shoulder the burden of price defence, and not surprisingly followed suit in declining to cut its production for the sake of the quota. Abu Dhabi's very light, sulphur-free oil was highly sought, and its main market was Asia. As was anticipated by us, the meeting with Sheikh Za'yed ended inconclusively, in exactly the same way as meetings with the other Gulf heads of state.

Resigned to this, we returned to the celebrations at which singers from Morocco and other areas were performing various songs that voiced the poetry of Mana Otaiba. Amidst all the cacophony, Minister Grisanti fell fast asleep, emitting a low but continuous snore. I envied the man's ability to take an hour's 'cat-nap' amidst so much noise. In our private jet flying between one country and another, he always slept then awoke refreshed and with an instant return of his jocularity. Sheikh Za'yed became so caught up in the festive atmosphere that in a state of conviviality he began handing out pieces of meat to his guests. It should never be forgotten that it is thanks to this amazing Bedouin's innate wisdom that he achieved a miracle converting the Emirates from a desert of dust and poor dwellings into a clean sparkling city with wide, tree-lined streets, spectacular skyscrapers, beautiful shops – a transformation in only 17 years into a booming economy. I first visited him in 1971 and I remember his very simple 'palace' then, but every time I visited Abu Dhabi I saw a remarkable transformation in modernity and progress.

Dubai seemed an even great miracle, as on my last trip there in the 1990s it already resembled Singapore or Hong Kong. How different when, back in 1971, after seeing Sheikh Za'yed during the inauguration of the United Arab Emirates, my Minister Hammadi and I went to Dubai, where we were met by a Mr Mehdi al-Tajer, an extremely rich man of enormous influence in Dubai (owing to his close relationship with the Emir). In his Arab *distasha* he looked very different from the 'shoe-shiner' image I first had of him. He took us to meet Sheikh Rashid Maktoum, who was sitting in the Customs office in his *distasha* and sandals, having no income other than customs' excise until Dubai developed its oil industry. It was well-known in those days how Dubai thrived on smuggling from Iran and Iraq, evident when Mehdi al-Tajer invited us to his sumptuous house for an elaborate dinner. When the pilot, who was to fly us back to Abu Dhabi, suddenly announced that the weather was too inclement for take-off, Mehdi al-Tajer very kindly offered to accommodate us in his house overnight, but Minister Hammadi, with his austere outlook, insisted that we stay at a hotel, which turned out to be very basic and rather sordid. The transformation since that year, 1971, comparing Dubai as it was then with the Dubai of today, seems nothing short of a miracle, sparkling with modern construction, commerce and pleasant amenities.

The year of our 1987 mission, after dealing with the UAE, the OPEC delegation had to fly to Tehran (Iran). With the Iran–Iraq war raging, we flew by private jet from Jeddah to Doha (Qatar) in order to proceed to Tehran. I explained to the OPEC president that I had grave reservations about accompanying them because of the war, especially in view of the fact that the Iranian oil minister had been taken hostage by the Iraqis, as I felt there was a risk that the Iranians could reciprocate with a retaliatory kidnapping. Given my Iraqi nationality, there was a likelihood of my becoming a target, and so I opted instead to return to Vienna, via Jeddah.

My decision gave rise to an awkward episode, which I should preface here with a mention of my dawning comprehension of Arturo Grisanti's antagonism towards me following this very incident. A member of the Venezuelan congress and a lawyer by training, Grisanti had a predilection for cracking malicious jokes, and suddenly began to accuse me of colluding with the Saudis and Kuwaitis to bring oil prices down so as to weaken Iran in its war

with Iraq – as lower prices for Iraq could be compensated by financial aid from other Gulf countries, while Iran did not benefit from
such aid. One day his remarks provoked me into a swift riposte:
'Excellency, this war between Iran and Iraq is not *my* war. I myself
do not believe in it. Besides, I think the problem of prices should
be dealt with on the basis of economics, not politics.' It was while
I was trying to understand his particular acrimony that I suddenly
realised the likely cause was an absurd incident that had blown up
out of nothing, all because of my precautionary decision not to join
the delegation's trip to Tehran back in 1971. It so happened that
Grisanti's wife had also declined that Doha–Tehran route, and it
was decided that she and I would both return to Jeddah in a private jet. While we were airborne I was reading a book about Islamic
military conquests, written by the famous English military commander, Sir John Bagot Glubb, known as 'Glubb Pasha', who in 1931
revolutionised the Arab Legion by creating a formidable Bedouin
force. I was so absorbed reading the book that I became oblivious
to the presence of the Venezuelan minister's wife, who took this as
an affront, as if I had deliberately ignored her. On landing, we were
met by the Venezuelan ambassador, to whom Grisanti's wife even
conveyed a certain displeasure at my inattention, though, of course,
no discourtesy was intended. I simply had no idea that Venezuelan
custom dictated that a man must fuss over a woman even while
travelling on a plane. For evermore my misinterpreted 'snub' was
reflected in the grudge Grisanti bore me, and ultimately even in
his vehement opposition to the extension of my term as Deputy
Secretary General.

Later that year, 1987, we embarked on our next trip which
was to North Africa to visit the OPEC countries of Algeria, Libya,
Nigeria and Gabon. It had long been my dream to meet Gaddafi,
as I was curious to see how this man, with his speech impediment,
had held Libya in his grip of absolute power for over 40 years yet
had eschewed the title of dictator, claiming instead that Libya was
indeed a *jemahria*, which means a country ruled by the mass of people, similar to a popular democracy. In this way nobody could hold
him to account, he evaded responsibility for his country despite
being the sole head of state. When he issued his famous 'Green
Book' it was hailed by the Libyan press as Gaddafi's great work
inspired by living in the desert.

Instead of Gaddafi, it was Libya's 'number two' who met us, Lieutenant Abdul Salam Jaloud, whom I had first met in the spring of 1971, and again later in December 1975, when he boarded our kidnapped aircraft, stepping in to intervene when we were taken hostage by Carlos the Jackal, when Jaloud and Carlos went into the cockpit leaving us passengers with our anxiety (as described in Chapter 7). Now more than 12 years later, Jaloud's manner, though somewhat calmer, still belied an uneasiness. Our quota meeting with him, as with the others, proved fruitless. Jaloud was prepared to discuss anything except quota compliance. Libyan production was actually stagnant at the time.

What struck me on this trip was the sad deterioration of Libya's once beautiful capital, Tripoli. I walked first thing in the morning along the promenade, just as I had in 1971 when in those days the city sparkled with character, and the elegant Italian marble balustrades of the promenade elegantly followed the sweep of the bay. But now, in 1987, I was dismayed by the air of neglect. The once clean pavements were now filthy and full of potholes, the bay had been converted into a port for cargo deliveries, and this marred its coastal beauty, spoiling the view of the sea beyond, which I had previously so admired. They took us to a modern hotel, where we stayed overnight. Its ugliness typified much of the city's new architecture. When I ordered room service, after a long delay a rudely mannered waiter brought in a tray with lukewarm tea and stale biscuits. This small example illustrates the deterioration, compared with 1971 when I stayed in a far less 'grand' hotel (belonging to the old regime) that had an excellent service and was far cleaner. I wondered what on earth the Libyan government had been doing, letting this once resplendent city become so ravaged, with only three million inhabitants and an 'oil revolution' with windfall revenues. Libya's oil revenues prior to Gaddafi's revolution did not exceed $3.8 million in mid-1973, at a time when the per-barrel oil price was $3; but by January 1981 the per-barrel price was $36, and the cumulative gross value of Libya's oil exports between 1970 and 1988 amounted to $170 billion.

The next day we left for Algiers, where we were conducted to President Ben Jedid's office by the Algerian Oil Minister, Belkacem Nabi. The Algerian President was most pleasant and quietly spoken, contrary to the tendency of his countrymen to speak very forcefully and with an overbearing self-assurance, as if Algeria were the centre of the universe. Certainly Algeria had been the focus of world attention when it reputedly sacrificed 'a million martyrs' in a war that shook France's Fourth Republic to its foundations, Algeria finally wresting its independence from the Fifth Republic in 1962. Our quiet, calm meeting with the President could not have been more different from that held with the Libyan Jaloud, who during the entire meeting never once desisted from his tirade condemning Western imperialism. The President did his best to respond positively to the OPEC delegation, though Algeria's official production numbers, as communicated to the OPEC Secretariat, did not match the estimates given in the petroleum press. On this score, there was an understandable confusion over the definition of the quota, as Algerian oil production numbers, before 1980, had included gas liquids which are produced together with crude oil. Algeria was later notified that these gas liquids should be excluded in the assessment of its oil production quota, which ought to be determined exclusively on the basis of crude oil only. Consequently Algeria's official production numbers, as received by the Secretariat, amounted to around 1.1 mbpd in 1979 but only 800 tbpd in 1981. This was also due to the fall in production capacity of that country. The motive behind Algeria's constant pressure to raise the oil price was the country's inability to increase its revenues through production volume.

Next, our OPEC delegation went to Nigeria. On arrival in Lagos we were informed that the President was away, and while Nigeria's Oil Minister, Rilwanu Lukman, joined by other OPEC ministers, attended a military parade in suffocating heat, I remained in my room, which at least had rudimentary air-conditioning and overlooked the parade. Later, our quota-compliance meeting was held with the President, who assured us of Nigeria's commitment, although the numbers published by the petroleum press indicated the contrary. A dinner party was held, which the ministers and I attended and which gave me an opportunity to chat to some Nigerian officers who had returned after working for OPEC.

I had first visited Nigeria back in 1972 with an Iraqi delegation headed by Minister Sa'doun Hammadi, on the occasion of the OPEC Conference of November 1972, held in Lagos, and inaugurated by David Gaoim in his military attire. He had just recently seized power by the usual means, a military coup, to which he later himself fell victim. I had never forgotten that earlier visit, as it was very special, being my first time in black Africa. Nor had I forgotten the suffocating humidity at the airport, being installed in a Mercedes car with no air-conditioning and sitting in it for two and a half hours while hardly moving along the traffic-gridlocked road from the airport to the hotel. Overcome with dizziness and nausea, almost fainting from the airlessness, on arrival at the hotel my priority was to have a shower and sleep, but in this I was thwarted by two burly Nigerians, my 'bodyguard' waiting to accompany me, who then insisted on remaining in my hotel room. One of them asked me what I would like to do now that I was in Lagos. When I expressed an interest in seeing the jungle, their reaction was of surprise, almost shock, as if I had made a gaffe. 'You mean the villages?' one of them asked me, in a polite attempt to help me redeem myself. I replied 'yes,' but was then told that the villages were remote. Having made one faux pas I then probably made another in telling them that in truth I preferred to be left alone to take a shower. After this, I explored in the vicinity of the hotel and found street-merchants selling artefacts, such as wood carvings, also giant python skins that repelled me. In my childhood, I had feared even watching a snake on screen, and my reptilian revulsion even prevented my enjoyment when the Iraqi ambassador later regaled us with horror stories of snake-hunts in Africa's jungle terrain. Accompanied by one of my two Nigerian 'bodyguards' on my walk through the city, I found the relative poverty and squalor of its inhabitants a distressing experience – partly a comparative reaction: judging conditions against those in my own native Iraq, which was still an affluent society at the time of my first trip to Lagos in 1972. (What also shocked me were the swarms of prostitutes and their blatant touting for clients, it being considered normal in Lagos hotels for them to knock at your door offering services. If one declined they often argued, and if you succeeded in ridding yourself of one, another would run after you down the hotel corridor or accost you in the lift.)

While at Lagos airport waiting to board our onward flight to Beirut we had a curious experience in the VIP departure lounge. Wondering what was causing the delay, we asked the Iraqi Ambassador who smiled and explained that one had to negotiate with customs staff who insisted on bribes before they let anyone through. Seeing our surprise, he added that this was very normal, and that we would not be able to achieve anything without bribery. Sure enough, someone then arrived from the Embassy and automatically paid an 'inducement' just so that we could retrieve our luggage. Once aboard our Lebanese Middle East Airlines flight, I felt surge of relief at being free from the ordeal of it all.

Our last African destination that year (1987) was Gabon, a short but very interesting trip. Libreville, the capital, is beautiful, with its long, sandy foreshore, and I felt a keen wish to stay for days to enjoy the beautiful scene. The cleanliness (in marked contrast to Lagos) was remarkable, as was the city's simplicity. My first visit had been over a decade earlier when I attended (as an observer) a meeting of the OPEC Fund for International Development. Also in mid-1975 OPEC had held a Conference in Libreville, when it was decided to accept Gabon's membership. On our last evening (before our flight to Paris), we were involved in a final, very protracted session with Gabon's Undersecretary for Oil, and someone intervened with an announcement that our aircraft was about to depart. At this, Gabon's Undersecretary for Oil boomed: 'Tell the pilot that he must wait until the meeting is over and that the plane cannot follow any schedule without the agreement of the Undersecretary!'

The most intriguing aspect of the 1987 trip was being in the company of President Omar Bongo, a short, jovial man who, with his constant laughter, reminded one of a pantomime figure. On one occasion Bongo sat in a coronation-type chair, higher than the normal level for a chair, so that one could not help but observe his amusing manner. Mr Nangwema, the former Secretary General, sat beside me while interpreting from French into English, and each time he finished a section of translation he took me by the hand and gently asked 'Fadhil, correct me if I am wrong... Is it good?' – and every time I nodded my approval, Omar Bongo shrieked with laughter. When he converted to Islam he had adopted the Islamic name of Omar.

After this final leg of our African schedule, our next trip was to Latin America, stopping first in Venezuela, whose President at the time was Carlos Andrés Pérez. Having made several trips to Caracas, I had been there ten years earlier during Carlos Pérez's previous presidential term (when I met him with Dr Ali Attiga, then Secretary General of OAPEC). According to the Venezuelan constitution, when the presidential term ends, the president cannot renominate himself for the presidency for ten years. It was in the late 1970s when President Pérez bestowed on me the Bolivar decoration for my active participation in OPEC while representing Iraq and presenting the reports of the Economic Commission to the Conference.

The Venezuelan Oil Minister at that time was Valentine Hernandes Acosta, and it is with great respect that I make specific mention of him, as his polite civilized manner, refinement, elegance and stature as an OPEC minister was special. Tragically he died prematurely from a heart attack. Indeed it was most tragic that, soon after his death, his widowed wife with two of their children died in a helicopter crash in Caracas. The last time I had seen Acosta was in Washington when he was the Venezuelan Ambassador and he invited me to his ample residence there. I appeared to be well known in the Venezuelan petroleum community, especially when my book *OPEC and the International Oil Industry: A Changing Structure* was translated into Spanish and met with approval in academic circles.

Later on our OPEC delegation's quota mission trip in 1987, it was the third time of my meeting President Peres, whom I now found much more relaxed. With pride and humour he claimed that Venezuela was the real sponsor of OPEC when it was founded in Baghdad in 1960, and while he conversed congenially with us he spoke of convening an OPEC Summit in Caracas, a plan that in effect encouraged him to co-operate with other OPEC countries concerning the the quota matter. Peres was especially pleasant to me and kind enough to help me in an attempt to acquire a Venezuelan passport in the summer of 1989 when, having finished my services for OPEC, I was experiencing problems with the Iraqi Embassy in Vienna over the renewal of my Iraqi passport, purely because of my decision to stay in Europe and avoid returning to Baghdad.

Next we flew to Quito, Ecuador. I had first visited this beautiful city, with its spectacular views, back in 1974, as head of the Iraqi delegation in my capacity as Undersecretary for the Oil Ministry – my Minister Hammadi having refrained from the trip because of respiratory problems caused by the extreme altitude, Quito being 10,000 feet above sea level. On that earlier 1974 trip we were received with a lot of fanfare and ceremony, Ecuador being on the point of its admission to OPEC as a new member, and each delegation chief was given honorary citizenship. The altitude did cause me a few health problems, and travellers to Quito should be advised to eat lightly, abstain from alcohol and remain longer in bed. We met the President at the Presidential Palace, a military man – prior to Ecuador's becoming a democracy. He was most congenial and gave us an exceptionally warm welcome. A dinner was held for the OPEC delegates, with much pomp and ceremony. After this, during the Conference deliberations, the Kuwaiti Oil Minister, Abdul Rahman-Ateeqi, fainted and was given medicine to help him breathe normally. That same evening a grand dinner was held for the delegations, and someone approached me with my seat number but it was for the wrong table. I noticed the delegation heads, of which I was part, being seated at the head table elsewhere. Irritated by this inappropriate seating error, and feeling tired, I decided to return to the hotel, where after dinner I read, as is my custom before falling asleep. Suddenly I had difficulty breathing. I called the hotel doctor who arrived with an electro-cardiogram. In his opinion it was a heart attack and I was rushed off to the hospital's intensive care unit, where the care given was exceptional. I had a strange presentiment that I would die in this land so far from my family and country, and was so grateful for (and shall never forget) the kindness of an Australian nurse, who was a deeply religious devotee of the Roman Catholic Church. She came every day to read to me from the Bible, in particular the Gospel according to St John, which I found both moving and comforting. She gave me a Spanish–English copy of the Bible, which I still have. I asked her what had brought her all this way from Australia. She replied: 'One day I opened the Old Testament and it fell open on the page where Abraham is told by God to leave his country, and that is what I did.'

After several blood tests and X-rays, a cardiologist told me that he disagreed with the diagnosis and that my breathing difficulty was not heart failure but a diaphragm problem. Kept in hospital for several days, I was very touched by the kind visit of a delegation from the Lebanese Arab community, bearing flowers and good wishes.

Returning to our 1987 quota-mission trip to Quito, our OPEC Ministerial delegation was accompanied by the Ecuadorian Oil Minister, Dr Santos, a very affable, refined person, who was also our Spanish-English interpreter. I knew him well from his former position as head of OPEC's Legal Department, and we had a good working relationship. We met the President of the Republic of Ecuador, after whose welcoming words Lukman began to explain the nature of our Ministerial Delegation's mission, which was to persuade all member countries to abide by their quotas. According to available information, Lukman said that Ecuador was one of those OPEC members that needed to cut production to comply with its quota. At these words the President, sitting at his table, grew furious: 'What are you saying? You want me to reduce Ecuador's oil production and lose my job as President of the Republic? Ecuador is a poor country with enormous economic problems. If you want to keep the prices high by restricting production in line with the quota system, you ought to go to the big rich producers of the Gulf, with their enormous financial capability; whereas we in Ecuador do not have enough money to meet the country's basic requirements. This must be some kind of joke.' Poor Minister Santos was visibly mortified having to translate word for word his President's angry outburst.

When this fruitless meeting was over, after a light lunch, we flew back to Venezuela, where we stayed two nights in Caracas before returning to Europe. Venezuela's Oil Minister Grisanti organised a dinner in the garden of the building where he had an apartment, which turned out to be too small for our number. This was a welcome sign of how this man was completely 'uncorrupted', and it impressed me, accustomed as I was to Venezuelan politicians living in the lap of luxury. When I saw Grisanti's flat, I found it most pleasant but refreshingly simple without any suggestion of an over-indulgent, lavish lifestyle. However, during the dinner Grisanti's wife could not conceal her continued irritation with me over my earlier 'neglect' when engrossed in reading on the flight to Vienna.

The final phase of our OPEC odyssey was Indonesia, where, after meeting President Suharto, we were conducted by the Oil Minister, Dr Subroto, to Bali to spend a day in that stunning sea-side city (which I knew well, as an OPEC Conference was held there back in the 1970s, as described in Chapter 2). Indonesian oil has a problem in being relatively limited and given the country's demographic density its enormously high local consumption comes at the expense of export volume. The consequent decline in exports to some extent justified Indonesia's non-compliance with the quota system, although, in reality, its limited production was of no great concern, as Indonesian oil is light and sulphur-free, qualities that always guarantee a market, especially given its geographical proximity to Japan, China, India and Australasia. Indonesia later became a net importer of oil and, as a consequence, left OPEC.

Regrettably, for all the expense involved on the 1987 'quota mission', the OPEC delegation returned absolutely empty-handed. Notwithstanding the marvel of travelling across the globe, meeting heads of state at significant events, sampling at first hand intriguingly different cultures and witnessing various phases of each country's development, that it would all end up as a 'mission impossible' was a foregone conclusion before we even embarked on the great expedition. Here was an example of OPEC's extravagance.

14

Dispelling myths about OPEC

Since its inception in 1960, and above all ever since the price shocks of the 1970s, OPEC has been mythologised by the media. It has been frequently, if inaccurately, depicted as an oil cartel that periodically holds the world economy to ransom; while another myth portrays OPEC as a lionised 'Third World power' that has undermined the hegemony of the West, from whose domination it has, at the very least, wrested its economic rights.

Of these myths, the one most commonly disseminated by the media, especially in the United States, is that OPEC is an oil cartel. Press reports invariably qualify any reference to the organisation with the phrase 'OPEC, the oil cartel...'.

In 1973, when OPEC countries assumed full control over the pricing of their oil (which, until 1973, was the domain of the concession holders), OPEC held a very dominant position. With over three-quarters of the world's oil reserves, in 1975 OPEC accounted for more than 87 per cent of world trade in crude oil, and its share of world oil supplies outside the US and FSU exceeded 70 per cent.

With the organisation flourishing in such favourable conditions, OPEC was well placed to have become an oil cartel – had it wanted to perform economically as one. The reality is, though, that OPEC has always conducted its affairs in a manner contrary to the modus operandi of cartelization, a precondition for which is the retention of a dominant share in the market so as to control trade and pricing. A cartel is typically hyper-attentive to its group's ability to secure continued growth in its market share, and a cartel's pricing policies first and foremost aim at *discouraging* competitors from taking a larger share in the market. OPEC, on the other hand, has systematically *encouraged* non-OPEC oil competitors to make inroads into the market at its own expense. Hence (as shown in Chapter 10) the 'new oil' boom from the 1970s onwards was exemplified by non-OPEC world oil production (excluding US and the FSU) jumping from 8.2 mbpd in 1975 to 17.1 mbpd in 1985 and, by 2005, to 26.3 mbpd.

In 1979 OPEC produced 31 mbpd, but because of its production and pricing policies, its production fell, by 1985, to around 15.5 mbpd. Although it has increased since then, OPEC's production now totals 3 mbpd less than its total in 1979, over 30 years ago. Its share in the non-FSU world market fell from 62 per cent in 1979 to 37 per cent in 1985. As we know, OPEC's price shocks forced consumers to reduce their oil dependence and in particular OPEC dependence, and the result was that world dependence on OPEC oil dwindled in favour of both non-OPEC oil and alternative energy sources (at that time primarily natural gas and nuclear energy). In this way, OPEC's share in the world's primary energy declined from 27 per cent in 1973 to 11 per cent in 1984, increasing to 16 per cent in 2005. Its own self-defeating policies led to this heavy loss in its share of world crude oil trade, which by 2003 had fallen to 40 per cent.

This demonstrates the way OPEC's production 'realities', like its pricing strategies, run counter to the basic operative rules of a cartel. Although cartel behaviour would typically give some priority to maximising profits through high prices, what takes precedence above all is ensuring that demand for its commodity does not fall below a certain level. A cartel would permit price rises as long as they had no negative impact on its dominant market share. If there is any risk of a higher price diminishing its market share, the 'cartel' cuts the price to discourage investment elsewhere. All this runs counter to OPEC's strategies.

Here one can note the irony of OPEC's production and pricing policies with their effect of practically 'inaugurating' the expansion of rival producers' new oil. Its policies fostered and promoted this rapidly expanding non-OPEC oil, almost as if OPEC's intention was to have its own world market share replaced by its rivals – such was its lack of concern.

Another cartel feature evidently lacking is OPEC's neglect to plan investment and production capacity in tandem with demand. Instead, its member countries plan investment and capacity to suit their own short-term financial requirements. I have described in the earlier chapters how the 'Seven Sisters' were able to meet sudden increases in oil demand during the concession era. With their regulatory control of the industry and inter-company exchanges, this group indeed exemplified facets of cartel conduct that were instrumental in achieving their skilled vertical and horizontal integration. As pointed out in Chapter 2, it was this regulatory integration that averted an oil crisis in 1951, when Mosaddegh's nationalisation measure caused a sudden interruption of Iran's oil supplies. The world oil market remained unaffected only because the various concession holders were able to fill the supply gap by increasing production from other areas, and this forestalled any oil crisis.

Regardless of their conflicting interests, the concession holders of the Seven Sisters demonstrated that where a difference arose – as occurred over crude requirements for BP and Esso, on the one hand, and Shell and CFP, on the other – they were able to smooth things over by involving inter-company exchanges.

This flexibility does not exist among OPEC's NOCs, which do not collectively consider production in relation to demand for their oil, and among whom conflicting interests are very marked.

Also, contrary to cartel behaviour, they lack co-ordination in any endeavour to formulate a joint vision of long-term planning of what is to be done in relation to market requirements. As has been noted previously, all endeavours to formulate a long-term strategy have failed. The only factor that unites OPEC's member countries with their diverse interests is their one common goal of an immediate short-term maximization of revenue.

Bearing all this in mind, evidently the notion that OPEC operates as a cartel needs to be consigned to the realm of myth. Ever since OPEC assumed full control of pricing its oil, its concerns have always contradicted those of any cartel model. Its pricing strategy is so preoccupied with national short-term financial needs, that a prominent representative of one of its member countries once commented to me that 'OPEC has become a prisoner of its member countries' budgets'.

Another non-cartel feature of OPEC is the geopolitical focus that often propels its actions. We have seen how oil prices have surged dramatically during geopolitical conflicts and regional wars. A cartel, by contrast, bases its policy decisions on commercial criteria alone. For instance, if cartel producers ever perceive that their market share looks shaky and risks benefitting competitors, they automatically adjust the commodity price downward to maintain their economic advantage. For this reason, strong demand is a *sine qua non* for a cartel to sustain its hegemony, as it is demand alone that enables it to control prices to its advantage. OPEC, by contrast, seeks price advantage always at the expense of market share, preferring instead to be the residual supplier, the supplier of last resort.

Composed as it is of countries with heterogeneous, often conflicting, economic and political interests, OPEC's ministerial representatives are politically driven, rather than setting socio-economic priorities. This is why OPEC collectively lacks a vision of what their long-term priorities ought to be, and of what the longer-term consequences of its pricing and production policies will be. I described earlier how OPEC's LTSC was doomed because OPEC ministers are in essence *politicians*, whose objectives (by definition) are fixed on gaining short-term results. When I asked a prominent member of OPEC about the effect of high prices on long-term demand for OPEC oil, he replied, 'In the long term I will not be here!' (rather reminding me of John Maynard Keynes's famous quip 'In the long run, we are all dead!').

The oil price escalations of 2005, 2006, 2007 and 2008 reflected the market's recognition of the fact that, in the face of a rampantly growing global oil demand, especially from Asia and in particular China, OPEC countries continued to neglect to invest part of their massive oil revenues in the expansion of production capacity. This was aggravated by an inadequate *light*-crude capacity among OPEC producers. With the exception of Saudi Arabia, OPEC has done nothing to reinvest its colossal oil revenues in drilling activities, which have remained stagnant if not in perpetual decline, ever since OPEC first took over the industry from the oil companies in 1973.

The situation is not helped by state ownership, the laggard approach of which gives no incentive for managing the oil industry on a commercial basis. Higher oil prices make it easy for any OPEC government's growing budgets but the failure to apprehend long-term effects of sustained high oil prices will jeopardise not only the world economy but OPEC's own future interests.

Notwithstanding this cautionary note, the old myth that OPEC is an inimical 'Third World' economic power has to be dispelled by the knowledge that it has never fundamentally imperilled Western interests. It was never established with the purpose of 'confronting' the oil companies but instead it set up a marriage of convenience between the two. We have already seen this (in Chapter 2) in the way that OPEC's formation, with its initial taxation and pricing strategies, became indispensable in avoiding unrestrained market chaos, and was a *sine qua non* for protecting the revenues of the oil-producing countries while consolidating the position of the major oil companies, at a time when a newly emerging free market threatened to undermine their oligopolistic status and market domination.

What made matters worse for the oil majors by the late 1950s was the Soviet Union's access to the new free market, offering crude oil exports at discounts. Until the mid-1950s, a free world oil market did not exist (beyond selling off surplus crude to companies with a crude deficit, as inter-company exchanges). But by the late 1950s independent oil companies were acquiring crude oil for oil refineries that needed it, which had led to a small but burgeoning free market. At the same time, new producing areas offered investment opportunities for independent oil companies on financial terms different from those prevailing in the Gulf. It was the new era of discounts, and this is what pushed Esso in 1959 to cut the posted price. It was the additional price cut the following year, in 1960, that triggered the formation of OPEC, which put an end to price cuts and brought countries into line with the financial system operating in the Gulf by using the posted price as a reference for taxation – instead of a realised market price as in the case of Indonesia, Algeria and, later, in Libya. Again, Chapter 2 explains in more detail how OPEC not only helped prevent the erosion of the major oil companies' market share (threatened by the emergence of new independent sellers, including the Soviet Union), but also in part regained for them their share losses.

In other words, OPEC's very existence reinforced the strength and profitability of the major oil companies in the 1960s, by reversing the trend of declining shares in both the upstream phase (crude oil production) and downstream phase (refining and distribution). Subsequent developments, beginning – as we have seen – in Libya with Gaddafi, led to an upward adjustment of the price and an increase in taxation from 50 per cent of the posted price to 55 per cent. This led to the beginning of an era of higher oil prices, which oil markets generally welcomed, and which saw the IOCs thrive. The very high cost of oil production in the USA, especially in the lower 48 states, could not continue with a low-price regime set against such high costs. In the early 1970s, oil companies began to intensify investments in expensive oil exploration outside the Middle East Gulf. In October 1970, BP's 'Forties' oil field was discovered in the North Sea, but before this high-cost venture came on stream in 1976, BP's escalating costs had turned out to be 2.5 times greater than originally estimated; and, contrary to the usual oil company practice of financing developments internally, BP had been forced into heavy borrowing.

In this way, despite its negative effects on the world economy, the price shock of 1973 helped the oil companies invest successfully in high-cost areas, with the object of diversifying oil supply sources and avoiding over-dependence on Gulf oil. This diversification was driven by the state involvement and 'oil nationalism' gaining ground in the producing countries. As mentioned earlier, OPEC's 1968 Resolution 90, the Declaratory Statement on Oil Policies in Member Countries, heralded the new phase of state involvement in exploration and development, independent of the oil companies; a trend that Iraq pioneered by nationalising the IPC in June 1972, following which the oil companies demonstrated their readiness to withdraw from the concession system and come to an amicable agreement with the Gulf countries.

The story of the nationalisation of Iraqi oil (told in Chapter 4) is significant. When the Iraqi government demanded higher production, the manner of the companies' representatives became unyielding, in such a way as to steer Saddam into nationalisation, as if they were tacitly behind a move that was avoidable had they simply conceded to the Iraqi government's request to increase production.

This transformation of the oil industry was instrumental in justifying higher prices, seen as essential in the light of growing oil demand and OPEC's lack of investment in additional capacity to meet it. Oil investments in Alaska, the North Sea, the Caspian Sea would never have come on stream without high prices. These new high-cost areas helped divert oil investments away from the Middle East. Fulfilment of this quest was already evident when OPEC tried, in early October 1973, to re-open negotiations on the former Tehran agreement of 1971, and the oil companies were adamant in their stand-off, refusing to renegotiate. I have described how George Piercy, President of Exxon (who at the time headed the companies' negotiating team), even pushed OPEC into taking its momentous, unilateral decision to reprice oil in October 1973. Had they wished to, the oil companies could, typically, have presented a counter-proposal to OPEC asking for an increase of 70 per cent. Instead, on 12 October 1973, in Vienna, they gave OPEC carte blanche to go ahead with its unilateral decision to 'fix' and substantially increase the oil price.

Then came the Kuwaiti meeting of 16 October 1973, followed by the Tehran meeting of December 1973, memorable for the Iranian Shah's zeal in raising the price from $5.40 to $11.50 per barrel. His minister, Amouzegar, in a bid for maximum prices, now made his extraordinary volte-face from his recent position.[1] Sheikh Yamani revealed (in several speeches) that when King Faisal of Saudi Arabia sent him (Yamani) as an envoy to the Shah of Iran to warn against such a hefty increase in the oil price, the Shah had asked why he was so bothered, given that the Americans were all for it – and that if Yamani wanted to verify this he should 'go and meet Henry Kissinger'. As mentioned in Chapter 5 (p.114) possible US complicity with the Shah over higher prices was reflected in American oil interests, about which oil expert, James Akins, then head of Oil Affairs in the US State Department, wrote revealingly in 'The Oil Crisis: This Time the Wolf is Here'.[2] Akins was reported as having emphasized the need for certain price targets: first $5, then $7 per barrel, in the interests of stimulating oil supplies from sources other than the Middle East.

What further supports the hypothesis that Western oil interests, for these reasons, favoured higher oil prices is a book entitled *A Century of War* by William Engdahl (1992),[3] in which we are told that the first price shock of 1973 was encouraged by the big oil companies and financial establishments. In his Chapter 'Running the World Economy in Reverse: Who Really Made the 1970s Oil Shocks?', Engdahl recounts how at a secret conference, held in the summer of 1972 at a Swedish resort, attended by representatives of major oil companies, banks and certain prominent politicians such as Henry Kissinger, a paper was presented by Walter Levy, a prominent oil economist, recommending an increase of 400 per cent in OPEC's oil revenues. This could not be achieved without quadrupling the oil price.

His argument behind this was that the American economy was passing through a critical phase after President Nixon's decision to de-link the value of the dollar to gold. As discussed in Chapter 3 (p.66), the 1944 Bretton Woods Agreement established a system of fixed rates to peg the major currencies to the US dollar, with the latter being linked to gold on the basis of $4 per ounce of pure gold. The dollar value, based on this agreement, was rapidly deteriorating, causing the US government to undertake two devaluations of the dollar. With this, there was a massive outflow of US dollars to Europe and the creation of Eurodollars.

In other words, the 1973 oil price shock, which increased OPEC's oil revenues by 400 per cent, served two purposes: (1) to create a massive increase in global demand for dollars, as oil prices were denominated in dollars; (2) more significantly, and as Kissinger allegedly pointed out, the sharp increase in OPEC producers' revenues would ultimately recycle oil money back to the West in the form of its export volumes: increased demand for imports of merchandise from the United States would stimulate the US economy and help the dollar. At the same time, the vast profits achieved by the oil companies from high oil prices in turn benefitted Western financial markets, with equities bolstered by the oil sector's surging profits.

These various events contest the notion that OPEC confronts the West as a Third World economic power. Already we have seen how, when the OPEC quota system collapsed in 1986, the ensuing de facto price war led the USA to intervene in the person of George Bush Senior, the then US Vice President, in order to protect the interests of American oil-producing states, for whom, unable to live with low prices, OPEC's quota system had been indispensable in securing a minimum price of $18 per barrel. As discussed earlier, the oil price collapse of 1986 was disastrous for the US oil industry and economy, and specifically for the financial sector of Texas.

As the OPEC countries, with their larger reserves, became keen to impede the rapid growth in the market share of non-OPEC oil, Sheikh Yamani tried to adopt an independent policy for Saudi Arabia, but was thwarted by American and British oil interests. From an objective and economic viewpoint, countries like Saudi

Arabia, with the world's largest reserves and the advantage of low production costs, are best placed, competitively speaking, to maximise revenues by achieving a far greater export volume, as opposed to seeking a high per-barrel income from the excessive prices achieved by curtailed production. Logically they would normally take steps to prevent higher-cost producers from acquiring an increased market share at their expense. In this respect, as mentioned earlier, history will record Sheikh Yamani's efforts to define Saudi Arabia's long-term economic interests, independently of the West, a goal that politics prevented his accomplishing.

At the time of the Asian financial crisis, in 1998 oil prices plummeted to less than $10 per barrel as a result of OPEC's decision (in Jakarta in 1997) to raise its production quotas by 10 per cent, inadvertently just when the stock build-up from weak oil demand was at a high level. This situation was aggravated by Venezuela's increase in production, far beyond its quota. It was Saudi Arabia that took the initiative in proposing that OPEC redress the situation with a quota cut. Then OPEC found itself at an impasse: it had based its earlier quota-cut decision on its member countries' *actual* higher production levels as reported in the specialised petroleum press. It emerged, for example, that there was a difference of 300,000 barrels between Iran's *reported* production and the so-called 'official' numbers communicated to the OPEC Secretariat.

During this period, in the late 1990s, everyone imagined that prices would continue to be weak, but one day an executive from an American financial establishment telephoned me from New York to say that there would soon be an agreement within OPEC to lift the price. When I queried his surmise his reply was that, given that larger revenues for OPEC countries encourage imports and that higher prices stimulate trade generally, an accord was about to be struck to satisfy Iran by reducing the production level of certain member countries, in particular Saudi Arabia. This compromise with Iran shows how, at a time when oil prices were extremely weak, higher prices were pursued for the sake of the oil industry and financial markets, where it was quite widely held that OPEC had become a channel through which to transfer wealth from the industrialised countries.

This point also illustrates how OPEC has never been entirely free to pursue its own long-term interests (if it ever chose to). In

1998, the then US Energy Secretary, Bill Richardson, made a tour of the Gulf states, during which he succeeded in striking up a deal to reverse upwards the then low-price trend, in order to conform with investment needs for high-cost American oil production.

OPEC pricing and production policies certainly aided the IEA with its aim to reduce dependence on OPEC oil. At this juncture it is interesting to note a seminar, to which I was invited in early 1982, organised at the John Hopkins Bologna Center in Italy, and at which there was a German economist, Dieter Schmidt, at the time attached to the IEA. In my paper, I reflected that OPEC's pricing strategies had encouraged conservationist policies among the consumer countries. My paper was edited by Professor Wilfrid L. Kohl,[4] and after I had finished my presentation, Dieter Schmidt commented that he was indeed puzzled to see OPEC policies in harmony with the conservationist policies of the consumers. His observation reflected the truth. The IEA had been founded under the guidance of Henry Kissinger, who for political reasons was resolute in his determination to reduce energy dependence on the Gulf. It was rumoured that he believed that the industrialised oil-consuming countries must have higher oil prices and that if OPEC ever failed to maintain a high price level (in the event of world market prices falling) high excise duties should be imposed on imported oil to sustain high prices in consuming countries.

15

Iraq's oil politics after Saddam

In the early days of the invasion of Iraq in March 2003 (before the subsequent fall of Baghdad in April that year) a meeting was held in Washington, sponsored by the US State Department, to discuss policy options for Iraq's oil industry following the fall of Saddam Hussein's regime. I was invited to that meeting along with other oil experts as well as engineers from Iraq, and also non-Iraqi oil experts such as Robert Ebel of the Center for Strategic and International Studies (CSIS) based in Washington.

At the meeting, which was moderated by Tom Warrick of the US State Department, I was quite outspoken about the necessity for IOCs to invest in Iraq and be provided with enough incentive to do so – on the basis that Iraq, following two devastating wars, had become far too impoverished for any degree of self-financing to undertake the huge investments needed to resuscitate its oil industry. Not only has it to regain its pre-Iran war (1980) production level of 4 mbpd but it also has to develop several giant oil fields discovered in the 1970s, development of which was prevented by the UN sanctions, imposed in 1990 after Saddam's invasion of Kuwait and not lifted until mid-April 2003 following the coalition invasion. Knowing the colossal capital outlay required, I was realistic in stressing the importance of increasing the inflow of foreign capital into Iraq by means of massive investments in its oil industry, commensurate with the country's gigantic oil potential. My position was that only a massive inflow of capital could reconstruct the destroyed infrastructure of Iraq's oil industry and thus rescue the economy from the impoverishment into which it had sunk. As oil is Iraq's only source of foreign earnings, a rapid increase in exports must remain a priority (with an immediate aim of restoring the oilfields' capacity to a 4 mbpd level).

Tom Warrick showed interest in my interventions and suggested that I might be interested in involving myself with formulating oil policies for the post-Saddam Iraqi government. Later the US State Department organised a meeting with Dr Condaleezza Rice, at that time the National Security Advisor. When I met this distinguished lady she expressed the opinion of the US government that my vast experience in oil, especially Iraqi oil, would benefit a post-Saddam Iraqi government. I thanked her, and in the politest way possible explained that, while I could express a willingness to be involved in an advisory way, I would have to refrain from involvement in any political capacity, such as accepting any official status in the new Iraqi government. The reason for my position was that I had no wish to take any part in a post-Saddam coalition-backed Iraqi government.

With my awareness of Iraq's highly complex politics and my observations of the political activities of Iraqi opposition groups that were now co-operating with the USA, I anticipated a series of political problems that Iraqis would have to face after the deposition of Saddam, notably their sectarian and ethnic divisions. My instinct was to remain apolitical and keep a distance from a political process that I feared could lead to social conflict and chaos.

Despite my clearly defined non-political position, one or two misinformed observers at the Washington meeting imputed to me a policy favouring the 'control' of Iraq's oil by Western oil companies. This puzzling and carelessly misjudged description became more serious in March 2005 with a prominent BBC Newsnight reporter alleging that I had given 'the green light in a secret meeting in London' for the 'sell-off' of Iraq's oil to foreign oil companies. This flagrant distortion of facts (which to this day remains a slanderous irritant on the Newsnight website and linked websites) was attributed to Mr Robert Ebel of the CSIS, based in Washington DC; yet when I later spoke to Ebel he denied all knowledge of ever attributing this stance to me. Such a notion was absurd. I was in no position to give any 'green light' and the very idea of Iraq being robbed of its oil wealth would be anathema to me, an unthinkable outrage redolent of the old concession era or a bygone era of nineteenth-century-style colonial plunder.

Later, in 2008, a national newspaper, The *Guardian*, took up exactly the same story in a report (13 October), corrected by me in a subsequent edition of that newspaper (24 October), two of its journalists having sourced their suppositions from the same websites. The *Guardian* also erroneously claimed that Iraq was about to hand over its oil reserves to multinational oil corporations. This complete 'myth' distorted the truth behind the Iraqi government's negotiations with the IOCs, falsely alleging that they constituted 'the biggest sale of oil assets ever ... 40 billion barrels of recoverable reserves up for offer in London' (13 October). Iraq's reserves are certainly not for sale. The two *Guardian* reporters responsible for this article were confused by the whole nature of 'risk service agreements', which do not give companies any ownership of Iraq's oil reserves. Genuine confusion may have arisen in the press because of the complicated way in which the oil companies were dealt with by the Iraqi Oil Ministry, which I shall discuss later in this chapter.

When the coalition forces invaded Iraq in March 2003, there was much debate and censure concerning motives, the most popular assertion being that the USA, which played a central strategic role throughout, sought to boost market supplies by ensuring that Iraq's oil was developed as rapidly as possible. But this has not happened, and so the accusation has never been vindicated.

There is no doubt that, for reasons related only to security of supplies, the USA would have welcomed the chance to have some influence on oil production in the Gulf region, but this does not necessarily mean that it invaded Iraq for the purpose of controlling Iraq's oil. Had the USA been seriously interested in Iraqi oil, the Bush administration could have achieved control simply by appointing key qualified experts to help run the ministry in order to boost the country's oil production, and yet it refrained from any interference.

Far from demonstrating that the US's focus of concern was primarily on Iraq's oil, on the contrary, it is now questionable whether there was any serious desire to increase substantially Iraq's oil output, given the glut that would impact on the market were Iraqi production capacity significantly expanded and speeded up. This would serve only to depress oil prices, which would be anathema for the IOCs and for most non-OPEC producers like the USA, who need high prices to sustain their high-cost oil production. Combined with weak oil-demand trends (from the last quarter of 2008 through 2009 and 2010) the case for substantial additional oil output from

Iraq (which OPEC cannot absorb without a further plunge in oil prices) would prove incompatible with the USA's avowed ambition of reducing dependence on imported oil from the Middle East Gulf, because the alternative of high-cost non-OPEC oil would prove too exorbitant to develop in the face of the sharp downward pressure on prices that an inevitable glut would exert if copious additional capacity were introduced from Iraq.

Again, this important point leads one to question the real strategic objective behind the 2003 invasion and to doubt that it was related to oil as much as to geopolitical strategy, given that military bases have been established by the USA in southern Iraq, similar to those in other Gulf countries. In this respect, arguments have often revolved round the powerful influence of the Neo-Conservative faction within the George W. Bush administration, with its determination to reshape the Middle East. With the complexity of the issues at stake, it is difficult to pin down precisely this latter motivation as the ultimate spur for invading Iraq, but no doubt history will, in time, judge.

Meanwhile, this view of the Bush administration's remapping mission in the Middle East evidently shows signs of being substantiated by information recently declassified following a freedom of information request. Reported in the press[1] in early July 2009, FBI accounts give credence to 'the view held by many regional experts that Saddam's weapons bluff was aimed not at the West but at his old enemy Iran'. While Saddam was awaiting his execution, the FBI held 20 formal interrogations and five 'conversational' interviews with him, during which he admitted that he had allowed the world to suspect that he was concealing weapons of mass destruction because he was anxious that Iran should not perceive Iraq as militarily weak. He also claimed his intention was to negotiate a security agreement with the USA to protect Iraq from the regional threat that Iran presented, doubtless an intention that he realised would cut no ice with a hostile Bush Administration that saw in Saddam a convenient expedient for the invasion. These revelations will no doubt prove critical when history reassesses the developments that seemed to propel the US-led invasion, given that the pretext for war arose with the Bush Administration's insistence that Saddam still possessed weapons of mass destruction and posed a real threat to international security.

In reality, the main menace from Saddam was that he endangered his own people. Thirty years of his tyrannical dictatorship had left Iraq like a wasteland. With his misconceived wars and arrant dishonesty towards the UN and its weapons inspectors, he inflicted his country with 13 years of UN sanctions, which left its economy in ruins, reduced from its relative wealth in 1980, with a per capita income of over USD$4,000,[2] to the rank of an impoverished country, with an abysmal 12 per cent of its 1980 level. The root of Iraq's dire economic plight lies in the sheer magnitude of its lost oil exports after the long period of UN sanctions, all on top of earlier export losses incurred by Saddam's eight-year war with Iran. By 2003, in just 23 years (from 1980 until the fall of the Saddam regime) Iraq's cumulative production losses amounted to over 19.4 bn/B: a volume calculated as the difference between Iraq's actual cumulative oil output compared with what it would have been assuming it had continued at its previous rate of 14.5 per cent of OPEC's total production (prior to the 1980–88 war with Iran).

Iraq's reconstruction and recovery from such enormous setbacks can be achieved only by rapid investment in new oil production and export capacity. This needs to be discussed in the context of OPEC and its quota system, bearing in mind that Iraqi oil production has remained outside the system ever since Saddam's invasion of Kuwait in August 1990 (when UN Sanctions were imposed).

To give the reader a clearer understanding of the importance of regenerating Iraq's damaged economy by means of increasing its oil production and export capacity: at the outbreak of the Iraq–Iran war, in September 1980, Iraq's oil production stood at 3.9 mbpd; and prior to that war Iraq had avowed a target of 5 mbpd, with the help of foreign oil companies on the basis of a 'buy-back' contract. But with the war raging, Iraq's oil exports then collapsed from 3.5 mbpd to only 750 tbpd, the reason for this being the destruction of the two key deepwater terminals: the Khor al-Amaya and the al-Bakr (after the fall of Saddam's regime, the latter terminal was renamed the 'al-Basra'). At the same time, the pipeline conducting Iraqi oil to the Eastern Mediterranean via Syria was blocked by Syria's former President Assad, who supported Iran throughout the war. All that was left for Iraq was the Turkish pipeline with its limited 750 tbpd capacity. Iraq later succeeded in doubling the Turkish pipeline's capacity while at the same time striking a deal with Saudi Arabia to have a pipeline linked with the Saudi system conducting oil to the Red Sea, so that by the end of the Iraq–Iran war Iraqi production was almost 3.5 mbpd.

Yet less than three years later Iraq's production dwindled drastically during heavy bombardment in the Gulf War of March and April 1991, provoked by Saddam's invasion of Kuwait and his defiance in the face of international mediation insisting on his withdrawal from this oil-producing neighbour. Facing a coalition composed of half a million troops from 27 countries, Iraq suffered heavy bombardment of its infrastructure and oil sector, with the result that its oil production fell from over 3.5 mbpd to 2.8 mbpd. Iraq was in fact producing far beyond the 'healthy' levels of 'sound production practices' and was also pumping surplus fuel oil from refineries, consequently damaging high-quality Kirkuk oil.

For the sake of economic recovery, increasing Iraq's oil production capacity commensurate with its oil potential must remain a priority; and for this it needs help in the form of adequate investment – a huge and rapid injection of the capital that can be provided by foreign oil companies to revitalise the country's oil industry – without, of course, *over*-investing in capacity expansion (a new complication that will be discussed further on in this chapter).

During the Saddam era, in 1995 the Iraqi Oil Ministry organised an international seminar, to which many in the oil industry outside Iraq were invited, and at which the Ministry presented a paper on its programme for increasing production to over 6 mbpd: a plan devised for raising production to over 4 mbpd from oil-producing fields and a remaining 2 mbpd capacity the development of four oil fields with reserves that had been discovered but not developed – the Majnoon, West Qurna, Halfaya and Nahar Umer. For developing these four oil fields the Saddam government envisaged co-operating with certain oil companies on the basis of a Production Sharing Agreement (PSA), a formula for foreign investment to provide the requisite capital for developing the fields, with the proviso that once each field commenced production the investor would have the right to recover his own expenditure by lifting crude in remuneration of costs (hence the term 'cost oil'), relative to the world market price. With the PSA formula, a company's extraction of this remunerative 'cost oil' would be subject to a ceiling of 40 per cent.

This PSA formula would also give the investor the right to acquire 'profit oil' in the form of 'booking reserves', which means obtaining guaranteed access (for the duration of the contract) to a certain percentage of the total production. The amount would be conditional on the fair and reasonable remuneration of capital investment and would depend on the current world market oil price. At the time when Lukoil and China National Oil Corporation (CNOC) signed a PSA contract agreement it was intended that the profit oil of 0.6 mbpd from West Qurna would not exceed 10 per cent. Negotiations with the two French companies, Total and Elf, before they merged, culminated with an agreement to develop two oil fields, the Majnoon and the Nahur Umr, with a total capacity of 1.1 mbpd. However, the imposition of UN sanctions in August 1990 intervened and this agreement with the French companies was not signed. The Ministry's report at the time gave details of each field, indicating that Iraq's capacity could exceed 6 mbpd in a matter of eight years.

After the fall of Saddam's regime in April 2003, Iraq's oil industry continued to suffer bombardment damage from sabotage and widespread looting, with a consequent loss in production capacity. The pipeline taking oil from the northern oil fields was constantly sabotaged by the anti-coalition insurgent forces. Basra oil production fell with the result that Iraq's overall production plummetted to only 2.5 mbpd, with exports of only around 1.5 mbpd, and this production level was achieved only thanks to the abatement of sabotage in the northern oil fields.

In the aftermath of the invasion there was a prolonged period during which the post-Saddam government professed no clear policy objectives for Iraq's oil, nor was there any unanimity, but at least there was a strong consensus of opinion that something had to be done to develop rapidly the country's huge oil potential to salvage it from the deterioration that had set in after Saddam's wars with Iran, Kuwait and the 13 years of UN sanctions. Iraq's severely dwindled oil production capacity was grave from the standpoint of its lost market share, and naturally the most immediate challenge to overcome was the task of addressing the issue of expanding that capacity (initially with the aim of developing a 4 mbpd capacity from the discovered oil fields). Yet when the Oil Ministry confronted this major task, it faced the greatest hurdle of all with its endeavours to promulgate a new Petroleum and Gas Law, a draft of which it first drew up in June 2006. Involving a prolonged central Parliamentary debate, the drafting of this crucial Law was impeded by the irreconcilable divergence of opinion that it aroused over Iraqi oil policy.

As a major component of the draft Oil and Gas Law involves opening the industry up to the IOCs (without whose capital investment, technology and managerial skills, Iraq would be unable to achieve its objectives), fierce political opposition ensued from various parliamentary groups who feared that negotiations with foreign investors (on the basis of the Saddam regime's former PSA model) could result in a reversion to the spectre of the former oil companies, tainted by the old concession system of the colonial past.

At first this vociferous opposition led the Ministry of Oil to negotiate contracts for 20-year periods with certain major oil companies. Protracted negotiations, conducted on the basis of first one formula and then another, meant that during an intervening period of six years (April 2003 until late 2009) political discord, combined with the Ministry's inertia, held up the investment plans, whether for increasing Iraq's production capacity by developing the new giant oil fields discovered in the 1970s or rehabilitating existing producing oilfields.

In the beginning the Oil Ministry was concerned primarily with two immediate issues.

First, the procedure for fields that are already producing oil. Here the Ministry initially would have been best advised to sign contracts immediately with internationally known oil service companies (like Haliburton and Schlumberger) simply to tackle the work required for increasing production capacity, which had declined for the reasons mentioned earlier. But instead, and much later, the Ministry negotiated with IOCs for a 20-year period, a form of contract unknown in the oil industry.

The second issue related to the discovered but undeveloped oil areas. For these, the Ministry, in an attempt to avoid the controversial PSA model, at first negotiated complicated long-term 'service contracts'. Yet, in the final analysis, these rounds of negotiations could weaken the role of the INOC and government participation.

The difficulty is that the Ministry entered into these negotiations involving a multitude of contracts and oil fields without adequate technical, financial or administrative expertise for supervising them. Here it should be remembered that during the Saddam regime, especially after two destructive wars, Iraq had suffered a massive brain haemorrhage of oil experts. After the coalition invasion, this tragic loss of the country's long-accumulated technical expertise remained a major problem.

Meanwhile, strong objections were – and still are – raised by those who fear old associations with foreign oil companies; and their pretext for preventing the re-entry of IOCs has been that this would contravene Iraq's oil nationalisation law. It is not the oil experts who emit this outcry, but over-politicised 'pseudo-experts' who echo the mistaken assumption described early on in this chapter: that any involvement of foreign companies will lead to a rip-off of Iraq's oil wealth.

This being the case, the outcome is that Iraq's important Oil and Gas Law has remained in abeyance since 2006. Even while these words are written in 2010, the Law still awaits Parliamentary endorsement.

An equally complex matter for the draft Oil Law is the province of Kurdistan and the extent to which it has a prerogative to negotiate deals with IOCs independently of the Ministry of Oil. The new Constitution, ratified by the Iraqi Parliament (15 October 2005), is bedevilled by a contradiction concerning oil activities that pertain to the Federal Ministry of Oil in Baghdad and those pertaining to the regional ministry in Kurdistan. Although the Constitution considers oil and gas to be the preserve of the entire nation, which means that the Federal Government Ministry is the ultimate decision maker for all Iraqi contracts, the Constitution also gives a prerogative to a regional government to issue its own law, but there is a contradiction in its statement that the regional government may overrule the Federal Government. Not surprisingly, the Federal Government has become embroiled in a series of conflicts with the Kurdistan authorities ever since the latter became engaged in drawing up over 20 contracts with as many companies – all based on the former PSA formula.

In essence the oil companies would be far more interested in investing in Iraq on the basis of Saddam's earlier negotiated (1995)

PSA formula. The Iraq Parliament's political mistrust of the PSA is arguably misplaced, as the PSA model, as explained, gives the right for IOCs to 'book' a part of Iraq's reserves – *not* in the context of any ownership but purely in the context of production, in order to have some guarantee of access to a small part of the reserves. The IOCs were instead offered a round of negotiations not for the PSA but for a more limited Service Contract Agreement, the terms of which are not sufficiently transparent. Despite its caution, the Ministry of Oil has come under fire from many engineers and other ministry staff. In this way, seven years have been wasted (since the fall of the Saddam regime until 2010) with political deadlock and incessant debates kept 'on the boil' over the Oil and Gas Law, which the Iraqi Parliament has still not endorsed, and the degree of political control to be exerted by Regional governments relative to the Federal Government.

In December 2009, notwithstanding these protracted policy disputes, the Oil Ministry revealed a new and staggering production target. This was the outcome of two rounds of negotiations with various IOCs, the first of which (in August 2009) had covered the development of 'supergiant' oilfields – Rumaila, West Qurna-1 and Zubair – with the aim of reaching a plateau of 6.3 mbpd by 2017. A subsequent (second) round of negotiations was conducted in December 2009 with a number of IOCs, mainly for the development of the oilfields that had been discovered but left undeveloped: the Majnoon, the Halfaya, West Qurna 2, Nahur Umr and others.

Having added Kurdistan's production target of 1 mbpd, the Oil Ministry signed a number of contracts (see Table 15.1) calculating a total production target of around 12 mbpd by 2017. This, if we exclude Iraq's current 2.5 mbpd production capacity, would need a vast capacity increment of over 9 mbpd.

Several geologists and engineers have expressed serious misgivings about the technical feasibility of such an immoderately high increment in production capacity in a mere seven years. A key issue in dispute is the durability of the peak or plateau phases of oil production, as many experts believe that it is very difficult to maintain such a high production level for the duration suggested by the Oil Ministry. Apart from this question of plateau durability, complexities and hitches over the capital outlay involved in the assembly

Table 15.1 Production capacity estimates according to timelines of contracts (mbpd)

	2011	2013*	2016–17**	2023	2027	2030
Rumaila	1.555	1.365	2.85	2.85		
Zubair	0.214	0.253	1.125	1.125		
WQ-1	0.286	0.338	2.325	2.325		
Total	**1.655**	**1.956**	**6.3**	**6.3**		
Majnoun	0.175	0.36	1.2	1.2	1.2	
WQ-2	0.12	0.375	1.25	1.25		1.25
Halfaya	0.07	0.135	0.45	0.45		0.45
Gharraf	0.035	0.067	0.225	0.225		0.225
East Baghdad	0.03	0.067	0.225	0.225	0.225	
Total	**0.43**	**1.004**	**3.35**	**3.35**		
Other fields	0.8	0.8	1	1		
KRG fields	0.5	1	1	1		
Total	**3.385**	**4.76**	**11.65**	**11.65**		

*2013 estimates based on an increase of 30 per cent of initial production in the producing fields and a similar percentage of the target plateau in the non-producing fields.

** Production plateau targets for second licensing round fields are assumptions.

Source: Middle East Economic Survey (MEES)[3]

of rigs, materials, managerial expertise – all of which are proving increasingly costly – could change the economics of the whole venture; as it is clear from signed contracts with the IOCs that there is no incentive for the companies to reduce such costs, as they are borne entirely by the Iraqi government.

Also of concern is the extent to which the IOC contracts are legally binding for the Iraqi government. In the opinion of the Oil Ministry, the legality of the agreements is recognised simply by their being endorsed by the Council of Ministers. However, several parliamentarians and jurists disagree with this notion on the basis that, because the new Oil and Gas Law has not been ratified, the validity of these contracts is not established without parliamentary endorsement of further legislation. Previous legislation, i.e. Law 97 of 1967, reserved oil industry investment rights exclusively for the

INOC. This is why, in order to sign an agreement in 1997 with the Russian oil company, Lukoil, to develop the West Qurna oilfield, the Iraqi government had to get the parliament of the day to ratify the contract as an 'exception' to the previous law. In the same way, the government still needs to pass a law through the present parliament to ratify the 2009 contracts signed with the IOCs; or, alternatively, wait until the Oil and Gas Law is finally approved by parliament.

As for the Oil Ministry's declared 12 mbpd production target, a major worry is the decline in oil demand and the amount of oil needed from OPEC member countries. Strong reservations are expressed by experts about the marketability of such a vast increment and the insurmountable difficulty to be caused for other OPEC countries, given that OPEC's *shut-in capacity* at present amounts to as much 6 mbpd, which, together with Iraq's projected increment, would give the organisation an impossible collective spare capacity exceeding 14 mbpd. A worrying aspect is, therefore, the Iraqi Ministry's apparent lack of forethought as to how this massive increment in Iraqi oil production capacity will find enough markets. The world oil market cannot absorb this extra capacity without a negative impact on oil prices over the next decade.

In any event, this situation rests on the growth of world oil demand and of oil supplies from outside OPEC. As the world's residual oil supplier, OPEC fills the gap in the market between global demand and non-OPEC supplies. By aiming to produce just enough oil to fill that gap, OPEC notionally bestows price stability to the world oil market. Producing more than that gap calls for would create an instant glut and downward price pressure; conversely if OPEC produces a lesser volume than is needed by the market gap, there would be an oil shortage and prices would rise. Although, historically speaking, OPEC has not been particularly adroit in balancing its production regulation in harmony with these two magnitudes, we recognise that, if it were not for OPEC's production restraints, price wars and market chaos would be rife.

Having established that the production-gap issue pivots on the future of global oil demand, it must be borne in mind that during the last five years demand trends have weakened significantly compared with the rampant demand characteristic of the first four years of the millennium. From September 2008, global recession has aggravated declining growth rates but although the world economy has improved marginally since, oil demand is expected to continue to be weak.

This long-term trend in downward demand may be clarified when we consider the following factors: first, the oil price surge in the first seven months of 2008, which peaked at $147 per barrel in July that year, caused a huge shock for consumers, leading to a sharp fall in consumption through increased efficiency in oil utilisation, especially gasoline and diesel oil, and a shift to alternatives: nuclear energy, biofuels, smaller vehicles with fuel-efficient engines, ultimately to the expanded production of hybrid and electric cars.

It is to be recalled that in the wake of the first two oil price shocks of the 1970s Western Europe and Japan rapidly reduced their oil dependency, and their rates of oil intensity (the amount needed for economic growth) have continued to fall. Today they consume even less oil than in 1975. It is now expected that with this recent (third) oil price shock, something similar will probably happen but on a global scale. Between 2004 and 2009 OECD oil demand has fallen dramatically, by 4 mbpd, while China's annual growth rates in consumption have come down by 6 per cent, from their 2000–04 level of over 10 per cent.

Second, the drive of the consuming countries, especially the USA, to reduce their dependence on imported oil for economic and geopolitical reasons is another factor. This policy having been adopted by George W. Bush and President Obama, action will follow to achieve set targets, involving oil production from tar sands, the development of non-conventional gas from shale and greater investment in nuclear energy, leading to a continued fall in fuel requirements.

A third factor that places political pressure on consuming less oil is the issue of climate change, fears of which fuel the endeavours of the consuming countries to cut back on oil consumption and reduce their CO_2 emissions. The increase in global warming remains a source of great concern, though it remains debatable in scientific circles.

Another critical component that will determine the degree of the world's need for OPEC oil is the future extent of non-OPEC world supplies, notably from Russia, China, Africa, Canada, Latin America (including Brazil which is set to become a major player) and eventually the Arctic Circle. On this subject there are widely

diverging views. 'Peak-oil' theorists predict a fall in world oil supplies because, from their point of view, world oil supplies have
already reached a plateau. Others hold that peak-oil theory completely disregards the impact of technology on enhancing recovery from existing oilfields and ignores the many discoveries of new
reserves. Also overlooked are the huge reserves of the Middle East
Gulf where (as shown in Chapter 12) there have been no serious
exploratory efforts, particularly in Iran and Iraq. For this reason
it could be assumed that non-OPEC oil supplies by 2020 could
increase instead of decrease.

If we take the trends of both global oil demand and non-OPEC
crude production, the increment in the required production from
OPEC to achieve market stability will be too small to absorb Iraq's
planned additional oil capacity. Tables 15.2 and 15.3 demonstrate
the trajectory of world demand movements.

According to the IEA's forecast[4] (shown in Table 15.3), the call on
OPEC crude oil production by 2020 will have increased by about 3
mbpd from the year 2008. The IEA estimate assumes a weak annual
growth in global oil demand and an increase in non-OPEC supply
of 3 mbpd. By comparison, the CGES forecast (shown in Table 15.2)
estimates, by 2020, an increment of 6.5 mbpd on the call for OPEC
oil, with the assumption of 1 per cent global demand growth per
annum, and an increase in non-OPEC supplies of 0.5 mbpd.

Table 15.2   CGES' projections – Base Case

	2008 mbpd	2015 mbpd	2020 mbpd	2008–2020 % change per annum
Global oil demand	86.0	90.9	96.5	1.0
of which China	7.9	10.0	11.2	2.9
Non-OPEC supply	49.4	50.8	50.0	0.1
of which processing				
gains	2.2	2.4	2.6	1.1
Other biofuels	0.4	0.7	1.0	7.6
OPEC NGLs	4.7	6.4	7.5	3.9
Call on OPEC (crude oil)	31.8	33.1	38.3	1.5

Source: CGES

Table 15.3 IEA's projections — Reference Case from medium term review

	2008 mbpd	2015 mbpd	2020 mbpd	2008–2020 % change per annum
Global oil demand	86.0	91.9	96.6	1.0
of which China	7.9	11.6	13.5	4.5
OECD oil supply	18.7	17.5	16.2	−1.2
Non-OECD oil supply	27.4	30.3	31.3	1.1
Processing gains	2.2	2.3	2.5	0.9
US ethanol output	0.6	1.0	1.3	6.4
Brazil ethanol output	0.4	0.7	0.9	6.7
Other biofuels	0.4	0.7	0.9	7.4
Total non-OPEC supply	49.8	52.5	53.1	0.5
OPEC NGLs	4.4	7.2	8.8	5.8
Call on OPEC (crude oil)	31.8	32.2	34.8	0.7

Source: CGES

This would imply that, in the interests of maintaining a world market balance and not creating undue downward pressure on world oil prices, OPEC's incremental production in the coming ten years should not exceed the range estimated by the IEA and CGES.

Notwithstanding that (as past experience shows) forecasts for future oil supply and demand invariably prove inaccurate, these estimates nevertheless illustrate an increment by 2020 in world demand for OPEC oil that would in all probability range between 3 mbpd and 6.5 mbpd. This level of demand would be far too small to absorb the huge expansion planned for Iraq's production capacity by the Iraqi Oil Ministry.

Bearing in mind that there is already 6 mbpd of idle capacity among OPEC countries, this could cause serious problems for OPEC, and a degree of conflict principally between Iraq and Saudi Arabia. Historically speaking, Iraq's OPEC quota share stood at 14.5 per cent, which means that, by 2020, its production limit could not exceed 5 mbpd. Yet this is less than half the production level sought by Iraq's Oil Ministry. The Ministry's plan would involve vast capital expenditure for an excessive production capacity, for which there may be no buyers, and this would create enormous problems economically for Iraq.

Given the following possible scenarios, we need to reflect on Iraq's conceivable options:

The first option predicates itself on the likelihood that Iraq's Oil Ministry will negotiate with OPEC for a higher quota share than its former 14.5 per cent share of OPEC's total production (excluding Angola and Gabon). The Oil Ministry has stated that Iraq would remain outside the quota system until its production exceeds 4 mbpd, at which point it would then commence discussion of its quota with OPEC. This would entail other OPEC members having to concede to Iraq's claim for a quota share higher than its former 14.5 per cent, and accordingly having to reduce their own quotas.

Iraq would argue the case that it sustained enormous losses in exports from the time of the Iran–Iraq war and above all during the 13 years of sanctions. Of Iraq's huge loss of market share, 75 per cent went to Saudi Arabia: that is to say 75 per cent of Iraq's cumulative export losses of 19.4 bn/B.

OPEC, conversely, would argue that its members, in particular Saudi Arabia, had to fill the supply gap caused by Iraq's wars and the UN sanctions, bearing in mind that Saudi Arabia had the idle capacity with which to replace Iraqi production. Had Saudi Arabia not done so, a sharp surge in oil prices would have ensued, causing market turbulence.

Given that OPEC member countries depend heavily on their quotas and are not prepared to sacrifice their own financial needs for the sake of Iraq, this first option, involving Iraq's increase of its historical quota share at the cost of reducing the shares of other OPEC members, would be highly problematic and unfeasible.

Second, were Iraq to proceed with selling its oil in line with the Ministry's latest plan to maximise production from high capacity, irrespective of the OPEC quota, this would cause market mayhem in the form of free-for-all price wars and a serious oil-price collapse. Bearing in mind that OPEC already has (without Iraq) around 6 mbpd of idle capacity which its member countries would aim to use, with each increasing its own production, clearly the attempt to seize the incremental call on its own oil (or higher share) would result in a damaging battle within OPEC.

Furthermore, for Iraq the inevitable collapse in oil prices would be self-defeating, as what it will have gained in expanded volume, it would then lose in value with low prices.

A very low price scenario would prove unacceptable for the world oil industry. When this type of free-for-all situation arose in 1986, as already mentioned, the collapse in oil prices from $25.28 to $7 and $8 per barrel was intolerable for the USA with its costly domestic production, and a large number of wells were shut down in Texas and other oil-producing states that same year. The then Vice President George Bush Snr, in the Reagan administration, intervened, requesting that Saudi Arabia reduce its production in order to achieve a minimum price of $18 per barrel (and OPEC agreed to adopt this price at the time).

At the same time, North Sea oil producers experienced similarly grave problems with their high production costs, and they collaborated in the effort to raise the oil price.

In 1998 oil prices collapsed again in the wake of the Asian financial crisis, and the US Secretary of Energy, Bill Richardson, visited the Gulf on a similar mission to raise oil prices, this time reaching a compromise deal with Iran as well as other Gulf producers.

A third option is the hypothetical scenario of a huge market glut if Iraq were to produce a massive 9 mbpd capacity increment – bearing in mind the Iraqi Oil Ministry's recent avowal of a target of around 12 mbpd by 2017. This presupposes that other OPEC members would be forced to minimise their own production quotas drastically enough to allow Iraq this immoderate output; and it would be Saudi Arabia that would have to bear the burden of OPEC's dramatic quota cutback.

However, Iraq is too weak politically and economically to embark on such a gamble with OPEC. The position of the USA could be crucial in this context, i.e. to what extent could the USA put pressure on the other OPEC countries to help Iraq increase its production quota to absorb the incremental capacity?

The options and scenarios so far suggested are extremely challenging and are likely to prove self-defeating, as Iraq could find itself left with 6 mbpd of idle capacity, on which it would have spent billions of dollars that are needed to salvage its damaged economy. The maintenance cost alone for such a huge idle capacity would be exorbitant.

It would seem that, so far, the Oil Ministry has inopportunely tied the country down to obligations that could endanger Iraq's future oil industry, and this would have a far-reaching negative impact on the country's economy. Of this the Oil Ministry seems extraordinarily unaware.

Fourth, as explained earlier, if we apply Iraq's historical production share of 14.5 per cent of OPEC's total to the two scenarios, represented in Tables 15.2 and 15.3, Iraq's share should not exceed 5.5–6.0 mbpd, which is about half that planned by the Oil Ministry.

Therefore, a fourth and very prudent option would be for the Oil Ministry to renegotiate and revise the IOC contracts so as to implement a plan for a more gradual capacity increase, one that bears in mind market developments and aims at avoiding a huge idle capacity. Even so, it is questionable whether the IOCs would be prepared to curb capacity significantly enough, as profitability of contracts depends on the construction of higher capacity.

To serve Iraq's best interests, the only way out for the Oil Ministry is to curb its ambitious strategy, avoid its present unrealistic commitments to the oil companies, with the object of reaching a more reasonable addition to its capacity. In other words, Iraq would do far better to reach an optimum plateau of no more than 6 mbpd, including the present production from Kirkuk and other oilfields.

The future of Iraq's oil industry will also depend to a great extent on the political developments that lie ahead, and what kind of regime will encourage or discourage investments in the country's oil industry.

Apart from the Kurdish problem, a major impediment to this future is the political instability inherent from the split between the two major Arab Islamic sects: a Shi'i majority and a Sunni minority. This split was a geographical and historical legacy, but it became intensely political and dangerously entrenched after the US-led coalition toppled Saddam's Sunni Ba'athist regime. Prior to this, Saddam's brutal dictatorship had ensured an absence of sectarian insurgency.

The Sunni legacy of political leadership had for centuries been the tradition in Iraq, which is how political and military power came to be vested in a Sunni minority. The Shi'i majority was marginalised, excluded from political power and permitted only a sphere of commerce and trade dealings. Imposed by the Sunni Turks, this socio-political formation became institutionalised throughout four centuries of the Ottoman Empire rule.

Following the collapse of the Ottoman Empire, the Shi'as remained disempowered. This was because, after the First World War, the 1919 Treaty of Versailles and 1920 San Remo Agreement, when the three former Ottoman Iraqi provinces became a British mandate (under a new monarchical regime), the British agreed that political and military power would continue to be vested in Sunni leadership. Although a minority, the Sunnis thus remained the ruling elite (especially in the military) until the fall of Saddam's Ba'athist regime. The Americans then installed a provisional political system predicated on a population redistribution: i.e. a quantitative, demographic percentage based on creed and ethnicity.

This new system profoundly disrupted the old ruling elite, by giving far greater representation to the Shi'a majority, and a critically low representation for the Sunni minority. This has caused a power imbalance that remains an impediment to political stability.

On 30 January 2005, Iraq held its first democratic national elections, but given the predominance of a Shi'i electorate, the Sunnis felt so acutely marginalised that they boycotted the elections. Not surprisingly the result was a landslide victory for the Shi'i majority and this consolidated Shi'i power in the hands of clerics, who formed a government headed by Nouri al-Maliki, the Secretary of the Shi'i religious Da'awa Party.

However, rule by the Shi'i clerics has been branded as far too sectarian for a country that has always been ruled by secular governments. Ever since the fall of the Ba'athist regime, when the Sunnis were for the first time divested of their political leadership, al-Maliki and his ruling coterie have proved unequal to the task of resolving the challenges of sectarianism and the legacy of the wars waged under Saddam's regime. There has been a catalogue of failures on the part of the Maliki administration: the gravest being that the huge petroleum revenues flowing into Iraq, especially during the years of very high oil prices (2006–08 and again in 2010), have been largely dissipated by unprecedented levels of corruption and mismanagement. Despite massive oil revenues during these years, the Shi'i government has not provided even the basic requirements of a society, such as security, functional utilities and services, like electricity, clean water, proper medical services and education.

The consequence of this was that Iraq's second democratic election, held on 7 March 2010, reflected the disappointment of the Iraqi people over the rule of the Shi'i clerics. By the same token it reflected the relative success for the moderate candidate Dr Iyad Allawi who, although a Shi'i, is a secularist. Allawi has earned electoral support from Sunni and secular elements of the political spectrum, as leader of the 'al-Iraqiya' group. But having gained a lead of only two seats, he did not obtain a large enough majority to form a government, and has been unable to steer Nouri al-Maliki into making headway with their proposed coalition. Endeavours by both to form a wide coalition headed by the Islamist al-Maliki, on the one hand, and secularist Allawi on the other, are blocked by Moqtada al-Sadr, the hardline leader of Shi'i insurgents, who (despite having only 40 out of 315 seats) aims to exclude Allawi on the basis of representing secular elements. In this al-Sadr has the firm backing of Iran. This has resulted in bitter political deadlock, a situation not conducive to forming a feasible government. The Iraqi people, instead of at last securing the government they elected democratically and deserve, are faced once again with corruption, bitter political disputes and the protracted deliberations of regionalist rivalry.

What exacerbates this situation are the incursions into Iraqi politics implicated on the part of Iran, Iraq's neighbouring regional power. Since the fall of the Saddam regime and consolidation of Shi'i power, Iran has scarcely veiled its ambitions for regional dominance, while its attempts to manipulate Iraq's political process remain blatantly intrusive.

Saudi Arabia and other Gulf countries and also Egypt have felt the mounting threat posed by the influence of a hardline Shi'i Iran, bolstered in its ambitions for regional dominance by its questionable uranium enrichment programme. Not surprisingly this Sunnite group of countries lends its support to Dr Iyad Allawi's secular 'Iraqiya' group and the Sunnis. In this vein, Iraq's political problems are destined to become more and more regionalist.

Given this politically precarious state of affairs, the colossal oil investment programme envisaged by the Iraqi government, and agreed with the IOCs in December 2009, may end up at best being delayed by sectarian conflict, or, worse: impeded and threatened by sabotage.

16

Epilogue

When I moved from OPEC (in July 1989) to the CGES, a London-based think-tank founded by Sheikh Ahmed Zaki Yamani, my keen interest in OPEC affairs in no way diminished, nor, needless to say, my passion for the oil industry. For this reason, throughout these chapters, my candid scrutiny of OPEC tends to infer what OPEC could have achieved had it pursued alternative policies as possessor of the world's bulk of cheap oil reserves; had it aimed at exerting a more positive influence on the world energy market to balance its quest for market dominance; and had it pursued its own long-term interests.

While my analysis of OPEC has been predicated on what OPEC *should be* for the sake of its long-term benefit, my approach has also been governed by an intellectual bias, allied to my preoccupation with OPEC's likely decisions in the light of market fundamentals. These intellectual and practical considerations have proved problematic, as my well-intentioned, constructive criticism is often misconstrued as 'destructive' by certain OPEC people, who, because I was with OPEC for a long time, regard my comments as a form of betrayal, as if my aim now is to defend the interests of the oil-consuming countries at OPEC's expense. But the reality is that I have OPEC's own interests at heart, and I strongly believe in an often quoted insightful dictum that 'if OPEC breaks up, a new OPEC must emerge' – an axiomatic admission that the petroleum industry must have some form of production regulation, without which the oil market would become an anarchic free-for-all, with resultant price wars, disinvestment and market chaos.

After the demise of the concession system and break-up of the Seven Sisters' international petroleum cartel, when the NOCs took over the upstream operation, a radically different system emerged in which the industry's integration, formerly ensured by the cartel's co-ordination, was now replaced by a totally *de-integrated* system. The reason for this is that the NOCs of OPEC member countries (with the exception of a few) have always remained cut off from the downstream operations of the consuming countries. In this way, the NOCs have been reduced to mere sellers of crude oil on a world commodities market. What has distanced them even more from the market has been their incorporation into the state, so that far from being purely commercial entities they are forever subjected to state politics and state priorities concerning financial needs.

In 1975, in an attempt to find some form of mutual co-operation among the NOCs, a meeting under my chairmanship was held in London, attended by Sheikh Ali al-Khalifa al-Sabah, then Undersecretary of Oil for Kuwait, and Nordine Ait Laoussine of Algeria. Predictably, recommendations arising from that meeting were later rejected by several member states, who regarded them as limiting state control over the oil industry. Before leaving for London (together with Dr Ramzi Salman, who was in charge of oil marketing) I had met Saddam Hussein to obtain his instructions, and during our meeting he could not have been clearer in affirming that this type of co-operation among OPEC's NOCs should in no way hamper or contravene our marketing and pricing procedures. Saddam's own assertion that 'if they impose certain oil price levels, they will restrict our freedom to formulate our own marketing and pricing policies' was a clear indication that he was opposed to Iraq's commitment to the NOC principle of co-operation.

But with so many OPEC member states opposed to our recommendations, the upshot of the 1975 London meeting served a final death blow to any hopes for a focused, interactive co-operation such as that which had characterised the industry's upstream during the oil companies' era. Instead, there was now a mix of various state political and economic requirements that would inevitably lead to an imperfect supply regulation system which, unable to cope with demand variations, would give rise to oil price instability. This inherent difficulty, which OPEC had to contend with by virtue of its composition, weakened over time the organisation's role as price stabiliser. Nevertheless, OPEC's supply regulation system could have done more to minimise price instability had the organisation followed an economically motivated rationale as exporters of a crucial world commodity. But this was not to be the case, the main reason being, as I have explained, the over-politicisation of the decision-making process within OPEC, which, ever since the oil price shocks of 1973, has increasingly linked itself with political events.

In this way, it is totally dissimilar to any commercial organisation, whose *raison d'être* would normally be allied to economic benefit. By contrast, OPEC's collective entity subjects its decision-making process to political demands from its member states, each articulating its own agenda of socio-political priorities. This heterogeneity of national interests hinders any economic rationale that would be exemplified by an objective examination of market fundamentals, and which alone can stabilise the oil market. Rather than planning longer-term targets to achieve price optimisation, what drives OPEC countries and brings them together is the short-term maximisation of oil revenues.

Understanding the structural transformation of the oil industry is the key to perceiving what OPEC stands for and what its limitations are in achieving oil price stability. We have seen in these chapters how OPEC's strategy, influenced by political pressures, soon eschewed commercial considerations, and how this led to huge oil price volatility. From the time the organisation took over oil pricing from the major oil companies – with the Kuwaiti decision of 16 October 1973 (coupled with the later demise of the concession system) – OPEC prices have soared: to begin with from just $2.50–$3.00 per barrel in mid-1973 to $36 per barrel in January 1981, an increase by a factor of 12 in less than eight years. The price would later spiral to $47 by 2004, and to $147 per barrel by July 2008, before plunging to $36 per barrel in December that year. Such a pattern of price instability has persisted ever since OPEC lost its earlier command of price formation.

This price volatility has been intensified by OPEC's penchant for not abiding by its own decisions, and by the futures market's interpretation of this pattern. Early on, the first precedence for ignoring its own declarations was OPEC's momentous decision of the 23rd December 1973 (in Tehran), the effect of which famously quadrupled the price of oil, and this was in direct contravention of its declaration only two months earlier in Kuwait (16th October 1973) when OPEC elected to take over the pricing of oil from the major companies and increase the posted or tax-reference price by 70 per cent. As already mentioned, the intention of this earlier 'Kuwaiti' decision of October 1973, was for the OPEC price to relate to the market but at a median point between the tax reference price of $5.10 and the real market price of $3.65. Then, as a result of pressure from the Shah of Iran – and with US acquiescence – the price increased irrespective of OPEC's October 1973 decision. When the oil embargo ended and supplies were resumed, OPEC ought to have reverted to its original decision to take the price back to $3.65 per barrel, but it did not – and the reason for this was purely political. Also the companies continued to buy oil at high prices, and sustained these high prices by lifting expensive oil and storing it.

One can argue that the Tehran price shock of 1973 was necessary to achieve a desirable halt to the habitual waste of very cheaply priced oil, and to arrest the rapid depletion of OPEC's oil reserves, over-consumption of which would have soon proved unsustainable in Western Europe, Japan and the USA. Notwithstanding that the price shock certainly ended the era of excessive waste of a depletable resource, OPEC's failure to abide by its October 1973 decision after the oil embargo was nonetheless entirely political (related, as shown, to US support of Israel during the Yom Kippur War).

Another instance of OPEC's non-observance of its own decisions arose in 1979 during the Iranian crisis, when the organisation decided in the summer of 1979 that the price of its oil should stand at $18 per barrel, as market prices were in chaos, reaching $40 per barrel as a result of Ayatollah Khomeini's revolution. At the same time a decision was made that member countries could add a maximum market premium of $2 per barrel to reflect the soaring market prices at that time; and it was further agreed that the price should not exceed $23.50 per barrel. Meanwhile, in an atmosphere of confusion over the price, member countries felt unrestrained in fixing their premiums. It was only a few months later, in mid-December 1979, that OPEC, at its conference in Caracas, decided that its oil should be priced at $28 per barrel (see Chapter 9).

Another example of unnecessary price volatility occurred at the time of the Conference in Bali, Indonesia, in December 1980, during which the OPEC oil price soared to $36 per barrel while Saudi Arabia held the price at $32 per barrel, thus creating a two-tiered price structure.

An equally serious and more recent case was when OPEC continually reneged on a decision (taken in March 2000 and reiterated in 2002) for an optimum price band that was to remain constant within a range of $22–$28 per barrel, so that if the market price exceeded the upper limit of $28 for a certain period, OPEC would automatically increase its production by 500 tbpd; and, conversely, if the price fell below the $22 mark for a certain period, OPEC would automatically cut its production by 500 tbpd. OPEC's decision was a sound one, taken in favour of price stability. Yet at its meeting in Algiers on 1 October 2004 – by which time accelerating demand from China and the USA had doubled prices to $47 and $49.45 p/b respectively for dated Brent and WTI – instead of abiding by its earlier decision and increasing production to ease the price downward, OPEC made a strange decision to cut production by 1 mbpd (which in reality amounted to 0.5 mbpd). In so doing, OPEC ignited a very sharp price escalation which by late July 2006 saw the oil price soar to $78 per barrel.

Over the following years OPEC's failure to ease the market with increased oil supplies fuelled over-speculation on the futures market, so that by July 2008 the price had spiralled to $147 per barrel. To the surprise of those who had begun to 'talk up' price expectations of $200 per barrel, the price proved unsustainable and a dramatic downward spiral and price collapse ensued in the last quarter of 2008, accompanied by a global financial crisis (which had begun earlier but worsened in September 2008 with the collapse of Lehman Bros.).

In terms of OPEC's role in the world oil market and in primary energy consumption, the most critical issue is the organisation's market share and world demand for its oil. As a result of its policies, oil industry growth shifted to other producers. According to the Oil and Gas Journal[1], core OPEC[2] production of crude oil was about 3 mbpd higher in 1973 than in 2009: i.e. 29.3 mbpd in 1973 and only 26.4 mbpd in 2009. This deterioration of the oil industry in OPEC countries is to be compared with the spectacular growth in output from non-OPEC producers: from 25.9 mbpd in 1973 to 44.1 mbpd in 2009.

Furthermore, this trend has deprived OPEC of its former role of world market price setter, as it is effectively only with a high market share (such as OPEC had in 1973, when its crude oil exports accounted for 87 per cent) that OPEC can play a dominant role in determining market trends. With OPEC's market share declining to 44 per cent in 2008 (according to the IEA), the world oil market became increasingly influenced by competitive traders and speculators on the futures market, where billions of US dollars exchange hands in paper oil barrels.

This means that OPEC's production cutbacks, which achieve a higher price level to suit member countries' budgets, have become the sole instrument that OPEC can deploy to affect world markets, and consequent sharp price movements – up or down, according to traders' perceptions of supply and demand – have come to dominate the market.

Another upshot of the contraction in OPEC's market share was that the oil market 'reference price' switched from 'Arab Light' to 'Brent' (a relatively small amount of oil) and WTI, both traded as benchmark crudes on the free market. It is ironic that the bulk of oil-trade pricing, even in OPEC oil, is now based on non-OPEC crudes (minus differentials in geographical location and quality) rather than on the Gulf's Arab Light, which was the old reference price until the mid-1980s, and which still represents the bulk of oil entering world trade.

With these developments, OPEC has become a world market *price-taker* as opposed to its earlier role of *price-maker*. Its declining market share has benefitted non-OPEC producers, whose oil production flourished thanks to OPEC's production and high-pricing policies. As we have seen, OPEC's share of world production has fallen substantially from 60 per cent in 1978 to 48 per cent in 2005 and to 41.7 per cent in 2009, as a result of the improved economics of investments in Alaska, the Caspian Sea and the North Sea and increased oil exports from Russia and central Asia. Despite these developments, there are those within OPEC who continue to dismiss the significance of market share so long as oil revenues increase; but the shrinkage of OPEC's market share amounts to the erosion of its economic power in terms of 'price-making'.

If OPEC keeps up its high-pricing policy this trend is bound to continue. The decline in its market share began with the oil price shocks of the 1970s and 1980s. Later, the sharp rise in oil demand from China and India, especially by 2006, regarded as the first year of the 'third oil price shock', caused prices to spiral out of control until – as we have seen – they peaked famously at $147 per barrel in

July 2008, before subsiding with the collapse of markets in the last quarter of that year.

Oil prices have since recovered through 2009–2010, but the impact of these price shocks on consumers swiftly changed the energy mix from oil to alternative energy sources, including natural gas and nuclear energy. As has been discussed, this was remarkably evident in Western Europe and Japan, both of which experienced a substantial decline in the share of oil in their total energy mix. Between 1973 and 2009, the share of oil in total primary energy consumption in Western Europe fell from over 58 per cent to 42 per cent. Over the same period, the share of natural gas and nuclear energy grew from 11.7 per cent to 37.6 per cent, respectively. In the case of Japan, during this period the decline in oil's share of primary energy consumption was even more marked, falling from 77.5 per cent to 43.6 per cent.

The shift towards improved energy utilisation in Western Europe and Japan has been more marked than in other parts of the world because the first oil price shock of 1973–1974 and the second shock of 1979 prompted stiff government measures, involving heavy taxation to enforce energy conservation, far tougher measures than those taken in the US and elsewhere. But with the world's "third price shock" in the first seven months of 2008, this pattern was already set to change in the US.

This being the case, the share of OPEC oil in the energy mix will inevitably shrink, a decline that will not be borne equally by OPEC members: Gulf oil having suffered far more than non-Gulf members, who enjoy secured markets for their limited resource base because of the higher quality of their oil.

Nevertheless, the most important oil within OPEC is Gulf oil because of its abundant 'low-cost' reserves, and the reduced world dependence on Gulf oil has been to the cost of the Gulf's market power, eroded over time and by degrees forfeited to other producers. The dependence of Western Europe on OPEC Gulf oil for meeting its total primary energy requirements continued to decline from 42 per cent in 1973 to only 10 per cent in 2009. Similarly the share of Gulf oil in Japan's energy requirements continued to fall, though to a lesser extent.

Among the major problems that OPEC faces as a residual supplier is its absence of vision for a long-term optimum price for oil, a vision that should shape a consistent decision-making process. We have seen how the work of the LTSC, chaired by Sheikh Yamani, was blown apart by market turbulence during Ayatollah Khomeini's revolution. Our LTSC's recommendations were accepted by the Conference but soon forsaken in the pursuit of high prices, far higher than those proposed by the Committee.

A major reason for a persistent lack of a long-term vision for optimum price movements is the fact that the long-term interests of OPEC's member countries vary so sharply. Algeria, a member country with limited oil reserves but with an important natural gas resource base, is always eager to gain the highest possible price for oil in order to secure the highest per barrel income in the short term, though it is not interested in the *volume* of its oil exports. Recently natural gas prices have become slightly detached from oil prices, but in a normal market a high oil price has always meant a high price for natural gas – on which Algeria depends far more than on its oil.

By contrast, Saudi Arabia should, in theory at least, be interested in long-term demand for its vast oil reserves. High oil prices are not in its long-term interests, tending to reduce its share in the world energy balance. Given these two countries' divergence of interests, their agreement over *long-term* strategy becomes ever-more problematical. Nevertheless, OPEC's guiding philosophy – the concept of pricing tactics that maximize oil revenue in the short-term – continues to bring the member states (including Saudi Arabia) together in broad agreement and enables the organisation to survive.

In April 2006, OPEC issued a pamphlet on its 'long-term strategy', and of particular interest is its phraseology in this document (a summary of an immense study on the subject, which remained unpublished), the tone of which varies according to the member country's needs. It is non-committal where it qualifies the OPEC price as 'fair', the concept of which is indefinable. OPEC's definition of 'fairness' is governed by what constitutes, in the words of the pamphlet, a 'fair rent to oil producers and is acceptable to the consumer'. World trade, however, is not based on a moral issue of fairness or unfairness, as the price on the free market follows basic laws of economics in being determined by the interaction of supply and demand. Alternatively, this could be a cartelised price, set by a powerful cartel in search of certain objectives related to profit-making. The only way to explain the pamphlet's vague definition of a 'fair price' was the organisation's need to seek price levels commensurate with the financial needs of its member countries. Yet its notion of a 'fair' price swiftly changed over time with subsequent price escalations.[3]

At a time when demand-growth was at its strongest between 2002–2004, OPEC claimed to be apprehensive that markets were insufficiently robust to warrant the cost of maintaining additional producing capacity, and challenged the criticism levelled at its investment policy in the upstream (i.e. its lack of investment in additional capacity) in the pamphlet mentioned above. In response to the oil-consuming countries' frequently expressed anxiety over the 'security of oil supply' and the need for a 'guarantee of supply', this pamphlet insists that from OPEC's standpoint any expenditure on new capacity should be conditional on a 'guarantee of demand' or 'security of demand' from consumer countries. This guarantee that OPEC has professed to seek is not practicable because most of the global economic system is based on market economics. The sole means by which governments of consuming countries can ever influence the market is by curtailing demand through taxing oil products at the consumer end. Governments can also mandate vehicle efficiency gains, as the USA has done, but there is nothing they can do to 'guarantee' demand, as this can only be influenced by market conditions.

The free-market economies that govern consuming countries are influenced by a plethora of factors, such as economic growth, technological change, changing consumer habits, prices, etc. Demand, above all, depends on the *price* of oil and on price elasticity: with higher prices demand will be lower, and with lower prices demand will be higher. If OPEC wishes to have a guarantee of demand, the only key to this is the oil price itself. The pamphlet at least showed where OPEC stood in its determination not to invest capital in new production capacity without a 'guarantee' of secured markets. Indeed OPEC's aversion to the cost of being dumped with unused capacity is entirely understandable, but during a sustained period of strong world demand for light crude, without OPEC's investment in adding light-crude capacity, the increased demand left OPEC capacity even tighter, as clearly shown by its own statistics concerning its level of drilling activities, which (as discussed in Chapter 12) remained stagnant over a long period of time, despite enormous oil revenues. While expenditure in OPEC countries naturally tends to prioritise socio-economic and political considerations, ploughing back some of their revenues into spare capacity should not be overlooked.

No doubt at the core of this reticence to invest in new capacity lies 'oil nationalism', as it alone explains why, when strong demand was a sustained feature (until the recession beginning in the last quarter of 2008), OPEC producers would neither take this investment risk nor permit foreign investors to do so.

OPEC's future will depend on these price movements, as a continued high-price regime will bolster the momentum of consumer endeavour to reduce dependence on oil. Of critical importance to OPEC is to observe the trend of decline in oil consumption within the OECD area, which accounts for more than 54 per cent of total world consumption. Between 2005 and 2009, oil consumption has declined by more than 4.1 mbpd, i.e. from 49.5 to 45.3 mbpd. Part of this significant decline is the result of the present global recession, as recessions inevitably denote lower consumption of commodities. However, for three years prior to the recession there had already been a pattern of decline in oil consumption, caused by the run of price spikes between 2005 and 2008, fuelled (as mentioned) by uncertainty over OPEC supplies and consequent over-speculation on the futures market.

Even in China, considered the main driver of growth in oil demand, there are altering trends in oil consumption, noticeably in the country's falling rates of incremental demand: from a high of over 10 per cent in 2004 to a recent 6 per cent in 2009–10. This is largely the result of the Chinese government's reduction of subsidies for transportation fuels, together with increased efficiency in energy utilisation, and also a drive in China to consume more coal, a resource which the country possesses in abundance.

Meanwhile, oil price volatility and the trend of decline in oil demand have been aggravated by factors other than market fundamentals, a major factor being the impact of geopolitical events which, if perceived by the markets as affecting the security of oil supplies, are powerfully influential in setting the market price. Terrorist attacks, events such as September 11 2001, and, more recently, political tensions over the emergence of Iran as a potential nuclear power and a regional threat, intensify anxieties concerning the dependence on the Middle East for imported oil.

Besides the impact of high prices on oil consumption, other factors have evidently combined to reinforce trends showing a reduced dependence on oil in the world energy mix. For example, while the global outcry against detrimental carbon emissions has gathered apace, with the long lead-time involved concerted efforts are being made to reduce oil consumption as a major source of CO_2 emissions contributing to global warming. Mounting concern and commitment at a serious political level, as exemplified by the European Union, spread in 2009 to the United States when Barack Obama took office as President, immediately becoming politically engaged in promoting the economic feasibility of alternative energy sources for both power-generation and transport – none of which can be achieved without higher energy prices.

The fact that the consumer countries have redoubled their efforts to reduce oil consumption, by means of efficient fuel utilisation and transferring to alternative energy sources, provides the clearest indication of a 'threat' posed by oil-price volatility to world oil demand, and thus to OPEC itself. In terms of *power generation*, oil's contribution is dwindling fast, particularly now that nuclear phobia (provoked by accidents in the 1980s, such as Chernobyl) has been eschewed in favour of a renewed faith in and reliance on nuclear energy, along with natural gas and a revival of coal production – the latter fostered by scientific research into 'clean coal' technology.

In the longer run, the dominance of oil (gasoline and diesel oil) in the *transportation sector* is also under threat, as the first priority in developed economies is to reduce the amount of oil consumption per mile. Ever since 2008's oil price shock, the US automobile industry has opted for smaller, more efficient cars, with a resulting sharp downward trend for large 'gas-guzzlers', such as SUVs.

The price shock of 2008 impelled oil consumers, especially in the transportation sector, into a new awareness, and US motorists, for example, became preoccupied with the new reality of having to pay over $4 per gallon. They now drive far less and use public transport far more. The fact that the per-barrel oil price fell from its July 2008 peak of $147 to $33–36 per barrel by the end of the last quarter of

2008, has hardly altered the pattern of conserving gasoline, as consumption of light distillate in 2009 was -0.3 per cent. while prices soon doubled within a few months, rebounding to $70 per barrel by June 2009, and continuing through 2010 at $75–80 per barrel. Market trends still indicate that oil price volatility will remain a permanent feature, although the range of volatility has narrowed during the present recession.

Equally long term is the eventual substitution of the oil component in transportation with alternative fuels, in particular the hybrid vehicle, production of which will in time become more affordable, thus commercially viable and increasingly commonplace. In Japan and the USA there is huge investment in the hybrid car, which combines a gasoline-driven engine with an electric motor. The replacement (or mixing) of gasoline with bio-fuels (mainly ethanol produced from the utilisation of vegetable oil or sugar cane) may well lose ground to this cleaner gasoline-electric hybrid car, which has become the most significant innovation so far in terms of fuel conservation. In October 2008, the US Congress announced the provision of $25 billion in low-interest loans for car manufacturers to invest in promoting production lines of, for example, the plug-in hybrid model. The electric car, already capable of a distance of 60 km on electricity alone, stands to benefit from an increasing distance range with plug-in technology, and also by means of the 'compressed battery' which will reduce the long time taken for battery recharging to the same brief time that it takes to fill a tank of petrol. Both will greatly reduce petrol consumption. In the USA, Ford announced in 2009 the imminent marketing of several zero-emissions vehicles and new plug-in hybrid models, and unveiled plans for an electric car with a range of up to 100 miles on a single charge, powered by an electric motor running on lithium-ion batteries. This was followed by Nissan, in August 2009 and March 2010, announcing the success of its Leaf electric model driving 100 miles on a single charge, to be available for purchase in late 2010. In the meantime, US scientific experts are making further breakthroughs with the more nascent technology of the hydrogen fuel cell. Although it will take time for such vehicles to replace the conventional internal combustion engine (the fuel efficiency of which has been greatly improved), these next-generation breakthroughs will make the electric car an attractive investment option as a car of the future.

Given greater economic feasibility, many of these proposed alternative energy and transportation projects will ultimately take off, helped along by OPEC's high-price regime and further driven by the incentives of fear over oil supply insecurity and the menace of global warming from excessive CO_2 levels, exacerbated by burning fossil fuels. Related to oil supply insecurity are obvious geopolitical factors, driving large areas of the world to reduce dependence on imported oil, especially Gulf oil.

When the events of September 11, 2001 ushered in an era of renewed fear of over-dependence on imported oil, especially in the case of the United States, US energy strategy during the Bush administration aimed at reducing and ultimately ceasing to import oil from the Middle East Gulf. In the 1980s and 1990s we saw OPEC losing its market share to non-OPEC oil, and now the future looks set to launch a new era in which OPEC may lose yet more of its market share to alternative fuels. It is only a matter of time, and the higher the oil price the shorter the lead-time.

In conclusion to this analysis of OPEC, and notwithstanding the discussion of its single flaw as a supply-regulator and price-stabiliser, the existence of OPEC remains crucial. Its survival is necessary for at least the next 30 years, or until such time as it takes to reach a level of commercial feasibility for the above alternative transportation technologies. During this period of transition, OPEC needs to endure as it has a vital part to play, bearing in mind that even an imperfect OPEC is better than none; as the absence of OPEC would cause a reversion to a chaotic free-for-all oil market – which, in today's market conditions, would damage world energy supplies and bring market anarchy.

Notes

Introduction

1. Mohammad Rezā Shāh Pahlavi's reign began during World War II, following the abdication of his father, Rezā Shāh (forced to abdicate by an Anglo-Soviet invasion in 1941, in the interests of securing oilfields for the allied cause).
2. The Seven Sisters, some of which were shareholders of the Iraq Petroleum Company, are discussed in Chapters 2 and 4.

1 The path that led me to the oil industry

1. This marked the end of the 37-year old Hashemite monarchy in Iraq. King Faisal II was killed in the 14 July revolution, having ruled Iraq from May 1935 to 14 July 1958. The monarchy had initially been successful from 1921 to 1933 under King Faisal I (Faysal ibn Husayn) who commanded respect as the former pan-Arab leader of the Arab Revolt against the Turks in 1918, in the First World War. He fostered unity among Sunni and Shi'a in the interests of pan-Arabism.

2 Why OPEC? Confrontation or common cause?

1. Use of the term 'international petroleum cartel' to describe the Seven Sisters first appeared in 'Development of Joint Control over Foreign Oil' as part of a report by the Subcommittee on Monopoly, presented to the US Senate in 1952.
2. The post-Mosaddegh government did not repeal Mosaddegh's nationalisation measure and thus retained ownership of the National Iranian Oil Company (NIOC) with the formation of a consortium,

managed on NIOC's behalf. This Iranian Consortium agreed to remit taxes and royalties to the government at percentages conforming with those elsewhere in the Gulf.

3. Penrose, Edith, *The Large International Firm in Developing Countries: The International Petroleum Industry* (London, 1968).

4. Enrico Mattei resuscitated and transformed Agip into the multinational ENI (originally Ente Nazionale Idrocarburi), sanctioned as a state monopoly by the Italian government in 1953.

5. *The Large International Firm*, p. 78.

6. Ibid.

3   New winds begin to blow

1. This civil war, 1962–1970, fought between royalists (supporting the Mutawakkilite Kingdom) and republicans, started when Abdullah Sallal staged a republican coup to depose King Imam al-Badr, who was supported by Saudi Arabia. The USSR and Egypt under Nasser supported the republicans.

2. *The Game of Nations: The Amorality of Power Politics* (New York, 1970).

3. Dr Abdul Amir al-Anbari, a colleague and friend, was working for the OPEC Secretariat during this period. He would later be appointed to important ambassadorial posts during the Saddam Hussein regime: as Iraq's Ambassador in London, Iraq's UN Ambassador and later as Ambassador in Paris.

4. Kim Roosevelt, Jr, grandson of President Theodore Roosevelt, orchestrated 'Operation Ajax', the *coup d'état* which, in August 1953, restored the Shah to Iran after toppling Mohammed Mosaddegh. The latter, elected democratically in 1951 as Iran's Prime Minister, had nationalised Iranian oil the same year (1951).

5. Described in terms of 'standard' API degrees, reflecting the specific gravity, crude oil is set on a scale from less than 10 to over 50. The heaviest oil, such as Californian oil and Canadian (tar) oil sands, would be below 20.API and 10.API respectively.

4   Iraq's oil politics: precursor of the demise of the concessions

1. Penrose, Edith T., *The Large International Firm in Developing Countries: The International Petroleum Industry* (London, 1968), pp.154–172.

2. Ibid., p.158–9.

3. Penrose, Edith & EF. *Iraq: International Relations and National Development* (London, 1978), pp.268–9.

4. ERAP later merged with Société Nationale des Pétroles (SNPA), in 1976

5 The Shah and OPEC's oil price frenzy

1. Akins, James E. 'The Oil Crisis: This Time the Wolf is Here', *Foreign Affairs*, vol. 51 (1973), pp.462–90. Also referred to in Parra, Francisco, *Oil Politics: A Modern History of Petroleum* (London, 2004), pp.147–8.

7 OPEC terrorised by the Jackal: the Carlos affair

1. Yallop, David, *To the Ends of the Earth* (London, 1993).

8 The OAPEC intermezzo and my exit from Saddam's regime

1. Karim's blunders, misjudgements and narrow interpretation of Ba'athist politics are described in Chapter 6.
2. In Iraq, a unique country of ethnic, religious, sectarian and linguistic heterogeneity, professional life is rarely based on merit but rather tends to reflect a certain prejudice resulting from the heterogeneous, socio-political structure. Arabs represent the vast majority, besides an important Kurdish minority (about one-fifth) which differ ethnically, speak another language and have different cultural aspirations. There is a smaller Turkish minority, again representing a different ethnicity and language. Among the Arab majority, the Shi'i (who represent 55–60 per cent of all Iraq) and the Arab Sunni minority (representing about 20 per cent), political power traditionally rested with the higher echelons of army officers from the Sunni sect. This imbalance was inherited from the Ottoman Empire and maintained during British colonial rule. Before the creation of the state of Israel, there was a significant Jewish community concentrated in Baghdad and Basra, which later migrated to Israel and elsewhere. The Christian community is also significant and integrated with other faiths.

9 Iran's Ayatolla drives the oil market mad

1. It would be almost three decades before China and India emerged as new, important players in the world oil industry.
2. Engdahl, F.W. *A Century of War: Anglo-American Oil Politics and the New World Order* (Concord, MA, 1993).

10   The backlash: OPEC is cornered

1. The Bali Conference (16 December 1980) and its two-tiered pricing system is described in the previous chapter.
2. Lajous was formerly Director General in Mexico's Ministry of Energy, later becoming President of Petrométrica and Senior Energy Advisor for Morgan Stanley, London.
3. After 1973, OPEC agreed on a price level based on a 'marker crude' – Arabian Light 34 API 1.7 per cent sulphur content, F.O.B. at Ras Tanura. Ras Tunura thus became the reference price for OPEC crude oil.
4. The Qur'an gives examples of a certain 'freedom in trade' and the obligation of the rich towards the deprived – an elementary method of wealth redistribution. I even recall a verse that declares that the deprived have a 'right' to the fortune of the rich, implying a financial obligation for the faithful to give part of their income to help the needy. 'Those who hoard gold and silver without spending them in accordance with the path of Islam shall be warned of hell fire.' Such verses from early eighth-century Islam may sound pertinent, or otherwise, in modern times.

12   OPEC quota-system throws reserves into dispute, fuelling 'peak-oil' theory

1. Indonesia suspended its OPEC membership in January 2009.
2. *Oil Production Capacity in the Gulf*, Vol IV 'IRAQ'. (London, 1997).
3. CGES, *Oil Production Capacity in the Gulf: I. The United Arab Emirates, II.* (London, 1994); *Saudi Arabia; A Compendium of Data. Saudi Arabia* (London 2002)
4. The Hubbert curve is a method for computing oil production rate from an assumed reserve base. It is named after the US geophysicist M. King Hubbert and his work in the 1950s and 1960s. The curve is basically a symmetric logistic function and Hubbert in the 1950s correctly predicted that US oil production would reach its peak rate by around 1970. See CGES, *Long-term Oil Supplies: Is a Global Crunch Inevitable?* (London, 2010).

14   Dispelling myths about OPEC

1. Ironically, only a few months earlier, at our OPEC meeting in Vienna, 28 June 1973 (as described in Chapter 5), Amouzegar had denounced as scandalous my proposal for a very moderate increase to the Tehran-

set price, and had attacked me for dishonouring the 1971 Tehran Agreement.

2. Akins, James E. "The Oil Crisis: This Time the Wolf is Here", *Foreign Affairs*, vol. 51 (1973), pp.462–90. Also referred to in Parra, Francisco, *Oil Politics: A Modern History of Petroleum* (London, 2004), pp.147–8.

3. Engdahl, F. William, *A Century of War: Anglo-American Oil Politics and the New World Order* (Concord, MA, 1993).

4. 'A Second Oil Crisis? A Producer's View of the Oil Developments of 1979', in Kohl, Wilfrid L. (ed.), *After the Second Oil Crisis: Energy Policies in Europe, America and Japan* (Lexington, 1982).

15 Iraq's oil politics after Saddam

1. *The Washington Post* and *The Times*, 3 July 2009.

2. In 1980, Iraq's per capita income was equivalent to Greece's, which, according to the IMF, was also USD$4,000.

3. *Middle East Economic Survey (MEES)* Vol. LII No. 51/52, 21/28 December 2009, pp. 26–29 (Initial oilfield data in MEES Vol. LII No. 45, 9 November 2009, pp 27–34).

4. *World Energy Outlook* (Paris, 2009)

16 Epilogue

1. *Oil & Gas Journal*, 22 June 2010.

2. 'Core OPEC' includes OPEC without Angola, Ecuador, Gabon or Indonesia.

3. After the collapse of the oil price during the Asian Financial Crisis of 1998–99, OPEC logically considered it fair to restore the price to the pre-crisis level of $18 per barrel. The 'fair price' notion was still plausible when OPEC increased it to $25 per barrel two years later. Soon, it reached $30 per barrel in 2002. In October 2004 the price leapt to $50 per barrel and, just after OPEC had announced that it considered $60 per barrel to be 'fair', by July 2006 it was $73.90 per barrel. OPEC then recommended a minimum price of $75 per barrel; but this definition of 'fairness' was challenged as inconsistent when the market price had doubled by July 2008, fuelled by speculators anticipating OPEC's continued tight production.

Selected Bibliography

Abdul Latif al-Shawaf. *Comments on the Case of Oil in Iraq.* (in Arabic) (Baghdad, 1966).

Abdullah Ismail. *The Case of Oil in Iraq.* (London, 1970) Adelman, M.A. *The Genie out of the Bottle. World Oil since 1970.* (Cambridge: MIT, 1995).

Akins, James E. 'The Oil Crisis: This Time the Wolf is Here' *Foreign Affairs,* Vol. 51 (1973): pp.462–90.

BP *Annual Statistical Reviews 1970–2009* (London: British Petroleum).

Centre for Global Energy Studies (CGES) www.cges.co.uk

CGES *A Compendium of Data – SAUDI ARABIA* (London, 2002).

CGES *Africa Oil and Gas Sourcebook* (London, 2010).

CGES *Annual Oil Market Forecast & Review2010* (London, 2010).

CGES *Are High Oil Prices Here to Stay? A Study of Oil Demand, Supply and Prices to 2020.* (London, 2006).

CGES *Canada's Oil Sands* (London, 2009).

CGES *GLOBAL OIL INSIGHT: Oil Market Prospects (Monthly).* (London, 2008–2010).

CGES *GLOBAL OIL INSIGHT: Industry Watch; Weekly Outlook* (London, 2008–2010).

CGES *GLOBAL OIL INSIGHT; Monthly Comment.* (London, 2008–2010).

CGES *GLOBAL OIL INSIGHT: Bi-montly Focus.* (London, 2008–2010)

CGES *Global Oil Reports (Quarterly)* (London, 1990–2007).

CGES *Long-term Oil Supplies – Is a Global Crunch Inevitable?* (London, 2010).

CGES *Middle East Overview. Oil and Gas, Economics, Politics* (London, 2005).

CGES *Monthly Oil Reports 1990–2010* (London, 1990–2010).

CGES *Oil in Fifteen Volumes* (London, 2000).

CGES *Oil Production Capacity in the Gulf: I. United Arab Emirates. II Saudi Arabia* (London, 1993).

CGES *Oil Production Costs in the North Sea* (London, 2001).

CGES *Post-Saddam Iraq: Oil and Gas, Economy, Finance & Politics* (London, 2004).

CGES *Product Price Report (Monthly)* (London, 2008–2010).

CGES *Russian Oil Demand. An analysis of Past, Present and Future/The Outlook for Russia's Economic Development and Oil Demand, 2010* (London, 2001).

CGES *Upstream Costs and the Price of Oil* (London, 2008).

CGES *Venezuela: Where Next? Oil, Economics, Politics.* (London, 2005).

CGES and Petrolog. *Oil Production Capacity in the Gulf,* Vol. 4, 'IRAQ'. (London, 1997).

CGES and associate, Dr Thamir Uqaili. *Hydrocarbon Exploration and Field Development in Iraq* (London, 2010).

Chalabi, F.J 'Iraqi Capacity Expansion Relative To World Oil Market Trends', in *Middle East Economic Survey,* Vol. 52, No. 51/52 21/28 December 2009, pp.26–29. (Nicosia, Cyprus, 2009).

Chalabi, F.J. *OPEC and the International Oil Industry: A Changing Structure.* (Oxford University Press, 1980).

Chalabi, F.J. *OPEC at the Crossroads.* (Oxford: Pergamon Press, 1989).

Copeland, Miles *The Game of Nations: The Amorality of Power Politics.* (New York: Simon & Schuster, 1970).

Engdahl, F. William, *A Century of War: Anglo-American Oil Politics and the New World Order.* (Concord, MA, 1993).

Frankel, Paul H. *Essentials of the Petroleum Industry: A Key to Oil Economics.* (London: Routledge, 1969).

Husari, Ruba 'The Rush for Oil: Iraq's Oil Capacity Potential and Regional Geopolitics' in *Middle East Economic Survey* Vol. 52, No. 45, 9 November 2009, pp.27–34. (Nicosia, Cyprus, 2009).

International Energy Agency World Energy Outlook (November 2009) (Paris, OECD/IEA, 2009).

International Monetary Fund (IMF) *International Financial Statistics Yearbook.* (Washington DC: IMF, 1997).

Kohl, Wilfrid L. (ed.) *After the Second Oil Crisis: Energy Policies in Europe, America and Japan.* (Lexington, 1982).

Mearsheimer, John J. and Walt, Stephen M. *The Israel Lobby and US Foreign Policy.* (London: Penguin, 2008).

PennWell. *Oil & Gas Journal.* (Tulsa, OK, USA, 2010).

OAPEC *Annual Statistical Reports 1970–2009.* (Saffat, Kuwait, 1970–2009).

OPEC *Annual Statistical Bulletins 1970–2009.* (Vienna, 1970–2009).

Penrose, Edith, *The Large International Firm in Developing Countries: The International Petroleum Industry.* (London: George Allen & Unwin, 1968).

Penrose, Edith & E.F. Penrose. *Iraq: International Relations and National Development.* (London: Ernest Benn, 1978).

Sampson, Anthony, *The Seven Sisters*. (London: Hodder & Stoughton, 1975).

Shikara, Ahmad A.R., *Iraqi Politics 1921–41: The Interaction Between Domestic Politics and Foreign Policy*. (London: Laam, 1987).

Yallop, David. *To the ends of the Earth*. (London: Jonathan Cape, 1993).

Yergin, Daniel. *The Prize: The Epic Quest for Oil, Money, and Power* (London: Simon & Schuster, 1991).

Glossary

Arab Light F.O.B. at 'Ras Tanura': As a port on the Gulf, Ras al Tanura (east Saudi Arabia) became the reference price for Arab Light crude oil as of 1973.

Benchmark crudes: These particular crude oils are used as 'reference' or 'marker' crudes in order to facilitate the pricing of the multitude of crudes that are differentiated by quality and location. The benchmark crudes achieved their status by becoming the reference crude in the three main futures markets. The primary benchmarks: US 'West Texas Intermediate' (WTI) and British North Sea Oil (Brent Blend) are very light and sulphur-free. Before 1986 the 'marker' crude was Arab Light free-on-board (F.O.B.) at 'Ras al Tanura', which OPEC's price system took as a basis for pricing other crudes.

downstream: Refineries and the distribution of oil products.

horizontal integration A system of cooperation among the major oil companies in the upstream, allowing the planning of crude oil production to suit the downstream (refining) needs of each company.

LNG: Liquified natural gas, predominantly methane.

marker crude: The grade of crude oil on which other crude prices are based.

oil concessions: A system prevailing (from the 1920s to 1970s) in the Middle East and Venezuela, by which the major oil companies were given over a long period the exclusive right to explore, find, develop and export crude oil; and according to which the companies jointly owned "an operating company" in each country, and held a monopoly among the producing/exporting companies. The concession system reflected the major oil companies' dominant position, supported by a colonial power structure in many host countries (such as Iraq).

Oil futures market: A derivatives market in which oil futures contracts are traded, involving the purchase/sale of crude oil or oil products for future delivery, months and even years ahead, at prices fixed 'today'. Hedgers wishing to 'lay off' the price risk when buying or selling physical oil at variable market prices, are able to take offsetting positions at fixed prices in the futures markets. Speculators, on the other hand, aim to profit from betting on the direction in which oil will be moving, without intending to offer or take delivery of physical oil when the contracts expire. Most contracts on the futures exchanges are settled with cash on expiry. Oil futures trading has become huge business: every day, more than ten times the physical oil consumed in the world is traded on futures exchanges. The two main oil futures markets are the New York Mercantile Exchange (NYMEX) and the Intercontinental Exchange, or ICE, in London. The first oil futures contract (for West Texas Intermediate oil, or WTI) was traded in 1983.

OPEC basket price: A "basket" of seven crudes set up as a reference price in January 1987 namely, *Sahara Blend* of Algeria; *Dubai Crude*; Saudi Arabia's *Arab Light*; *Minas* of Indonesia; *Bonny Light* of Nigeria; *Tia Inana* of Venezuela; *Isthmus* of Mexico.

per-barrel income: Oil revenue per barrel of oil for the producer, after the cost of production.

posted price: A fictitious fixed price set by the major oil companies (until 1971). It served as a reference point for calculating taxes and royalties paid by them to the host countries. It also served as a reference price for inter-company exchange. By the end of the 1950s, the posted price served as a basis for discounts in the free market which had started to develop. The concept of 'posted prices' disappeared as a result of the Tehran Agreement of February 1971.

PSA: Production Sharing Agreement: a long-term contract between an oil-producing country and a foreign investor, by which the latter undertakes the risk of spending capital for oil exploration and the development of discovered oilfields. Once the field's production begins, the foreign investor has a right to recover his capital expenditure in the form of lifting 'cost oil' at international prices. Besides this, the investor has a right to lift a percentage of oil, called 'profit oil'. The latter is determined according to the degree of capital risk and other factors.

royalties expensing: The 1952 "fifty-fifty" agreement (between the governments and the oil companies) decreed that the government share was calculated at 50% of the posted price. In 1964, OPEC declared to the companies that the 50% was to include *both tax and royalties*, and that the investor was to pay a 12.5% royalty to the landowner irrespective of taxable profits. OPEC asked the companies to pay first the 12.5% royalty and then 50% tax on the profits. The companies conceded to this with the proviso that the royalty be "expensed" as the part of their costs (given that the government share is 50% of profit minus costs).

Seven Sisters: Seven major international oil companies which, until the early 1970s, controlled all oil operations in the world oil industry outside the US and Former Soviet Union. Also referred to as the international petroleum cartel, they were Anglo-Iranian Oil Company (forerunner of BP), Royal Dutch Shell, Compagnie Française de Pétrole (CFP/Total), and the American companies: Gulf, and the Aramco partners Standard Oil of New Jersey (later Esso/Exxon), Mobil, SOCAL (Chevron), Texaco. These major oil companies were inter-related in an integrated cartel system that prevented a free world market trade in oil until the end of the 1960s.

shut-in capacity: unused oil-production capacity.

stripper wells: very low-volume oil wells.

upstream: The upstream phase of the oil industry is crude oil production, i.e. investments made in exploring, finding and developing crude oil.

vertical integration: A system by which each operating company obtained crude oil, destined for its own refineries, so as to plan crude oil production in line with the needs of those refineries.

Chronology of key historical events affecting the oil industry

1960 (16 September) Foundation of the Organization of Petroleum Exporting Countries (OPEC) announced in Baghdad by the five major oil-producing countries, Iran, Iraq, Kuwait, Saudi Arabia and Venezuela.

1961 Qatar joined OPEC, followed by Indonesia, Libya (1963), the Emirates of Abu Dhabi (1968), Algeria (1969), Nigeria (1971), Ecuador (1973) and Gabon (1975). The latter two members left OPEC in the 1990s, but Ecuador rejoined in 2008.

1968 (24 June) Vienna OPEC issued a 'declaratory statement of petroleum policy in member countries', a historical turning point, as it laid down basic principles that would later influence all major events of the 1970s. The statement emphasised the right of producing countries to fix the price of their oil, in an endeavour to give a greater role for the state in the development of hydrocarbon resources, and to give the state the right to participate in concession-holding agreements. The emphasis was on amending the concession system in the light of changing circumstances.

1967 (5–17 June) The Six Day War, involving Israel against its neighbouring states Egypt, Syria and Jordan.

1970 (9–12 December) OPEC Conference, Caracas, Venezuela. A decision is made to negotiate collectively with the oil companies to establish a general increase in posted prices and to raise the tax ratio from 50% to 55% of the posted price.

1971 (3–4 February) Tehran, Iran: The Tehran Agreement (to be of five years' duration and then renegotiated) was the outcome of this first round of negotiations with the oil companies, conducted by delegates from the six OPEC member countries bordering the Gulf – namely Iran, Iraq, Kuwait, Saudi Arabia, Qatar and the UAE. Besides price

and tax amendments, the Tehran Agreement provided for the adjustment of the price upward (on an annual basis) to reflect the impact of
world inflation, together with a fixed annual increase.

1972 and 1973 Two successive devaluations of the US dollar led to two
further agreements (in Geneva) to adjust prices and preserve the
purchasing power of the barrel, denominated in US dollars, against
other currencies. Known as the 'Geneva Agreements' ('Geneva 1' and
'Geneva 2') these two agreements laid down the formulae with which
to correct the oil price (agreed in the 1971 Tehran Agreement) – whether
upward or downward – in relation to the movement of the US dollar
value relative to other major currencies: UK sterling, French, Swiss and
Belgian francs, the Deutschmark, Italian lira and Japanese yen.

1973 (12 October) Vienna: OPEC decided to reopen negotiations with the
companies to revise upward the oil price set by the Tehran Agreement
of February 1971, as prevailing market prices now far exceeded the
Tehran-agreed price. Negotiations with the companies failed, and
OPEC ministers decide to hold a meeting (16 October in Kuwait) to
fix the price of its oil unilaterally and independently of the oil companies' participation, thus implementing for the first time OPEC's key
Resolution 90 of June 1968.

—— (6–26 October) 'Yom Kippur' Arab–Israeli War, involving Israel,
backed by the USA, against Egypt and Syria, backed by a coalition
of Arab states.

—— (16 October) Kuwait: Sheraton Hotel: OPEC decided to uphold
Resolution no. 90 of 1968 and henceforth set the price of its own
oil. Gulf members decided to increase the oil price by 70 per cent,
on the $5.40, and that Gulf market prices would now determine
corresponding levels of posted prices.

—— (17 October) Kuwait: at a meeting at OAPEC's headquarters the Arab
Gulf OPEC member-states decided to impose an oil embargo, by
which oil production was cut as a gesture of support for Egypt.

1973 (24 December) Tehran: OPEC's ordinary (winter) meeting. Spurred
on by the Arab oil embargo, the Shah of Iran pushed for increasing the price by 140 per cent from $5.40 to $10.84 per barrel (a total
increase of 400 per cent relative to the 1971 Tehran Agreement).

1979 (January–February) After months of petroleum industry strikes in
Iran, forcing oil prices upward to an unparalleled level, in January
1979, the exiled Ayatollah Khomeini arrived in Iran to great acclaim.
The Iranian Revolution and political coup was immediate.

—— (20 December) Caracas: OPEC's official prices having soared to over
$24 per barrel, OPEC members continued with price increments.

1980 (15–16 December): Bali, Indonesia: the majority of OPEC members decided to fix the price of OPEC oil at $36 per barrel. Saudi Arabia refused to raise the price beyond $32 per barrel, giving rise to a two-tiered pricing system.

1983 (14 March) London: OPEC extraordinary meeting at which OPEC officially adopted a production quota system to defend the oil price in view of the continued decline in demand for OPEC oil, in the face of competition from non-OPEC oil. OPEC's fixed price was reduced to $28 per barrel. A fixed production level was allocated to each member-country except Saudi Arabia, which chose to be OPEC's swing producer (upwards or downwards at a level of 5 mbpd). Given this role, Saudi Arabia's share in OPEC's quota system continually declined, so that the country soon opted to abandon the quota system.

1985 The extent of the petroleum backlash is evident when, by 1985, OPEC total production had already fallen by half, from 31 mbpd.

1986 A 'free-for-all' market prevailed with the rapid rise in Saudi Arabia's production, culminating in oil price collapse in July, with Arab Light selling at less than $8 per barrel.

—— Pressure group forms within OPEC (and among other countries) to push Saudi Arabia into readopting the quota system with a fixed price for its oil at $18 per barrel.

1987 (20 January) OPEC changes its pricing system. Saudi Arabian 'light' as a reference price for other OPEC crudes is replaced with a basket of seven crudes as a reference price, namely: Sahara Blend of Algeria; Dubai Crude; Saudi Arabia's Arab Light; Minas of Indonesia; Bonny Light of Nigeria; Tia Inana of Venezuela; Isthmus of Mexico. However, by 1988 OPEC had effectively abandoned the fixed price system.

1990 (August) Iraq invaded Kuwait. Oil prices rose steeply. UN sanctions imposed on Iraq.

1991 (January) Gulf War with Iraq.

1997 (September) A Climate Change Convention formalised the Kyoto Protocol, compelling signatory nations to set a deadline for reducing CO_2 emissions to diminish global warming. This favours the adoption of alternative, cleaner energies.

2000 (March) At its ministerial meeting in March, OPEC set up a price-band mechanism, according to which OPEC prices below $22 per barrel or above $28 per barrel would after a period be subject to production adjustments, upwards or downwards.

2001 OPEC suspended for several months its $22–28 price band in the wake of the events of September 11, citing stability in the market as more important than OPEC's optimum price target.

2003 (20 March–13 December) Second Gulf War: the invasion of Iraq, and the fall of Saddam Hussein's Ba'athist regime. Coalition combat operations continued until 2009 (ending for the UK on 30/4/2009, with the US drawdown on 31/8/2010).

2005 (31 January) The new Iraqi Government holds its first democratic parliamentary elections.

2008 (11 July) Oil prices peaked at $147 per barrel. From 2003 onwards prices began spiralling with OPEC's tight production capacity in the face of increased demand from China and India, combined with a resultant over-speculation on the futures market, and culminated in an unsustainable peak of $147 per barrel. This heralded an oil price collapse lasting nearly six months, a global recession and reduced oil demand, while reviving technological efforts in alternative energy sources. From April 2009, oil prices recovered, and through 2010 continues to keep within the same range of $70–$80 per barrel.

—— (27 October) Iraqi Parliament Committee failed to back Oil and Gas Laws as part of new Constitution. At the same time Iraq's Ministry of Oil continues to neglect improvement of the country's oil production.

2009 (August and December) Iraq's Oil Ministry finally conducts negotiations with the IOCs (in two rounds) to sign contracts for the development of the country's major oilfields, with a view to increasing Iraq's production capacity to about 12 mbpd by 2017.

2010 (7 March): al-Maliki's Government holds Iraq's second democratic parliamentary elections.

—— (20 April): a blowout at BP's Deepwater Horizon rig, caused by oil and gas escaping at high pressure from a well a mile below the surface of Gulf of Mexico, was a major challenge for BP and other industry experts in plugging tons of gushing oil. This resulted in attempts to restrict offshore drilling and to ban deepwater drilling, with the US Interior Secretary, Ken Salazar, urging Federal court to prolong President Obama's six-month moratorium on deepwater drilling. One certain factor that prevents a ban is the fear of fallout from economic damage that this would cause. By 12 July a provisional cap with valves was installed to contain the leak, until two drilled relief wells permanently shut off the pressure.

Index